To Sheila —
Hope there is room
for this among your
dance trophies. Read it
in good health.
Al Cartwright

The Best of Al Cartwright

Serendipity Press
Wilmington, Delaware

ISBN   0-914988-01-8

Library of Congress Catalog Card Number: 74-17236

The stories comprising this anthology originally appeared in the Wilmington News-Journal newspapers.

PRINTED IN THE UNITED STATES OF AMERICA
Designed by Edward J. Bonner
Consultant: Robert A. Livingston

To the former Mary Renninger, with apologies for an unprintable anthology of headaches; to Mary Jane, Debbie, Laurie and Dr. & Mrs. Albert Cartwright, Jr.; to my grandsons, Steve, Scott and Greg, whom I hereby officially acknowledge. And a nomination for MCP (Most Courageous Publisher) to Jack van Urk.

Publisher's Note

As the title A'La Carte promises, here is a book of articles, reflections and observations about people and places. The author, Al Cartwright, is a master craftsman with words and characterizations. His stories are certain to interest and intrigue every reader.

Whether you have a desire for the ritual of a Tokyo bath; wish to sit in on celebrity interviews; follow the baseball circuit; ride in a police car; join a heckler at a company stockholders' meeting or just observe the vicissitudes and frailties of active individuals—you have it here, and much more.

The country's top-drawer newsmen and authors assert that Al Cartwright consistently writes rings around most columnists. This is why he has won so many national awards.

The book is packed with absorbing anecdotes, deftly seasoned with a mixture of empathy and whimsy. What impressed me most was Cartwright's understanding of diverse subjects, and his varied skill in treating each. He mixes the ordinary and extraordinary with unique clarity and humour.

Al Cartwright is especially good at presenting the idiosyncrasies of people and interpreting their significance. He puts people into perspective—and he does it with considerable grace and style.

We feel privileged to publish "A'La Carte—The Best of Al Cartwright."

J. Blan van Urk

Foreword

by Jimmy Breslin

Among enormous dividends received for living in a city such as New York is the vast number of services, small services, varied and specialized services, available to you at almost any time you happen to be awake. One of these services—to me it is probably the most important one—is the newsstand at Times Square which carries the daily newspapers of almost every place in the nation. Through all my time in my city, the nights end with the cab pulling up to this big newsstand.

"Chicago," I call out to the guy.

"Which *Chickago*?" the newsstand guy says.

"The Chicago with Royko, The Daily News."

He snaps a Chicago Daily News from the rack. I have Mike Royko to read.

"Seattle!" I say next.

"Which one? We got two Seattles."

"The one with Emmett Watson. What is it, the P-I?"

"Seattle Post-Intelligencer," the newsstand guy says. His hand goes into the rack, past San Antonio and Des Moines and out comes a Seattle P-I. I now have Emmett Watson.

"Wilmington!" I tell him.

"Morning or Evening?"

"Evening. The Journal. Cartwright."

Out it comes, and now I can read Al Cartwright before I go to sleep.

Therefore, I am quite familiar with the person, the style, the eye and the clarity which is spread over the pages of this book. Clarity; don't pass by that word too quickly. Al Cartwright is one of those people who does not make a mystery out of the story he is telling you. If he writes of a man called Claudie Nix, Cartwright tells you immediately that Claudie Nix "was shot and killed as he drove in Delaware, near Harrington. This was during the nationwide shutdown by independent truck drivers." The facts established, Cartwright now can go on and deal in the coldness of the topic. The reader can move along with Cartwright too, and not have to slow and frown and pause and wonder and go back to try and find out what the thing is all about.

The style basically is known as journalism, and it is a very old and a very fine style. Of a recent couple of years, the style was considered obsolete by a group of writers who came up with a Madison Avenue catchword, "New Journalism", which is a mixture of fancy and fact, dazzling flights of ego disguised as personal opinion and, quite often, meanings so hidden that I never could find them. For some reason, they used to list J. Breslin as one of the New Journalists and I never knew what the hell they were talking about, but I never bothered to argue it out because I knew that time handles all fads. And so in June of 1972, two young reporters from the Washington Post, Woodward and Bernstein, went out to cover a burglary in Washington, and they covered a burglary the way I learned to cover a burglary and the way Al Cartwright learned to cover a burglary and when they were through, Woodward and Bernstein, they had helped put a President onto the street and people stopped going around talking about New Journalism. And we are left with what always was: The plain, hard, informative journalism of an Al Cartwright.

We are left with a writer who can go to people and sit and listen and sort out of their conversations such delights to the eye and ear as this passage from the story Al Cartwright tells of Boom Boom Felsburg:

"When I was a kid," he once told me, "I saw an old guy trying to beat the horses at Havre De Grace. He needed a shave, bad; he had a little stump of a cigar stuck in his teeth, holes in his elbows, run-down heels. I pitied the guy and I said to myself, 'I'll never get that way.' Well, this summer I walked past a full-length mirror at Delaware Park and I saw the old guy again. It was me!"

And we are left with a writer who, of a cold Sunday morning in December, the day before Christmas, gets on the bus that takes wives and mothers to the state prison at Smyrna. This shows you why journalism, the old journalism of the Al Cartwrights, is one of the highest of callings. There is no constituency for prisons in this country. People do not care about prison buildings, nor do they care about the people inside the buildings. It is usually impossible, therefore, for any sensible legislation to bring prisons out of the 19th century. Politicians never attempt anything that is not possible. So a man in prison is left with a woman somewhere, poor and helpless, and maybe a child or two, worrying about him. And a journalist like Al Cartwright.

In this piece, about taking the bus to Smyrna, Cartwright does what he is supposed to do, what his trade calls for: he spends time trying to understand and catch the feeling of the helpless.

Read the Smyrna piece carefully. Read the part about Warren, the young, barefoot prisoner needling the guards; read that part a couple of times. It is brilliant observing by Cartwright. He caught the child-like maneuvers of the prisoner as he played with the chairs in the visiting room, testing, taunting, exasperating the guard. Child-like is the proper description. For a prisoner in jail is the same as a young child forced to stay inside the house on a rainy day. When we understand this, perhaps we can begin to think of prisoners as men who have not grown, who are dangerously sick. And then perhaps, someday, we can begin to see if there might be better ways to quarantine and attempt to cure prisoners than just throwing them into a locked cage.

If it ever happens, it will be because an Al Cartwright went to prison and he brought with him the abilities of his trade: to see and distill, to hear and understand, and to feel life as it is.

There is one other thing, I'd like to point out. Through the pages of this book you will not find any instances in which Cartwright attempts to show that Cartwright is brilliant. He is too busy concentrating on other people— which is always the way of people of deep intelligence.

Contents

A Better Table

This is a true story. Wild horses couldn't drag the guy's name out of me.

He is a Prominent Delaware Businessman. Let us call him Prodelbus for short.

Mr. Prodelbus makes frequent trips to New York. Business takes him here. A couple of kinds. Business-business, and also monkey business. The reasons for the trip are not necessarily in that order.

The monkey business has to do with a girl friend in the big city. For Mr. Prodelbus, you see, is also a prominent Delaware Married Man.

There was this recent evening when, business-business completed, Mr. Prodelbus programmed the other kind. There would be a nice dinner, then the theater, and then some genuine monkey business.

Mr. Prodelbus took his girl friend to Leone's, which is one of the big restaurant attractions in New York. They hurl grapes, cheese, wine at you in Roman-feast fashion. It is a little too touristic for my tastes, but who am I to quarrel with the ghost of Mama Leone?

Mr. Prodelbus and his friend are seated. He sighs with comfort. It has been a good day. It will be a great night.

Leone's is busy, as usual. This is good for Mr. Prodelbus. He and his friend are but two faceless faces in the crowd.

The maitre d' approaches.

"Your name, sir?" he asks.

"P. D. Prodelbus."

The maitre d' beams. "Ah, Mr. Prodelbus, by all means. Let us get you a better table. A man of your distinction deserves a better table. This way, please."

Mr. Prodelbus looks at his friend and shrugs. He has eaten at Leone's before, but not so often that the help should recognize him and take extra care of him. But this is New York, he reminds himself; everybody has his hand out. The maitre d' is thinking tip.

The couple is escorted to a new table in the back of the restaurant. It is on a little balcony, a couple of steps up from the main floor.

It is a nice table, at that, with a view of the whole joint. It is bathed in a soft light. Mr. Prodelbus notices that the other tables on the balcony also have this unique lighting effect.

Mr. Prodelbus, though, would rather look at his girl friend. He reaches across the table and holds her hands. They talk. She is the understanding type.

Mr. Prodelbus senses someone standing at his side. He starts to give a drink order and then checks himself, for this cannot be the waitress. He is right. It is a tall, attractive young woman. Very attractive. Mr. Prodelbus would call her a beautiful broad.

"Mr. Prodelbus," she says excitedly, "how are you? How have you been?"

Mr. Prodelbus is not overwhelmed by the originality of the greeting, but he is speechless. He thinks, hard, but still cannot recognize the broad—uh, lady. He does not wish to appear stupid. In fact, he does not wish to appear at all, in the presence of some one who might know him.

"I'm fine," he manages, finally, smiling weakly. "And you?"

The lady seems to grasp his discomfort.

"Don't you know me?" she says, with a pleasant little laugh. "I'm Gail. Don't you remember taking me to dinner last week? Oh, those martinis! I haven't had one since. They do the darndest things to me."

By this time Mr. Prodelbus' girl friend has turned to ice. She is looking stilettos at both Gail and her big spender from Delaware.

"Jennifer says to say hello to you, too," Gail continues. Then, as if noticing Mr. Prodelbus' girl friend for the first time, she gives a slight gasp, puts her hand to her mouth and leaves.

Mr. Prodelbus exhales and reaches for his girl friend's hands. "Honey, you aren't going to believe this, but I never saw that broad—uh, girl—before in my life."

He is right. The girl friend does not believe it. She gives him much mouth. How dare he cheat on her in her town? Why didn't you call me when you were in New York last week?

Gail returns, and hands a card to Mr. Prodelbus. "Here is my new phone number. Forget the other one. Call me the next time you're in New York? Promise?"

Before Mr. Prodelbus can promise, or defend himself, Gail is gone.

And that starts Round 2 at the "nice table". The girl friend now is definitely stirred up. She has turned from an indignant green to an aggressive red, and Mr. Prodelbus can only stammer, when there is an opening.

"Pardon me, sir."

There is another stranger at the table. A man.

"Do you know who I am?" the stranger asks.

Mr. Prodelbus, his great night in shreds, looks at the man and nods yes and says no. Who could this be—Gail's husband?

No, but it is almost that bad. In case you haven't guessed it by now, the man is Allen Funt. The Candid Camera man. Mr. Prodelbus, his girl friend, Gail and assorted remarks had been on Candid Camera.

Mr. Prodelbus can get a chuckle out of it now.

"Man, I was nervous enough before Funt came over," he said. "Now I find out I'm on Candid Camera and I'm really sweating. All I can think of is everybody in Wilmington tuning it in.

"Funt said he would need my signature, and he would pay me, for the right to use the scene. I told him he didn't have enough money to pay me. I didn't sign anything, of course. But I'd like to buy the tape, just to make sure. Funt told me the table was bugged—a mike in the flowers. All the arguments were recorded."

They moved Mr. Prodelbus and his girl friend to the next table, and waited for two more patsies to enter. They turned out to be newlyweds. Gail went into her act and the bride almost went into tears.

"We could hear what was going on," Mr. Prodelbus said. "It really was hilarious—from that angle."

Mr. Prodelbus has learned his lesson. His experience has been fruitful, a powerful reminder that he is a married man, with commitments.

Now when he takes his New York girl friend out to dinner he always frisks the centerpiece.

Tokyo Bath

This was one of the highlights of the 1964 Olympics. You can always see a 100-yard dash.

T OKYO—I just had a bath.

About time, you say?

True. This was a Japanese bath, and I had been putting it off. It takes some courage.

A young lady gives you the bath. It's an old Japanese custom. And here the United States has been wasting its time importing transistor radios.

This was something that just had to be done. Going back to the mill without a first-hand report on the Japanese baths, after all those dares, would be like returning from Miami without a tan.

You got the name of the bathhouse from a match box, furnished by a cleanly New York newspaperman. This is how you find places in Tokyo—via match box. You take one from a restaurant that seems worthy of an encore, or someone hands you a new one by way of recommendation, and you hand it to the taxi driver. Instant communication.

So come with us to Miharabashi Toruko Center, which doesn't sound like a bathhouse. But that's what it said on the match box, and that's what it turned out to be.

It was on a little street off the Ginza, the gay neon way. The time was 3 p.m. You walked down stairs into a little lobby, where a Japanese guy was watching Olympics judo on television. He jumped up, bowed the client to a desk and disappeared. A thin lady at the desk relieved me of 1,300 yen ($3.64).

Pretty soon the lady scrubber, or masseuse, or something, showed up. You had been braced for the Tamara Press type. Surprise. As the saying goes, not bad. Short, on the chubby side, pleasant face, maybe 23, 24, nice hairdo. Wearing white sleeveless blouse over white shorts.

She said "Please" like "Pleece" and you followed her down a hall. She opened a door on the left that had a little window in it. You entered and you were there—gad, inside a real Japanese bathhouse bathroom. You felt as if you were halfway up Mt. Fuji.

She said her name was Ake-ah, when she laboriously spelled it out, it turned out to Eika.

The room was like 10x20 feet, half wood, half tile. There was a radio, with the judo broadcast on, a fan, ventilator, telephone, massage table. The far end contained a steambox and a small triangular bathtub. What, no life-guard?

Eika ran the water.

"Take off?" I said, waving what was meant to be a casual hand at my apparel. She nodded. I took off—the clothes, that is. She helped hang them on hooks. Everything came off but the glasses, which remained on in the interest of complete reporting.

This may be an old Japanese custom, but to an American rookie, it was about as uncustomary as you can get.

Eika waved me to the open steambox. I sat down, and she put three wooden lids on it and a towel around the neck aperture. There I broiled for 10 minutes. Every now and then she'd ask "Too hot?" and I'd say no, hoping she was impressed with the ruggedness of Americans. It really was hot. In fact, it was murder, and cramped.

Now and then Eika would put a cool washcloth to my perspiring brow. Bless you, my child.

Steambox time was over. I stepped out, every move a picture. She motioned for me to sit down on a tiny rubber stool. I felt like Wilt Chamberlain astride a Dachshund.

Eika broke out the soap and a rough washcloth, and lathered. She dipped water out of the tub with a pink plastic pan and rinsed me off several times. There was even a shampoo, which took practically no time at all out of the one-hour limit. The glasses had to come off for this, but Eika assured me she was still in the room.

The next step was the tub, as high as the steambox. The water was semi-hot. I sat there and soaked while Eika listened to the Japanese judo announcer. Funny what runs through your mind at a time like this. Things like:

(a) Wonder what the king is doing tonight?

(b) Whatever happened to Noah Beery Jr.

(c) Suppose somebody peeps in the window?

No one peeped. Eika pointed to a towel on the floor, the Japanese sign for everybody out of the pool. I got out and she toweled me, but not with the one that was on the floor. This was a class place.

5

"Back massage?" she announced and asked at the same time, and aimed me at the table. Eika gave the massage through a towel-sized sheet. Small talk took place. She wanted to know where I was from. I asked her "How old?" and she said "No speak" and busted out laughing. Gad, these Americans are hilarious.

Eika said "Excuse" and the next thing I knew she was walking on my back in her bare feet, which is probably the best way. Her feet slid slowly off at the waist, like a crazy form of artificial respiration. Then she resumed walking clear up to the neck. How's that song go? "Icy footsteps up and down my spine."

"Heavy?" she asked. No, I grunted—and lied. Eika felt as if she had been having too many seconds of fried rice. Wonder if they hand you a gold medal on the way out?

Eika completed her hike, jumped down and finished the massage after kindly switching the jubo jibber to a station that was playing American music. Doris Day was singing "My Foolish Heart". Eika said she liked American songs—"but not know too good". I had the ridiculous inclination to ask her to dance, but figured it wouldn't look too good. She was awfully short.

One more plunge into the tub and that was it. I dried and dressed with her assistance, and asked Eika if I could copy the sign on the wall. She didn't understand, so I copied it anyhow:

"Introduction of Your Turkish Bath.

"Effective for Your Health and Beauty.

"WELCOME SIR.

"Take the Vapor Bath first. You will sweat for 10 to 15 minutes.

"Washing your Body and Hair will be served after you sweat.

"Complete Washing will then be served in ordinary bath or shower.

"Massaging will be served after Washing (15-20 minutes).

"Full course will be completed after setting your hair and face.

"No tip can be received here, for the service charge of the hostess is already paid at the Front Desk.

"Please, offer anything to Manager without hesitation."

The last item convulsed me. I was still giggling on the way out, although the fact that the whole bit was over was sort of relaxing, too. I slipped Eika 500 yen ($1.30) as she followed me out, but she gave it to the thin lady.

Eika bowed and said the Japanese thank you: "Ah-ri-gah-toh."

Dol-ee-tah-shi-mah-shi-teh, Eika. You are welcome.

Cleaner, more wordly I taxied back to my hotel. I was halfway home before I realized I had been taken.

Hey, Eika—you never set the hair and face!

The Rumor

I enjoyed tracking down this story. It made me feel like a newspaperman again, instead of a columnist. There is a difference.

It is a finger of Eastern Shore Maryland reaching into the Chesapeake Bay. There are neighboring villages on the finger, like rings, named Wenona, Deal Island, Chance and Dames Quarter.

I was on an airplane over Europe when I first heard the story that was traced to that area. The Air Force sergeant couldn't swear to the facts. He could only swear. He was relaying it as told by relatives, and he was excited about it.

The sergeant was from Chincoteague, which is Delmarva, Virginia. The story had been passed clear across the peninsula.

"This preacher in Maryland," the sergeant said in the crew's quarters on the cargo plane out of Dover, "he brought a man back to life on a boat and the man sent him a check for $750,000. What's more, the man changed his will to take care of the preacher even more."

The sergeant knew no names. All he knew was that the preacher was aboard the ferry from Crisfield to Smith Island when one of the passengers was stricken with a heart attack. His heart stopped beating.

The preacher punched him on the chest, the story continued, and the passenger revived. They turned the ferry around and put him in a hospital on the mainland. A few days later, the preacher opened his mail and there was this check "in appreciation" for $750,000.

The sergeant had me hooked. I asked him if he had any idea how I could pursue the story. He gave me his mother's name, and an aunt's name, on Chincoteague Island. He had heard it from them.

I contacted the aunt. She identified the minister as the Rev. Dewey Crockett, Methodist, and formerly of her area, but she didn't know where he lived. She had a few amendments to the anecdote. He had been piloting the ferry, which he did on his days off from the church duties. And he was using some of the gift money to build a youth center on Tangier Island, where he had been born and raised.

She had heard the story from her son, who lived in Exmore, Va. I called the son. He related just about what his mother had told me.

"But I don't know if it is true," he cautioned. "The story's been bouncing around these parts, and you hear different versions of how much money was involved. I don't know if you'll get anything out of the preacher if you do reach him. Those Tangier Crocketts aren't much for talking to outsiders."

He said Crockett had been transferred from a local charge to "somewhere in Maryland". I checked with the conference office in Salisbury. Yes, there was a Rev. Dewey Crockett. He had a church in Deal Island.

I telephoned for several days before I got an answer. It was Crockett. I told him the story I had heard. He listened patiently. Then he told me what actually had happened. He is 26, and his voice is slow and pleasant, like the lifestyle of his land, and deep.

What I had heard, he said, was inaccurate but basically true. Especially inaccurate was that $750,000.

There was no ferry ride. Crockett is not a ferry pilot.

It happened in August. A private boat was sailing from Wenona across Tangier Sound to South Marsh Island. There were three other people on it: Horace Webster of Deal Island, a member of the preacher's congregation, Webster's friend David Israel of Washington, and the preacher's younger brother, Dennis, of Tangier.

"They were taking Dennis to their gun club on South Marsh, where he was to start a new job as cook," Crockett said. "I went along for the ride. I met Mr. Israel for the first time. He lives in Washington, a man 74 years old; president, I believe, of an engineering company.

"We neared the island and transferred to a smaller boat. Mr. Israel slipped and sprained his ankle, badly. Perhaps that was the origin of the trouble. A little later he collapsed, unconscious, and his face turned purple. There was no pulse. I used to work in a hospital as a medical technican, and I massaged his heart. There wasn't much room in the little boat. It had no effect. I took my fist and hit him over the heart, hard as I could. He came to.

"We got him back in the main boat and returned to shore. My wife is a registered nurse. She took Mr. Israel's blood pressure and we rushed him to Dr. (E.C.) Nutter's office in Dames Quarter. He said Mr. Israel had suffered a heart block, and told us he would have died had not it been for the sudden shock of the punch.

"Dr. Nutter, after the examination, advised Mr. Israel to go home to Washington and check into a hospital. This he did. I heard recently, through

Mr. Webster, that he still is under doctor's care. He is resting in a summer home in Hot Springs, Va."

I mentioned the rumor about the cash gift.

"I did receive a financial gift from Mr. Israel, the following week," he said. "The rumors—and we've heard them—have blown it up, out of proportion. It is a large gift for my wife and me; not so large for some other people. But it is nothing like $750,000. And I know nothing about a new youth building on Tangier.

"I think it best not to mention the amount, in fairness to Mr. Israel. We look on it as a friendship tie, more than a gift. You could call it a small love gift, of appreciation. The fact I was able to help—that's the thing."

I told him people also were saying Israel rewrote his will to include Crockett.

"I really don't know what he intends to do," the pastor said. "But Mr. Webster told me if we ever needed anything, he was sure Mr. Israel wouldn't forget us."

And so the young, life-saving preacher from remote Tangier Island, where two-thirds of the population are Crocketts, goes his way, serving his three churches in Deal Island, Chance and Wenona.

This should quiet the rumors, but I doubt it.

Lorelei

Carol Channing kills me. She is what musical comedy is all about. I saw the show and went backstage and she beamed "Oh yes, you're the one who asked the provocative questions." I bet she says that to all the columnists.

I told Carol Channing I had read a story that alleged she was a big pain in the cast.

The cast of "Lorelei," which is the sequel, or something, to her "Gentlemen Prefer Blondes" of 24 years ago. It now is playing Philadelphia on its long way to New York, and en route it is experiencing more changes than the White House varsity.

The story came out of Los Angeles a couple of weeks ago.

Carol Channing, clad all in red, was pouring from the biggest flask I've ever seen. Sterling silver, and it is optional equipment with a Rolls Royce. Her husband bought it for her at an antique shop—the flask, not the car. It looks like something Jackie Gleason would carry as standard equipment.

But what was in it was spring water. Carol Channing carries her own water, and also her own food, on tour. She broke out a broiled pork chop and some rice from her huge red and white tote bag at this press luncheon at John Wanamaker in Philadelphia.

The flask paused in mid-pour when I mentioned the story. Carol Channing is all eyes, and as she turned to me—I cleverly had positioned the local talent—even the eyes seemed to have eyes.

"I heard about the story, but I didn't see it," she said. "What did it say?"

I had fetched excerpts. A comedy writer named Kenny Solms, who had been hired to update the book, said that Carol was making like a dictator. "An actress should never take over a production, and she has. They're letting her act as chief. It's an egomaniac thing, and that might be good for her, but it's not good for the show."

The story also said that through Los Angeles, "the cast's morale reportedly hit an all-time low because of crash changes that were all aimed at focusing the show more exclusively on Carol Channing."

Miss Channing blinked. It was the first time I ever heard false lashes.

"Mr. Solms no longer is with the show," she said.

"That figures," I said, "but does he have a case? Are you an egomaniac?"

The taller-than-I blonde didn't hesitate.

"Of course I'm an egomaniac," she said, "and I'm delighted to be called one. It gives me character. The story is good, because it is controversial. I've been sitting here like a sweet blob, answering the usual questions, and I'm glad you came up with this one.

"Mr. Solms has the sound of someone who has been fired, wouldn't you say? He has a case—from his point of view. I think you can tell if a person is an egomaniac when you see her, or him, work. If you don't like her, she's an egomaniac. If you like her, she isn't. He obviously didn't like me.

"And as far as the cast's having a low morale—come and see the show and judge for yourself."

"I'll level with you. There hasn't been a day we haven't rehearsed since the show opened—and it's an 11-month, 18-city tour. We rehearse at 11 a.m. for a night show and at 10 a.m. for a matinee, and I spend hours working with the cast.

"If I'm good and the cast is lousy, what kind of a show is that? Julie Andrews taught me that theory, when we were making 'Thoroughly Modern Millie'. She is a perfectionist who wants everybody in the picture, not just herself, to be as fine as possible. This was the third straight movie she made—right after 'Mary Poppins' and 'Hawaii'. She was red-hot, and went from one right into the other. She finally got a day off, while they did close-ups of me. And do you know she came in that day, anyhow, because she knew I wouldn't be as relaxed working with her stand-in?"

It was mentioned that people might think she was pouring vodka, not water, from the flask.

"Gee, I hope they do," she said. "I'm tired of being thought of as a Christian Science girl, which is what I am. It annoys me. Anything to get out of the rut—even the vodka rumor. I'm allergic to sprays and insecticides in foods, and the chlorine in water—that's why I carry my own. Eight shows a week, you have to be careful."

It is all right with me if Carol Channing is an egomaniac, or a dictator, and she can drink all the vodka she wants, if she wants, because she is one of the great entertainers of my time. She cracks me up with those wide-eyed, wide-smiled expressions and that voice that ranges from a scratchy purr to a balcony-shaker. Incidentally, she says we all should sit in the balcony at a musical comedy, to appreciate the choreography. "Orchestra seats are for tourists."

This 51-year-old mother of a Williams College junior is queen of the musical halls, and queen of the road. The original Dolly Levi, she played "Hello, Dolly" more than 1,200 times through four years and never missed a show. She is Louise Gehrig.

I suggested her "Dolly" stand-in might have won a Tony as Most Frustrated Actress.

"She was Bibi Osterwald," Carol said. "When we took the show on tour, I told her she could come along if she wanted, but she'd never get to play. She decided not to go. Lorelei doesn't have an understudy, either. People ask me if I don't get sick and tired, doing the same thing night after night. There is no possibility of that. I love the character; it completely overcomes the way you might feel physically. The greatest compliment in the world is to be told you look like you love the part, and I do."

She played "Dolly" with bronchitis and a microphone in North Carolina ("Is there a Charlotte? That's where it was") and in her bare feet in Miami— she had injured a toe on the beach.

She "wanted to jump out the window" when they picked Barbra Streisand for the movie "Dolly".

"But the film director, Ernest Lehman, didn't want Gower Champion, either," she said, "and Gower had choreographed even the scenery for 'Dolly'. I was convinced he was going to make an anti-Dolly movie, and I was right. He changed it every place possible. It wasn't Barbra's fault the movie flopped—and even closed the studio. It had a pace like 'Sound of Music', when it should have been treated with a fast, farce pace."

Carol's now matronly Lorelei Lee is still maintaining musically that "Diamonds Are A Girl's Best Friend". She was wearing what looked like a three-tiered diamond ring on her left pinky, and I was about to ask her the value when she slipped off the top tier and gave it to me. It is direct from a variety store, and she hands them out as mementos. A touch of class. And glass.

Man From Anna

You never know. I went to Delaware Park to write about something else and while I was at it, talked to Buddy Raines for a rainy-day column. This was it—and it won the first Annual Thoroughbred Racing Associations' Award. I'm sure glad it rained.

Contrary to bad information from the corrals, Buddy Raines has not been around horses longer than Barney Google.

It just seems that way, even to Raines.

And no wonder. The trainer for Brandywine Stable, which is the home team at Delaware Park, played with horses instead of other kids as a young'n.

At 11, he was out in the world working for his keep as an exercise boy.

That was 33 years ago, and he's been in the thoroughbred racing industry ever since. Donald Ross's ringmaster can't remember when there wasn't a horse in a day of his life.

He sprawls on a lawn chair during a morning lull at Stanton Downs, loses himself in the past under a cowboy hat and takes you back to what is known as the hard way.

"Hard way is right," declares the small and wiry Raines.

"People ask me why I don't strike out on my own, and open up a big public stable like Hirsch Jacobs, or Frank Bonsal.

"I don't mind admitting the reason: I'm scared. I'm scared to go to work for myself. It takes so much money as a personal investment, and I had it so rough getting where I am, that I part myself from the idea right away. I'm afraid to look back.

"It is much more secure to just okay bills instead of paying them, and I'd just as soon keep it that way. However, my attachment to Brandywine goes much deeper than that. I have no reason for wanting to leave here. Mr. Ross is as fine an owner to work for as you can find."

It's no wonder Buddy Raines has a way with the critters. He was brought up in the horse-tradin' center of Wayne County, Ill.—"that's what my middle initial stands for. 'W' for Wayne."

The town was Anna, but they referred to the community as Bishopville because Hal Bishop ran his big horse auction there. Bishop, Jr., now is a prosperous trainer on the Chicago-New Orleans wheel. His father was Buddy's father's boss.

"When I was 8, I was ridin' along on those long-distance horse-sellin' excursions," recollected the man now known on the entry blanks as Virgil W. Raines. "I once rode from Iowa to Nashville, mostly just joggin' along and eatin', trying to keep up.

"We'd take a pack of 50 Clydesdales, for instance, and sell 'em in Tennessee. Then we'd make a deal for mine mules, and sell those on the way back. We'd have maybe 15 of them in a string, snapped to a rope hangin' from the back of a wagon.

"Horse-tradin' then was big business, and it almost amounted to a carnival. Like along the banks of the Mississippi. People would come for hundreds of miles to make a deal. I can still see those bankers with their checkered vests and log chains and big hats, comin' in for a week-end to swap horses and play cards.

"They'd try to match wits with the pros, but they didn't have much chance. Those slickers made their living that way. They had to be better than the other guys to get along. Money wasn't always involved. There would be even-up swaps, two horses for one, all kinds of deals.

"My father was pretty good at it. He put one over on a guy one time, swapped him a stiff horse for a couple of good ones by fast talkin'. My mother was a religious person, and she complained that the deal wasn't right, because the Bible said 'Thou shall not cheat thy neighbor'.

"My father just told her, 'Maybe so—but there's nothin' in there that says you can't outwit him.' "

And the good people of Anna were proud of their possessions and their skills. Buddy can recall the town character pulling aside the boy Raines and demanding that he admire his shiny, sassy string of horses.

"See them?" the puffed-up native swaggered. "All mine—just through tradin'. And all I started with was a pocket knife!"

But long before he was 12, young Buddy had shaken the road dust of Illinois off his bare feet. His parents busted up, and the boy went to live with a man called Dayton—horseman, of course. Then he boarded with another named Landgrave, all the while workin' horses.

"I just stayed with whoever fed me, and you know where I wound up? In Newark, Del." Raines continued. "Bob Smith, the late trainer for Brookmeade, and Sunny Jim Fitzsimmons ran a big public stable there, and they took me on as an exercise boy and a potential jockey.

"Before that, though, I first came East to work in Laurel, Md., for Commander J. K. L. Ross, who had the first Triple Crown Winner in Sir Barton. He had a big place on what is now the Laurel trotting track. My pay was a dollar, every Saturday night. And it was there that I went to school for the first time—sixth and seventh grades it was, I think. But Mrs. Smith, who saw to it that I went, got killed in a bicycle accident and I just sort of stopped school."

Brookmeade and Brandywine—in some 30 years around the tracks, those have been Raines' only associations—"and I've never lost a day's pay with either outfit."

Smith turned him into a jockey with Brookmeade, all right, but apparently neither party ever was quite convinced that a rider programmed as V. Raines was headed for immortality.

"I was terrible," Buddy confessed. "But I had company.

"There's a bunch of us trainers who were the worst jockeys in the world. Fellows like Bill Winfrey with Vanderbilt; Sherrill Ward, who trains Summer Tan; Bill McGee, others. We've got a standing gag among ourselves, that we'll be bug riders as long as we live."

The Flying Whale

The jet set, with hash marks. The world's largest plane left Dover, Del., for Germany on a Thursday and we were back home Sunday night. The return flight included a stop in the Azores. I was in the cockpit as we approached the United States and the view made me feel like an airborne Columbus.

FRANKFURT-ON-MAIN, Germany—I am standing on the runway, taking still another doubting look at the largest aircraft in the world, and for still another time I am groping for ways to describe it. Where is Jack Hunter, Wilmington's own Blue Max, when I need him?

The C5 Galaxy has fetched me 4,055 miles from the Dover Air Force Base. Well, not exactly just me. Me and like 120,000 pounds of cargo, on a representative flight to a Rhein-Main Air Base here that is so busy with military and commercial planes, it almost seems ready to take off itself.

Rhein-Main, named after two rivers that both rhyme with "fine," is where the Zeppelins flew out of in the 1930s. The field also was the staging area for Hitler's western-front fighters and bombers before he was rudely interrupted.

Now the stuffed cargo whales from the Delaware home of the 436th Military Airlift Wing fly in and out of Rhein-Main as though it were a taxi service.

You can put 58 Cadillacs in that belly. The Galaxy is 247 feet long and the wing span is 222 feet and its maximum takeoff weight is 382 tons and there are 28 wheels on its landing gear and so on into the statistics. But you still have to see it, to fly it, to believe it, and even now I'm not too sure it's for real. There are thinkers like the Wisconsin senator who do not approve of its $56 million-per-copy reality, but the Air Force guys swear by it.

I join the crew in Dover at 2:45 a.m. for the briefing. The aircraft commander is Major Mark Sabey, 35, of Fort Lauderdale, Fla. He looks like

Dick Selma, the pitcher, a handicap that worries me but briefly. The crew normally is eight, but there are extras going along in training and examining capacities. The commander himself will be evaluated by another major, Tom Dennis of Cincinnati.

There will be a stop in Mildenhall, England. I learn there will be 28 passengers on the second story of the plane, military people or dependents. However, I never get to see the passengers because their compartment is aft and separated from the crew's quarters, where I am to ride, just behind the cockpit. All passenger seats face the tail. I, too, rode backwards most of the trip. A safety measure.

I listen to a recorded briefing about the Central European Buffer Zone, the stretch that lets you know you're near Communist territory.

("Give only name, rank and serial number. Talk only to Russian commissioned officers, since the United States does not recognize the East German government.") I wonder if the Russians would settle for my zip code.

My orders identify me as flying MMO, which stands for MAC (Military Airlift Command) Mission Observer. My guide is Lt. Ron Bell of the Information Office at Dover, who is flying ACM, or Additional Crew Member. Bell is 30, from Evansville, Ind. He has recently returned from a 30-day leave which amounted to a cross-country tour with his wife and four children in a VW Fastback, so there is no way this flight can be rigorous to him.

I am not supposed to see several crew members checking out sidearms and stashing them inside their flight fatigues, but I do. The fatigues, also known as MAC pajamas, have zippered pockets all over them.

Most everybody orders a 75-cent snack box and, civilian sport that I am, I go for one, too. There will be coffee, but no additional food, on the plane.

We are aboard at 4:30 a.m., and the plane begins to taxi around 6. Sgt. Mike Martin of Brunswick, Maine, gives me an emergency briefing about ditching procedures, etc., then equips me with a headset so I can hear the cockpit communication.

There is an amusing interchange in which I learn how a little old paper towel helped to get the monster into the skies. The commander has started engines 1 through 4 and now I hear him say: "It's too dark to be taxi-ing around in this fog. We're going to have to open these windows. Anyone got a towel?"

Crew member: "I'll go back and get you some paper towels." He does, and apparently reaches out and begins wiping the mist off the cockpit windows.

Commander: "Be real careful you don't drop that out the window. The engines are running.

The takeoff is long, about a mile and a half, and this is when you really begin wondering if the whale can fly. But it can; noisily, but beautifully. We head north to Nova Scotia, from there to follow a latitude line almost directly to England. There, the plane will unload some cargo and take on a new 8,000 pounds.

Master Sgt. Ray Birch of Chincoteague, Va., a Vietnam veteran, is the primary loadmaster. He tells me the plane is only 500 pounds short of its 712,500 maximum, and that the big item aboard is an engine for another C5, weighing 20,000 pounds. The cargo is on 36 pallets, or portable platforms, wheeled in and out of the plane. The engine is taking up five pallets.

Master Sgt. Chuck Fluharty of Harmony, Md., the assistant standardization flight engineer, invites me to the cockpit and attempts to explain the battery of computers, switches, knobs and dials. They are between, above, and in front of the pilot and co-pilot, and before the navigator and engineer.

Some seven hours after we have left Dover, we see coast of England. It is to be a four-hour stop at Mildenhall. One tire is flat, and there is some engine trouble, this in addition to the cargo exchange. There is dinner at the base, but only Bell and I are permitted to have anything alcoholic. The beer hits the spot.

It is night when we cross the English Channel, a thrilling, moonlit sight from the cockpit. Major Sabey points out Dover, Calais, Dunkirk, Brussels. The lights of the cities form jewelry in the darkness.

Local time in Frankfurt is after midnight when we land, or five hours past Dover time. It has been a 13-hour trip with but a few hours' nap, but I am not too groggy to be intrigued, all over again, by the Galaxy at rest. It actually kneels to accommodate the big loading wagons, which invade it under a nose that is now pointed directly skyward or through the long bays that have opened in the tail.

I'm here, and I still don't believe it.

Her Best Pitch

Or, Backstage at the Burlesque. I wonder who's catching her now?

T here isn't much to tell, really.

All that happened was that the young lady took off all her underwear and tossed it to me.

What else can I say?

Just this: Eat your hearts out, peasants. Enough of this false worldliness.

Bobbye Mack's underwear also is her outerwear when she is at work, because Bobbye is a strip-teaser.

There I was poised in the wings, ready to field her clothing as she tantalizingly removed it for The Playhouse audience.

Bobbye strips with the "This Was Burlesque" show. She is billed as "The Las Vegas Baby Doll" because she is big out that way. Her home town is Lowell, Mass., and you can't do much with that. "The Lowell Baby Doll" doesn't ring. I would like to propose "The Lass From Mass." as having possibilities.

Her mentor is Ann Corio, who was America's Sweetheart (Burley Department) many moves ago. Miss Corio is the star, chaplain, choreographer, m.c., inspiration, director, den mother and straight woman with the troupe. I adore her.

It was Miss Corio, bless her, and Mike Iannucci who set up an evening backstage for me. Iannucci is the producer of the 10-year-old review, a William Bendix-looking guy who is experiencing an Old Home Week. He is a former West Chester State football player.

They suggested that while I was at it, I could be a "catcher" for one of the strippers, to help me get, well, the feel of burlesque. I acquiesced.

I had been watching the show's doll-babies and chuckling at Jerry Lester and the other dirty-old-men comics, from the dimly lighted area off Stage Right, as we in show biz call it.

Late in the first act, Miss Corio introduced me to Miss Mack, who is blonde, shortish, sultry-voiced and a very nice person, all over. Even her handshake is firm. She was about ready to do her solo, dressed in a lot of black stuff.

They turned me over to my catching coach, a tall young man named Thom Kirby, the show technician. He doubles as a catcher. He took me Stage Left and Ann had her dresser, Mrs. Edie Conley, tag along for moral support.

"Good luck. I'll give you a rating when you're through," said Ann.

Kirby told me to snuggle my back against the drape and to the audience in the "Two" zone. One more step, and I would have been in the act.

"Hold your arms like this," he instructed, left hand head-high, right hand at waist. I felt like the deep receiver in an adagio act.

Bobbye began her thing as the orchestra played "Blue Champagne," or something. She swished around the stage sexily, humming and saying little unintelligible things. You could see she was good. Ann Corio enlists no dogs.

Bobbye unzipped what she later told me was "a crepe negligee, with black maribou trim." She sidled towards me and handed, not threw it, to me. I draped it over my left shoulder, as taught. A dozen or so teases later, Bobbye came over with something else, "a black lace gown with beige crepe." It was surprisingly heavy. Mrs. Conley relieved me of both items.

The Las Vegas Baby Doll now was down to pasties and what I would call a long half-slip. It turned out to be a "nylon panel." She eventually gave it to me and spoke as she glided by: "We're in Wilmington, Delaware, dahling." I'll never forget her words.

Kirby told me I could relax for five minutes because Bobbye would be performing that long before "she removes her jock strap."

Her what?

Kirby repeated the term. "That's what everybody calls it, strippers included. Anyhow, this will be the exciting part for you. Sometimes she throws it wild and it hits the floor but don't worry."

I didn't. I merely perspired. I felt somebody holding my right wrist. It was Ann Corio.

"Just checking your pulse," she laughed.

Kirby moved me against another drape, in the "One" zone, the first off the footlights.

I rechecked Bobbye's scene and she was reduced to the narrow, highly cut, diaper that was to be my last fielding chance. This she actually threw to me, about a 3-yarder, and I thought I caught it rather adroitly.

"You're hired," Bobbye cracked into the wings and she continued to midstage to wrap up, or un-wrap up, her performance. All that was between her and an "X" rating were the pasties, her shoes and an almost invisible G-string which I had been told about.

I guess I got a good rating. I asked Miss Corio to autograph a program and she wrote "to the greatest catcher since Yogi Berra."

I owe it all to my pitcher.

Gregory Peck

*I'm a pushover for movie stars. And when they turn
out to be nice people, like this one, I'm really sent.*

The interview with Gregory Peck was scheduled for 10:30
yesterday morning, which was wonderful—except they forgot to tell Gregory
Peck.

But he was courteous enough to give me some time, anyway. He was here
for the meeting of the Presidentially-appointed National Council of the Arts.
I am counting on more arty members of the staff to fill you in on what happened.

A nice lady gave Peck my message and my dilemma, and he broke himself
away from the morning session in the Hotel du Pont's Du Barry Room. He
came out to tell me he had to leave town at 5 p.m. and was deeply interested
in the day's meetings, but could give me about 15 minutes if that would be
enough. It had to be.

"Sometimes these public relations people get things a little mixed up,"
Peck said as we headed for the dining room and coffee.

Heads turned. I had the feeling they weren't turning for me. There is no
mistaking Gregory Peck. He looked as if he had walked right off the TV
screen and Saturday night's "Mirage" re-run. Tall, ruggedly handsome, with
that slow, deep voice, a ready and genuine smile. Conservatively dressed.

I wish I could say I heard somebody ask "Who's the guy with Cartwright?"
but I really didn't.

The archives say Gregory Peck is 56. I didn't bring that up, but during the
conversation he mentioned he was "on the shady side of 50 and the sunny side
of 60."

He now is on a producing kick. His "The Trial of the Catonsville Nine" opens in New York next week. Another property, "Dove", is in the writing stage, and the way Peck sounds, he is in love with its possibilities. It is the true story of a boy—it was expanded from a National Geographic series—who sailed around the world in a 24-foot sloop. There is this girl he met on the Fiji Islands. "Dove" is the name of the boat. It is a love story.

"How about Gregory Peck appearing in a love story again, on the sunny side of 60 as you say?" I asked. "Are you still interested in scripts where you wind up with the girl?"

A sense of humor is among Gregory Peck's endless attributes.

"A mature girl—yes," he answered. "I'm not interested in chasing them in the movies, as I did 20 years ago. An occasional windfall would be all right—like if they knock on my door. I check out the scripts now and then. I'll be playing less-romantic roles. Character roles, more mature roles. I will play my age, because I am happy with my age. I have no desire to be a leading man any more. Besides, this is no day or age for old-fashioned love stories."

It is the day and age for profanity and undressing in gamey movies.

"Yes, and I don't like it. I will have nothing to do with it," Peck commented. "In a sense, the public gets the movies it deserves. They can always stay away. But they don't stay away. They go in large numbers.

"I do think, however, the current trend in moviemaking is running its course. It's just exhibitionism. The public seems to be saying 'Okay, we've seen it all; now show me a little art.' There are signs the better film makers, having experimented with this new freedom, are swinging back to better products with modern approaches. The fast-buck guys with the porno movies will go on, I'm afraid. They might as well be in the sausage business, the stuff they turn out."

Peck speaks so deliberately, I made the mistake of interrupting with a fresh question several times because I thought he was through with the old one. He wasn't this time.

"I will say some movies are good because they opened new areas of subject matters. When you swing back from extremes, something good comes with you, like a new freedom of thinking. The breakdown of rigid taboos, for example, that were based on nothing logical, has to be a good thing. In this respect, films like 'Carnal Knowledge', 'Bonnie and Clyde', 'A Clockwork Orange', were contributory."

I asked the distinguished visitor what was the saltiest thing he had ever said in the movies. He thought.

"I may have called somebody a bitch once," he said. "And I might have God-damned something once, but that's about it. I wouldn't go beyond that. I don't think I have corrupted the youth of America. I did have a scene in bed with a lady."

"Congratulations," I said.

"Thank you," Peck said with a nod. "Very nice, too."

Peck won an Oscar in 1962 for "To Kill a Mockingbird". The award indicates this is the best thing he has ever done.

"I found it the most satisfying," he said, "because it was more like me than anything I have done. Good acting is not versatility. It's depth. This is why Bogart, Cooper, Tracy, Cagney, made such deep impressions on the public. They were interesting men with depth and character. The public is more interested in this than mimicry or the ability to wear false noses.

"I was prepared not to win the Oscar. I don't want to appear overly modest, but I liked the chances of Jack Lemmon because of 'Wine and Roses'."

I asked if there was a leading lady who stuck out in his mind more than any other.

"That's an intriguing way of putting the question," Peck laughed. Come to think of it, it was. I tried again. "Were any of your leading ladies worthy of an Oscar for her performance?"

Peck said it still was an uncomfortable question for him to field. He told the story about Khrushchev on his tour of the United States, when reporters persisted in asking him about his crushing of the Hungarian student revolt while he kept talking about the corn in Iowa or all the cars on our freeways. When they wanted to know why he was so evasive, Khrushchev said, "You ask the questions you want, I give the answers I want."

Peck did say Ava Gardner was "my favorite girl. I made three pictures with her: 'Kilimanjaro', 'On the Beach', 'The Great Sinner'. Ava never won an Oscar, but she is just great to work with. If she comes up with a rich, varied role, she still could win the award."

But just why was Ava his favorite female costar?

Peck rattled off what sounded almost like the Boy Scout motto: "Because she is a terrific girl, honest, generous, down to earth, not vain, beautiful, smart. Is that a good reason?"

It was. It was time for Peck to go back to his meetings—he had given me 30 minutes—and I managed to ease in a query about his political activity. He has been a celebrity-type speaker for Democratic candidates over the years.

"I might make some appearances during the Presidential campaign, when I see who the candidate is," he said. "No, I'm not going to pick out a favorite. I'm not super-active politically. Like all the rest of us, I'm interested. If I believe in a man, I will support him, Democrat or Republican. Usually, it's been a Democrat."

The only other time he was in Wilmington, Peck recalled as he obliged autograph hunters in the lobby, was 1941.

"We opened here in a play called 'Punch and Julie', and the name will give you an idea of its merit," he said. "The great Jane Cowl was in it. We went on to Washington and died in Baltimore. We never did make it to the Henry Miller Theater.

And that was Sunday morning with Gregory Peck. You may remember him. He used to row for the University of California crew.

Claudie's Town

There was violence on the highways early in 1974, and trucker Claudie Nix, minding his own business, drove right into it and was murdered. What a waste of what investigation was to reveal was a fine human being. I went to South Carolina to talk to his family.

S T. STEPHEN, S.C.—You just sit at a window booth in Vilda's Restaurant and the view is State Highway 52. On the other side is a sign that says Albany Felt Works. A road leads to the plant, about a mile to the east.

Claudie Nix drove the Felt Works' tractor-trailer out of that road the first Monday afternoon in February, the start of his weekly run to the home factory in Albany, N.Y.

He turned right. Nix would cross the Santee River and pick up I-95 at Florence.

St. Stephen never saw Claudie Nix alive after that. He was shot and killed the next night as he drove in Delaware, near Harrington. This was during the nationwide shutdown by independent truck drivers.

Someone who thought trucks shouldn't be on the road because the price of diesel fuel was too high fired a bullet from a car and it went through the vent window and into Nix's heart.

That was four months ago. Police say they have no suspects.

Claudie Nix, 50, was to be identified as the father of six children and a deeply religious man. He had been adopted and raised by his grandparents. He was not an independent driver, but an employe of Albany.

I paid the lunch bill at Vilda's and drove to the Felt Works, a neat, sprawling, low brick building. With a payroll of 250, it is the leading industry in this torpid town of 1,800. It is a town split by the Seaboard Coast Line tracks. The mayor, who runs the Texaco station on the south end, just got himself reelected by attracting 264 votes of a total turnout of 449.

The plant makes felt for machinery used by paper companies, felt that acts as a sponge and filter. Nix was in Delaware because he had picked up some raw materials at Du Pont's Seaford plant.

A fellow by the name of Keith Harris now drives for Albany. He applied for the vacancy. The company had nobody in reserve because Claudie had the job for as long as he wanted it and everybody knew that.

"Claudie was our only driver, and in two years he established himself as the best one we've ever had," said the personnel manager, Robert Wall. Wall was on a college recruiting trip in North Carolina at the time of the slaying. "I think he was as satisfied with us as we were with him. A fine employe, a fine man.

"We leased the truck, our only truck. This was a brand-new one, only a couple of hundred miles on it, and the first time Claudie drove it north. He had taken it home to put new bed linen on the sleeper in the cab. It still hasn't been repaired—Harris is driving another one."

Claudie Nix always took a Bible with him. The Bible was his billfold. He put his credentials, his money in it.

Wall smiled. "Claudie would leave on a Monday and come back on a Friday every week, and in the summer if he didn't get back too late, he'd show up for our plant softball games Saturday morning. He pitched. One game last year, I had not done particularly well at shortstop behind him. I missed several balls. Claudie called time, walked over to his pickup truck and came back with a fishnet—for me."

Claudie's widow was waiting for me. The appointment with her had been set up by the Rev. Robert Mullinax, pastor of The Church of God, where Claudie taught a Bible class, sang and played the guitar.

They were all waiting for me, all the Nixes, crowding the cozy mobile home on the unlabeled street. Larry, 16, and Cheryl, 12, lived at home. Linda 27, Claudette 22, Michael 21 and Nina 19 are married and live nearby.

Two of the four grandchildren also were there, and the preacher and his wife. Everybody but Claudie.

Elouise Nix is a warm, ample woman, and it is a blessing she has this nice big family. And that they have each other.

The preacher had told me "Elouise is doing well," but I could sense she had a strong grip on her emotions. If this wound is to be healed, there has not been nearly enough time.

"You know, I tried to get Claudie to take the week off—that very week," she said, "as a vacation. I wanted him to take off because of the strike. I thought it would blow over after that. But he wouldn't. He told me he wasn't going to hurt anybody, and nobody would bother him.

"I always worried, every time he went on the road; more so this time. But Claudie loved his job. He had tried other things over the years, but he was more satisfied doing this."

She said she was not especially interested in seeing that his killer got capital punishment. Only that he be found. "He's got his punishment coming, without that. The FBI told us the only name they had turned in as a suspect was somebody who is mentally sick. If he is that sick, he needs to be put away, where he won't hurt people."

Nina, the 19-year-old who looks like a junior high student, wrote a letter "to the man who killed our father" and asked him to surrender, sending it to the Delaware State Police. "We don't want this man running loose. He may shoot a man with a houseful of little children next time. That would be more tragic than the first time."

Her letter reflected some of her father's religious beliefs. All the children signed it.

"I got the idea from my aunt, Mom's sister, who wrote to the Seaford paper in your state," Nina said, bouncing her child on her knees. "I told Linda what I wanted to do and she said go ahead, to write it like I thought. They all read it and accepted it and signed it."

As the atmosphere relaxed, the kids showed me the family albums and the scrapbook of clippings about their father's death. They even have a copy of the State Police investigator's summary to the Governor, which closes with the defeating "However, at this time, we have no idea who committed this crime. End of report."

I asked the preacher to show me his church and the cemetery. The cinder-block wing under construction, he explained, was to be the new Sunday school in Nix's honor.

Claudie and Elouise Nix sang in a trio at services, right up to the day before he left on his last trip. Now Michael, Nina and Claudette sing. Mrs. Nix listens. A few blocks away, there are artificial flowers on the grave, including the guitar shaped arrangement the church sent.

The price of diesel fuel—whatever happened to that?

The Office Nine

*I like to kid around with My Beloved Phillies. I went into my
Art Buchwald trance and concocted this during the ball players'
threatened strike right before spring training in 1969.
Incidentally, Ruly Carpenter now can pitch all he wants. He's
the club president.*

The scene is the office of the Phillies' president in Connie Mack
Stadium. The time is high noon. Assembled are assorted Phillies' brass.

President Bob Carpenter calls for order: "Gentlemen, this is an emergency
meeting. As you know, the ball players have voted not to report to spring
training unless their pension demands are met. Are there any suggestions
what we will use for ball players at Clearwater?"

General Manager John Quinn: "Bob . . ."

Carpenter: "Mr. Quinn, you are out of order. It has been suggested—by
me—that we, ourselves, man the dikes. In the interest of public relations and
season-ticket sales—after all, we have to have SOMETHING to sell—we
will go to Florida and put on uniforms and work out every day and give interviews."

Secretary-Treasurer George Harrison: "This sounds like an extreme
measure. Why don't we just defer spring training until the dispute is settled?"

Carpenter: "You, of all people, should ask that. When I said emergency, I
wasn't kidding. The ball players' strike is bad enough. What is worse is that
we have paid the Clearwater hotel bill in advance. American Plan, yet."

Harrison: "Oh."

Carpenter: "The ayes have it. I would now like to hear you volunteer for
the position you prefer to play."

Sales Director Frank Powell: "I volunteer to be in charge of the press
room, dinner reservations and cocktail hours."

Carpenter: "You take the word 'play' too literally, Mr. Powell. You will be the right fielder."

Powell: "Good, I have an old pair of sunglasses. Whose uniform should I wear?"

Carpenter: "With that boiler, you will wear the uniforms of Short, Ryan and Fryman. A seamstress will combine them. The hotel has assured me she goes with the bill."

Assistant Secretary-Treasurer Ruly Carpenter: "I volunteer to pitch."

Carpenter: "Sorry, son, that position is spoken for."

Ruly Carpenter: "By whom, dear old Dad?—as if I didn't know."

Carpenter: "By me, son, O heir to my estate and all things material. Any questions?"

Ruly Carpenter: "But, dear old Dad, you couldn't get the ball over the plate even when you were in shape, back at Tower Hill. I, at least, am of a more recent Tower Hill vintage and I've been playing handball every day and—"

Carpenter: "Should I repeat the heir bit?"

Ruly Carpenter: "I volunteer to play third base."

Carpenter: "Mr. Owens, you will catch."

Farm Director Paul Owens: "But I'm left-handed. I played first base in the minors. Can't I play first base?"

Carpenter: "We cannot sell any season tickets with a left-handed first baseman. You will be a drawing card."

John Quinn: "I volunteer to trade myself for three junior executives."

Carpenter: "No chance. We need your experience. Besides, think of the fan appeal of a second baseman in suspenders."

Quinn: "I'll get killed."

Carpenter: "On second thought, second base is no place for suspenders— you'll get all tangled up in them on pivot throws. You are the center fielder."

Publicity Director Larry Shenk: "I volunteer to spell Mr. Quinn in the out- field."

Carpenter: "Anything to do with spelling, you're out. You are the burly, aggressive first baseman."

Traveling Secretary Charley Meister: "Put me down for second base."

Carpenter: "Fine. I can already see the headline: 'Cookie Meister, 250- pound Keystone Sacker . . .' "

Meister: "Is it all right if I smoke cigars in spring training?"

Carpenter: "Yes, but only on the field. I can't stand a smokey clubhouse."

Harrison: "I will take a shot at left field, but who's going to watch over the expenses?"

Carpenter: "You are. You will have plenty of time to do your paper work in left field, with me pitching. You will not get a ball all day."

Ruly Carpenter (mumbling): "And neither will the catcher."

Carpenter: "We still need a shortstop, and there are only eight of us here. Anybody else in the front office we can use?"

Powell: "Well, we have a janitor, the elevator man, three secretaries and—oh, yes, the girl in charge of the hot-line telephone to your wife."

Carpenter: "That's it! She's the shortstop."

Powell: "The girl, sir?"

Carpenter: "No—my wife. The National League's first coeducational family club! Look at the ink those lady jockeys get—a lady shortstop will be a sensation."

Ruly Carpenter: "You'll never get Mom out in that sun. This is getting ridiculous. Why don't we just give the ball players what they want?"

Carpenter: "You have just talked yourself into batting ninth, son—and you might blow the will, too. Give in, indeed! Besides, I'm starting to like the sound of this ball club. The way we've been going, it might be an improvement. I just can't wait to hook up with Walter O'Malley in an old-fashioned mound duel."

Ruly Carpenter: "Oh, brother."

The meeting adjourns. Pitcher and catcher will report Feb. 21, the rest of the squad March 1. Tradition, you know.

52,000 Weddings

I'm not much for gambling, Las Vegas type. I went out there and got my kicks doing stories like this. The slot machines didn't get a quarter.

LAS VEGAS—There are five Yellow Pages of them.

Wedding chapels. No appointment necessary. Open 24 hours. Armed with a license from the Clark County Courthouse, you can get yourself merged, immediately, at a chapel. No waiting period, no blood test.

Not for nothing do they call this "The Marriage Capital of the World". 52,000 ceremonies here last year. A thousand a week. In the old days, you'd call it Elkton West.

At the Little White Chapel, if you mention the ad in the telephone book, you get a free tape recording of the ceremony.

At Cupid's Wedding Chapel, "we arrange everything for a beautiful & lasting marriage, including flowers, photos, rings and recordings."

There is a Hitching Post Wedding Chapel, of course. "Personal and payroll checks accepted" at the Silver Bell. The Sweetheart Desert Bell offers "dressing room, free corsages and gift."

All of them handle major credit cards. That's nice. Right from the start, the couple gets a charge. They might as well get used to it.

I picked out the Courthouse Chapel to scout. Uniquely named, it is right across the street from the downtown courthouse, on the corner of Bridger Ave. and Casino Center Boulevard. Next door to it is Alfred Becker, Law Offices. Then Barbara and Dave's Bail Bonds. Then the In and Out Coffee Shop, and that also could serve as the name of a chapel.

I wound up going to a wedding. Matter of fact, I was the whole audience.

The owners, Mr. and Mrs. Elvis Olds, were on duty. He is 28 and prefers the nickname of Jerry. She is Pat Olds, and they bought the business from her father with the money Jerry made selling insurance.

They are a nice couple. It took them a little while to relax; they said they were sensitive about bad publicity their profession has received over the years.

Olds admitted some of it was warranted.

"Some of our competition, they do things we don't like," he said. "They are gougers, for one thing. They will charge what they think the traffic will bear. They have cab drivers and motel clerks on their payroll, then include this cost in what they're charging the couple to get married."

There were artificial corsages displayed on a wall. A refrigerated case of orchid corsages. A display of rings.

Mrs. Olds said she had been on duty since 8 a.m. Now it was 2 p.m., and she had five weddings. All of them were walk-ins. She had one appointment for this day, at 7 p.m. She said they performed 1,500-2,000 ceremonies last year.

The price is $20, plus $1.50 for two witnesses. If you want rings or flowers or corsages or photos, they are extra. You can buy a garter for $3 and a veil for $10.

The license costs from $6 to $16, depending upon when it is purchased at the courthouse, which also never closes. You can get married in the courthouse, if you choose, by what is known as a civil commissioner, who could be a night watchman or a clerk. They have taken the performance rights away from Justices of the Peace.

A couple entered. I'd say they were around 45 years old. He wore a short-sleeved shirt on a cold day, she a red dress. Pat Olds said they catered mostly to "average people," and this couple qualified.

Mrs. Olds greeted them and asked to see the license. She then addressed him as C. C. and her as Doris, and asked them about the weather in Pomona, Calif.

The couple sat down as Mrs. Olds telephoned for a minister.

Then C. C. thought of something. "How much is this going to cost?"

$23 and whatever he cared to give the minister, he was told.

"How are you doing in the casinos?" Mrs. Olds asked.

C. C. said he didn't gamble, and Mrs. Olds said well, he was gambling right now, wasn't he?

"Not really," he replied. "This is different. This is our second time around, to each other."

The minister arrived in minutes. Jimmy B. Terrell, evangelist, Church of Christ. Young. Mustache and glasses. Olive suit.

"C. C." he asked, "how many rings are we using?"

To which C. C. replied, "None."

The three of them took four steps and they were in the chapel. Olds motioned that it was all right for me to join them.

The room was like 9-by-12. There were seven tiny, white-upholstered pews.

A bible, an arch covered with white satin, two candelabra.

The minister performed the ceremony without using a book. Just as he started with "In the presence of God . . . " organ music came through a speaker. "O Promise Me", followed by "I Love You Truly". Softly, and scratchily.

C. C. and Doris kissed and I congratulated them: I thought I had earned $1.50 as a witness, but what the proprietors witness for this charge is the marriage license, not the ceremony.

On the way out, Terrell told me he is on call for six or seven chapels. This one had taken about five minutes.

Lana Turner got married in this chapel, among many other places. So did Mickey Rooney, and likewise. Lana married her No. 7 at 2 o'clock in the morning. Mrs. Olds said Lana's husband keeps calling the chapel to pinpoint the time of the marriage. Seems he is trying to prove Lana's divorce from No. 6 really hadn't been final at the time.

Jerry Olds told me about the young fellow who came in with his bride-to-be, showed the license and then asked to use the men's room.

"I told him it was in the back," Olds said. "He went there and we haven't seen him since. He kept on going."

One shaky fellow of 35, who had been under the impression he was a confirmed bachelor, forgot to wear socks and his shoes didn't match. There have been ceremonies in which a witness carried a shotgun. This was for pictorial purposes, but very obviously appropriate, nonetheless.

Broderick Crawford served as best man at his son's wedding. George Segal made a movie here last fall. "Love in Blume" and Warner Brothers paid the Courthouse Chapel a fee for using it in a 40-second scene that took six hours to film.

"We get happy people in here, for the most part." Mrs. Olds said. "Some, they look like they couldn't care less. We've had young couples marry and soon as the ceremony is over, the parents grab their son or daughter and take them off in opposite directions. Incidentally, the marriage laws here are lenient, but the boy still has to be 21 and the girl 18. Either that, or show us notarized proof of consent."

The Olds themselves were married in a chapel. The Silver Bell. The minister was Jerry's cousin, so that was free. Pat's father picked up the tab. The Silver Bell is bigger, they told me; more room for guests.

Outside was a little "garden" they use when the weather's warm, mostly for pictures. Olds said it might not look it, but he had $6,000 worth of concrete in it. He was right. It didn't look it.

The Courthouse Chapel thinks of everything. They even have a Spanish-speaking minister on call.

Well, almost everything. I thought of something after I left. I may try to corner the market. I will install the rice concession in all the chapels.

Bring Soap

My next reincarnation, I want to be a travel writer. They get to go to places like this all the time. This was what is known as a junket. Club Mediterranee was trying to impress newspeople that this spot off Tunis would be just the thing for American tourists. With me, the club succeeded. It was fantastic.

D'JERBA LA DOUCE, TUNISIA—Anyone for Tunis? I came all this way just so I could use that line. I didn't dare try it on the natives, though, for fear they might slip a little ground pottery into my roast lamb with couscous.

But how does that glamorous dateline grab you? "All this way" is really that. D'jerba La Douce—no relation to Irma, they tell me—is an island in the Mediterranean off the southeast coast of Tunisia. On the map it is shaped like a tiny United States.

They are trying to make a Miami Beach out of D'jerba, and I can only deduce that somebody must be mad at the island. I hope they fall short.

Air France flew a bunch of newspaper and magazine people out of New York to take a look at the local version of Club Mediterranee's "modern vacation village". We came by way of Paris and Tunis, the capital of Tunisia, which is 600 miles to the north, and the last leg was by Air Tunisia. While we were here, Air France inaugurated direct Paris-D'jerba service. I can't believe they would go to that extreme to exterminate my Tunis line.

I was sort of an imposter in the gang, which was dominated by travel writers. Horace Sutton sent his secretary, Dena Kaye, who turns out to be Danny Kaye's daughter. They impressed me.

"Haven't seen you since Guam," one said to another in the lounge at Kennedy Airport.

Or . . . "Didn't we make the Martinque trip together?"

I tried to cover up the only sticker on my suitcase. It said Hershey, Pa.

First, let me lay a little Club Mediterranee on you. It is a Paris based international vacation organization, with 60 "villages" in 18 countries, mostly Europe. They call it a club because you join for $10 single and $14 family, and this makes the vacations available. There are villages in Egypt and Tahiti and Morocco and Majorca and all over and they're still building them, like filling stations, at the rate of three a year. One of their few disasters was an American experiment, a French type ski resort at Bear Valley, Calif., that didn't cut it.

Exotic vacations at bargain prices, is the party line. After only a short time on D'jerba, I found it to be out of this world, literally. They even ask you not to bring a radio. No T.V. No newspapers.

"The idea," said Mike Mooney of London, a virile kewpie doll of a social director, "is to get the guest close to nature, as far as possible from the machine age and everyday life."

Bring your own soap and towels. No tipping. No room service. Not even a room key. The package includes three daily meals with all the wine you can absorb, and the use of all sports and recreational facilities, plus instruction. You take a tennis lesson or a swimming lesson, no extra charge. I spoke to several guests from France and they said the all-inclusive sports program was the thing that sold them. You swim either in one of the biggest pools I've ever seen, or the amazingly clear and shallow sea. I did manage to hit the sports department with one question they couldn't answer: how come no diving board? Maybe you have to bring your own.

I discovered Club Mediterranee has a reputation as resorts that appeal to swingers and that it is not too difficult to get swung.

"Yes, we know of these rumors," said Mooney in answer to my leer, "and we don't try to deny it and neither do we advertise it. People make of it what they want to."

In other words, no house detectives need apply.

They have coeducational, all-out sun bathing, if that is your thing, on roofs. "Bronzage integral." they call it, French for tan all-over. No cameras permitted. I went up on a roof on a pretext that now escapes me. I saw some all-out girls on the next roof and a chicken guy, in trunks on another. I decided they needed a new orgy director and almost applied.

The club on D'jerba can accommodate 600 people; this week, there must have been 400. I handicapped the majority to be married couples in their late 20s or early 30s, mostly French. They are beautiful specimens. The bikini is very big. Make that very small, and especially on the guys with their revoltingly flat stomachs.

The club has 800,000 members in Europe and 60,000 in the U.S. and Canada, and sells 300,000 packages a year. It is going after more American members, which is why we were there. There is one staffer from the U.S., a water-ski instructor from Boise, Idaho, named John Radcliffe. He is a professional snowskier who had gone to France for advanced training and wound up job hunting. Only weeks-new to the D'jerba scene, he carries a little dictionary with him.

They are going to need more English-speaking staffers if they want American trade, and this they have in mind. The only American guests here were Norman and Marge Kurtz, from New York. He's an attorney who also is in the rock-music business—Jethro Tull is a client—and they had gone to Paris on business and been touted on the side-trip to D'jerba. I encountered them on the beach.

"Seems to be a great spot," Kurtz said when I asked for an opinion, "but I do miss the English language. Americans like to feel in, you know. With nobody to talk to, they're out. But there is certainly enough to do and no pressure to do it—the tennis, the discotheque, the theater, the swimming, the sailing, the shops. I agree they have a beautiful clientele. I see a few uncles and nieces, but I get the feeling, like you, most of 'em are Mr. and Mrs."

Marge Kurtz had a complaint there were "too many pretty men" on the scene. She had caught the staff's show in the 600-seat theater the night before and agreed with me there were like two too many female impersonations. But this, I understand, is as much a part of continental entertainment as our stand-up comic.

The staff is Beautiful People. G. O.s, they call them, an abbreviation for "gentile organisateur," or nice staff members. The guests are G. M.s for "gentile membre." The G. O.s stand at the bar with you and eat with you and there is no "sir" nor "madam" from them. They dress up in their camp stuff at night and it's almost too much. The guys come swirling in with their capes and robes and caftans and their token and charming English, and there is no mistaking a liberal sprinkling of gayness. One G. O. looked exactly like a French Joe Namath. You mix them with the formally informal attire of the French guest, and . . . well, I just stared and reached for another Tunisian beer.

Speaking of bars, no money changes hands. You do it with pop beads, from a necklace or a bracelet you buy for either $15 or $10 in dinar. A dinar is $2.12. I started out wearing a necklace that became a choker on the third night.

D'jerba's club is 15 months old. It is the second one on the island. The first, still operating, is one of the pioneer or "traditional" villages. All living accommodations first were under tent, and now are straw huts. No electricity. The fun is the beach and cookouts, not to mention the huts. This setup had to inspire the "swinging" reputation.

In the modern village, the whitewashed-masonry bungalows form a labyrinth that drove me crazy. Just when I've learned how to find my pad, it's time to leave the island. But they are nice quarters. Old-worldish. Adjoining courtyard. Twin beds, private bathroom, bottled water. Positively no single occupancy.

The sun always shines, mostly hot. Chilly at nights. The meals are feasts. The lunches are gastronomical orgies. They did much better when they didn't try to appease the Americans. Like, the "American chicken" (fried) was at best a near-miss, and the steak fought back and was saved only by the French fries and the pizza course. You had to be a grown man to drink the Turkish-type coffee. Man, was that rugged. And you drink it from soup bowls.

The prices? The two week packages for D'jerba, from New York, are $626 for the low season, $669 for the peak. I recommend the joint.

They took us on a side tour, to the eerie, rocky deserts and the cave-dwellers and the centuries-old plains of Tunisia, to another time and still another world. It was like putting down a copy of Playboy and picking up the Bible.

Troopers Mourn

The next lawmen to be gunned down in my area had been in this very funeral procession for the Delaware trooper. Two town policemen from Kennett Square, Pa. were ambushed and slain, less than a year later.

The aluminum threshhold must have been loose, for it clanked whenever a policeman's boot struck it.

In they marched, 1,100 of them, two-by-two, into the church. They uncovered and held hats or helmets over their hearts. Coming in from the dark and rainy day—funereal, is what the weather was—they muddied the red rug inside the door and then they were on flagstone and then inside the sanctuary and they went single-file down the right-hand aisle. The green carpeting muffled their steps.

The remains of Trooper Dave Yarrington were in a flag-covered casket in front of the altar. It couldn't be open, because it was a bullet smashing into the left side of his face that had killed him. There were two framed photographs atop the casket—a wedding picture, one of Yarrington in uniform.

"File past the casket without stopping and keep your hat over your left breast until seated," was one of the "Ground Rules" that had been read to them at the assembly point at Brandywine Raceway, 5 miles away.

It took 30 solemnly awesome minutes for the troopers from seven states and the policemen with patches that said Yonkers and Chester and Bethany Beach and Winslow and Trenton and dozens of other places, to pass the casket. One stopped. He knelt, quickly. Some looked at the photographs as they passed.

1,100 policemen, and what I was thinking I was afraid to say. But it was said in the patrol car, riding to the cemetery.

Bill Fugate, who is the captain of the Penny Hill barracks, Troop 1, was in the front seat with his lieutenant-driver, Pete Steil. There were 300 cars with headlights on, roof lights whirling. It was a magnificent sight and it made you shiver, and I'll never forget it.

"It came to me during the services," said Fugate, "that I didn't have any tears in my eyes. I guess we're all cried out."

Steil said the words I had been thinking, "Yes, until the next time. Who, and when?"

Fugate, who was shot himself six years ago, said what worried him were the turnpikes, the freeways. "There are so many criminals using them. And you stop 'em in so many isolated areas."

Who, and when? Was the next Ron Carey or Dave Yarrington marching in that second beautiful display of respect? No wonder people may have been cried out. Two burials in four days for two morally powerful young troopers, young husbands, young fathers, killed so senselessly.

Who, and when? The questions are obscene, but inescapable. The pastor didn't want them to be asked again, in his strong sermon about a gentle, sensitive 24-year-old. Asa C. Martin demanded we "put men on the bench in the halls of justice who dwell in fear of God and enforce the law, even to the point of capital punishment."

The anger, the tears, they are draining, and they are binding. The long line of cars going down Shipley Road to the church passed grade-school children lined up on a sidewalk, and I saw teachers biting their lips and crying. I watched the troopers in the honor guard outside the church standing at attention with wet eyes. On Red Oak Road near the cemetery, an old man on a corner bared his head and wept.

"There is more good coming out of this than I could ever believe," Fugate said as he noticed the old man. "The pendulum is swinging the other way. You wouldn't believe the number of kids bringing in cans of coins for the Carey-Yarrington fund. And the people who called in, offering rooms in their homes for visiting police."

The fury abates. Bill Fugate had returned from a Florida-Bahamas holiday vacation at 5 p.m. on a Monday and at 2:30 the next morning there was this call from Dan Bramble at the barracks. Ron Carey was shot. Also Trooper Yarrington. Carey mentioned first because he was Troop 1's man.

The commander hustled to his office. Carey was dead. For the next 14 hours, two days removed from Disney World, Fugate was engaged in the futile manhunt for the two-bit desperado from Ohio and his two-bit girlfriend.

"The first thing you think of," the tall captain recalled, "Is get 'em—and you hope somebody gets to 'em before you do. But time goes on, and you lose your anger. You hope the Lord will take care of things.

"I get the feeling something more is involved in this than just this earth. Look at all the million-to-one shots. The two troopers backing into a holdup. The perpetrators' car going 90 miles an hour and stopping without an accident on a road that was a sea of mud. Their getting cordoned off, and getting away. Then the man getting shot in the back of the head in another highway chase."

Yesterday morning at Troop 1, they tried hard to evade what was past and what was coming up. There was kidding about putting out an APB for a tardy trooper, about getting the patrol cars washed on a rainy day, about hats that might fail inspection. Irv Smith, the sergeant who is an ex-Marine and who too soon was about to command his second honor guard, picked up the triangularly packed flag from the bookcase, the one that was to cover the casket. There was no way to escape the clock.

"It's getting to the point where we have to clown a little—this is getting to us," Fugate said as he put on his jacket. "We've been hard on our wives, our friends, through all this."

At a time like this, a commanding officer must wish he was a car salesman, or an accountant.

"It's not like that," the captain said. "What happens is that everybody blames himself. Like the application investigator, the one who okayed the boys for service. Or me, for giving Carey that assignment that put him in the area."

The troopers headed for the raceway, leaving a token force. The detectives stayed behind, still working on the case. Troopers from Delaware, Pennsylvania and Maryland all were involved, and nobody has had time to sit down and critique all the information. Like just how were the troopers shot and could this answer possibly prevent another man from being killed, or wounded?

Trooper Carey will not be replaced in Troop 1 nor Dave Yarrington in Troop 6. The reason is manpower, or lack of it. But they are irreplaceable. The pastor said it: "This double tragedy is really a greater loss than we can sustain as a state and as a nation. We lost two God-fearing defenders of the law who knew how to mingle mercy with justice . . . their deaths have reduced the ranks of the godly by two too many."

This day the rifles were fired and the "Taps" were played for David C. Yarrington. They buried him on a rainy day in Silverbrook Cemetery and you wept for him and the pale girl widow who leaned hard on her trooper escort.

The thousand-plus policeman marched silently from the graveside, in waves, and Lancaster Avenue became alive with their four-abreast cars and their spinning red lights. They drove home to seven states and the questions went with them.

Who, and when?

Naked City, Ind.

This is how you, uh, cover a contest in a nudist camp. And was it ever camp. To show you what an all-around sport I have become, I flew to this event from the Democratic convention in Miami Beach.

With some startling exceptions, it looked like a crowd that might have been gathered around an exhibit at the Harrington Fair. Six-deep at the perimeter, the sun beating on them, they stared.

The startling exceptions weren't wearing clothes. Neither were what they were staring at.

This was a nudist camp called Naked City in the Indiana woods about a two-hour drive south from Chicago. I came to stare, too, at the first Miss Nude World Beauty Pageant.

There must have been a couple of thousand people sitting and standing around the "Sun Dial", a concrete circle in the middle of which protrudes a big, gilded, inverted female leg, bent at the knee. They had paid $10 a couple or $10 a single male or $5 a single female. They even socked the newspapermen $5. A cover charge?

You could undress in your car, if you wanted, and walk in naked and stick around to play volleyball, bounce on the ever-popular trampolines or swim in the pool. Deeper in the camp were the tents, the cabins and the trailers that the regulars use.

The naked people were startling only until you got used to them, which I never did. Me, I choked up. I didn't undress (where could I have clipped my pen?) and neither did most customers, who came to see, not to be seen.

I almost broke up at my first nude. He was a sourfaced old guy, wearing nothing but white socks and black shoes. Each sock had a lump in it. Either he needs a surgeon, I deduced, or this is how he carries his money. Anyhow, he was standing there arms akimbo and this nice folksy, dressed couple walked up and asked him how to get to the restaurant.

He unfolded his arms and pointed and got into a conversation with them and it was the silliest sight you ever saw. The nice couple thanked him and headed for the Adam and Eve Restaurant.

They have this headquarters called the Roundhouse, with mirrors for outside walls, and several Miss Nude World entries were posing in front of them. Cameras, of course, were all over the place, but you weren't allowed to use them in the camping area. Each girl was attached to the string of a large pink balloon that designated her "country." One contestant was Miss Nude Upper Volta and she was hefty enough to be the whole Volta. The girls just had to be from show biz, I figured. Go-go dancers, exotic dancers, that league.

The show was billed for 1 p.m. and it was more than an hour late starting. They must have had trouble finding coat hangers, maybe, in the undressing room. The wait was interminable. I cased the crowd. There was one naked guy who looked like Walter Cronkite sitting on the cement with those just outside the plastic barrier, camera ready. I checked him out later, when the sun really began boiling, and he had shifted to his haunches.

I saw some half-naked girls in the audience—topless—and one completely naked, holding hands with a naked boyfriend. Most of the all-outers, the regulars, were back in the woods.

At 1 p.m., the only action was several naked officials milling around chairs and the microphone. A guy in clothes distributed printed pictures of Suzanne Pritchard, "North America's No. 1 Sex Bomb, 4-feet-10, 44-23-34." Her agent's name was listed. He said she was going to be a judge.

At 1:20, there came an announcement that Jim Fisher had lost his wallet. Then we were told the show was being delayed because they were waiting for a limousine and also a helicopter bringing in such judges as June Wilkinson, Johnny Ray and Archie of the Hee-Haw Show.

They sent out Miss Nude America 1971 to walk around the Sun Dial posing and waving and plastically smiling. Valerie-somebody, and she cheated. She wore the bottom half of a bikini. I must admit the rest of her was disturbing. A record played "Miss Nude America" ("All she wears is a big smile, for her kiss I'd walk a mile"). Take that, Bert Parks.

Suzanne Pritchard, the kid with the 44, took a turn, wearing only pumps and a flowered G-string. I think it was a geranium. Short and blonde and round and most definitely a 44. To give you an idea of how long the wait was, people eventually got bored looking at Suzanne. There were four more appeals for Jim Fisher's wallet and Jim even made a personal appearance. They sent around Valerie and Suzanne four times each and they introduced Valerie's naked husband.

At 1:46 a helicopter landed dustily and the emcee asked for a big hand for it. I saw a naked guy in the audience squirming on a metal chair. The crowd was starting to growl. At 2:07 the judges appeared, led by June Wilkinson in red slacks and a very busy halter.

Finally, at 2:09, here came the girls and their balloons. They circled the floor and sat in an arc on backless chairs with orange webbing. I itemized the chests and divided by two and got a total of 26 candidates.

I'll say one thing for the contest. They don't fool around with talent. All each girl had to do was walk in front of the crowd, pirouette for the judges, and sit down. Meantime, the emcee was giving you inside stuff that told you what the girls were really like.

Did you know that Miss Nude Sweden's favorite politician is Angela Davis? And that Miss Greece's favorite number is 3?

You gleaned the true international flavor of the event with the very first turn in the alphabetical procession. Miss Australia, the emcee said, is from Indianapolis. For each girl, there was an alleged national anthem played. Most of them sounded like Hit Dirges of 1938, and if that was the Marseillaise they played for Miss France, then I'm Charles Boyer.

The girls were very watchable. The emcee happened to mention that Miss Nude Ireland was 34 years old, which explained what there was about her I liked. After the first six introductions, or from Miss Egypt on, the girls had hot seat marks on their fannies. I hope you appreciate this reporting.

The judges took more than 20 minutes to vote and they kept playing those funeral records and did things like introduce Mr. Nude America, who was wearing sunglasses. Both Valerie and Suzanne took bows—and it wasn't easy—for the umpteenth time.

Finally, the big news. Four runnersup, and now, Miss Nude World: Miss Canada!

I think everybody approved. She was a cute, small blonde with a pixie haircut. They gave her a flower spray and a green ribbon and she climbed to the top of a ladder with wheels on it and the four runnersup stood on the stairs. I saw this tableau from the rear and it was very effective.

Mr. Nude America took off his shades and gave Miss Nude World a big kiss. Then the owner of the camp, who is a paraplegic named Dick Drost, had Miss Nude World sit on his lap and they toured the Sun Dial in his wheelchair. It was about this time that I wished I were some place else.

First, though, I had to get the information on the winner. I went into the crowded Roundhouse. There was a naked guy in the whirlpool and a naked great-grandmother type was selling souvenirs. I pushed my way into the office and confronted Miss Nude World, nee Miss Canada.

I know you will find this hard to accept, but she is a stripper. Her stage name—are you ready?—is Vegas Jones. She is 21 and she is from Portsmouth, Va., which is only a few miles from Montreal. She is single, 36-24-35. She likes Burt Reynolds, seafood, George McGovern, baseball and the Alka-Seltzer commercials. Her pet peeve is an Afghan. I forgot to ask whether she meant the dog, the robe or anybody from Afghanistan. She would most like to be marooned with Peter Fonda. I looked in her eyes all during the interview. I didn't want to be uncouth. She has green eyes.

Vegas Jones now is $500 richer. She will get another $500 if she shows up to crown next year's winner. Each girl who entered got $50. That's not bad, considering what they saved on costumes.

Mike Royko

The interview—this is the second half of it— originally was scheduled for my hotel in Chicago. Mike Royko's car broke down and I wound up talking to him in his office. The way he writes, the rest of us should be selling aluminum siding. His only weakness is his car.

CHICAGO—Mike Royko gave me an answer I didn't expect, which I should have expected.

"How does it feel to win a Pulitzer?" was the question. I had asked it more or less as a disguised and tardy congratulation.

The strong-man columnist of the Chicago Daily News and a syndicated string that includes the Evening Journal, won a Pulitzer Prize last year.

You know how he felt to receive the most distinguished award in the business? "Flat."

"I liked having it out there as a dream, still waiting to be won," Royko said.

"I was surprised I won it. I don't want to sound arrogant, but I thought I'd get it in 1969. That's the first year they included a category for columnists. They gave it to Marquis Childs.

"1968 was the best year I ever had. I wrote up a storm. I wrote all the big stories. I worked hard. There was so much going on, life was simple. I wrote 20 straight columns on the Democratic convention here.

"By contrast, 1971 was a tough year. Not a lot doing, not a political year. No cities burning. No assassinations. All that had happened in '68, and I saw what the other guys were writing about them and I thought I did better."

I looked around the cluttered little office for an Oscar, or something. A Joseph?

"The Pulitzer must be the least ceremonial award of them all," Royko said. "You'd get a better-looking trophy from West Cupcake Teachers College. What you get is a scroll and a check for a thou'. But the important thing you win is that for the rest of your life, you're identified with a Pulitzer.

"In a way, I could have done without it and preferred that it come later. So much was happening to me otherwise in an ego-puffing way. The book was a best-seller. The column with a Chicago dateline was being accepted nationally."

The book was "Boss: Richard J. Daley of Chicago". Royko long has been the boil on the well-publicized fanny of the mayor and patronage emperor. They talked him into doing his probing in book form. It sold 100,000 and another 750,000 in paperback. Chicagoans lined up to buy it.

I asked the author if "Boss" had made him a rich man.

"Well, I paid for an awful lot of missions over Hanoi," said Royko, a known dove. "Every April, I would go down to the corner accountant and pay him 10 bucks to make out my income tax. Then I write a book and I'm talking to tax lawyers. I have eliminated one worry: I have set up my kids' college education. But I spend money fast. My wife and I had a grand tour of Europe last summer. The boat trip, the works."

A Chicago group is making a musical comedy out of "Boss". A movie would be tougher. They'd need Daley's permission. I asked Royko which actor he'd prefer in the title role. He mentioned first Rod Steiger, then eliminated him because "Steiger is always playing Steiger". Then he went on to Brando, Gleason, George C. Scott.

"You know, once they convinced me I should write the book, I was enthusiastic," he said. "I was curious to see if I could write one. 2,000 words was the longest piece I had ever written for the paper. It became fun to write something and not think about the length, or the daily deadline.

"And what a racket these authors have. A guy writes a book a year and he can live off it, meantime doing a magazine piece or two for walking-around money. A very nice life. I'd like to do another—I've roughed out some ideas. But I wouldn't attempt to do it while getting out a daily column. I was really tired for a year. The after-effect."

All of a sudden, there was Mike Royko on a promotional tour.

"I had done enough moonlighting on TV and radio here to be comfortable at it," he said. "Everybody who writes a column in Chicago pops up on some kind of talk show, and I had been a regular panelist on a TV interview show.

"I'll tell you when it felt strange. There I was standing in the wings of the Cavett show in New York, ready to go on and plug the book, and the band starts playing 'Chicago' to usher me in. I didn't know whether to do a buck-and-wing, or what. Everything has to be show biz, I guess."

Royko does not do public speaking. He does not like this "celebrity crap" that goes with success. He can break 80 but they can't drag him to a celebrity golf tournament. They wanted him to endorse a beer. "I have tasted that beer," was his answer, "and it stinks."

The son of a Polish mother and a tavern-keeping, Polish-Ukrainian father, Royko joined the Daily News staff in 1959 as a rewrite man. A college dropout, he had gone into the Air Force and in the last year of his hitch, was assigned to a base newspaper. Then he went to work for a chain of neighborhood papers here. In 1956, he joined the City News Bureau, which he described as "a local wire service, a combination news agency and training ground."

He was 26 when he came to the Daily News. Four years later, he started writing two columns a week in addition to his country-government beat. He became a full-time columnist in 1964.

"Jan. 1 is the date I celebrate the start of a regular column," he said. "And every year, the whole town holds parties the night before. Isn't that nice of them?"

Royko wrote a column on Lyndon Johnson's abdication that received a tremendous play and inspired 2,000 readers to write him letters.

"I felt sorry for Johnson when he decided not to run again, even though I was against the war," Royko said. "I agreed with his decision. But the viciousness of youth's stand against the guy repelled me. I was in a bar when the word came in, and all the young people cheered. They were totally unforgiving. That's what I wrote about."

Royko's expression of his feelings after the Dr. King assassination drew a similar amount of mail.

"I guess the one that pleased me most professionally," Royko said, "was when they tossed Daley out at the convention in Miami beach. I had 90 minutes to write a column and dictate it for the first edition. Everyone told me it was a helluva column. It made me feel like a pro, like I could still make it on the rewrite bank."

Royko is pleased with the national acceptance of his column, if only to dispel a theory that irritated him: That you had to be in New York or Washington to write one. ("What happens to people in Chicago could happen to anybody anywhere"). He comes up with so many little guys-in-trouble stories and so many obviously investigative columns, I felt he must have a stable of paid informers.

"I never paid anybody for tips," Royko said. "My best sources are the 200,000 readers. I get tips from ordinary people. They call me because they know I'll do something about their problems, or their friends' problems. Oh, there are people in government I can call for information, but my bread-and-butter is the average guy."

He does have an assistant, either a young man or woman who helps him dig. He is partial to hiring the non-college type who is industrious, intelligent and has an instinct for the business, because he does not have a degree himself. After a year and a half, Royko passes his helper on to the newsroom staff and recruits another.

Royko loves his work and Chicago. In a way, he has to love the cartoon politician Mayor Daley, too. Daley is half his act.

I wondered if Mrs. Royko loved his work, too.

"No," he replied, "she would rather I do something else. If I went home and told her I was quitting to start teaching journalism at Northwestern, she'd be delighted. The long hours, the pressures of this job, she doesn't like. And I'm sure she still thinks of the pickets around our house, the brick through the window. I don't dare mention the possibility of another book, and no more days off for a while. She'd get nervous as hell."

One more question. I wanted to know if he could describe the Daley administration in a word.

Royko thought for a while.

"The word," he said, "is Daley."

His kind of town, Chicago is. My kind of writer, Royko is.

The Lady Caddy

I didn't get around to playing golf in Japan my first trip there, for the Olympics. I made up for it in 1971. The gal caddies must have been good for my game. I haven't come close to a 103 since.

TOKYO—My caddy wore a bonnet and red gloves, and was strictly embraceable.

No, I haven't been over here too long. My caddy wasn't gay. She was a she.

They do not have male caddies on Japan's golf courses. I asked the club manager how come, and he said, "I personally would not have them. All they would want to do is play golf."

This was at the Ibaraki Golf Club, two hours north of Tokyo through impossible traffic, both ways. You must love golf to tackle this. Hideo Nishioka does. He was my host for the day. He is a tailor. I got to know him during the 1964 Olympics and it wasn't easy, because he doesn't speak English.

He contacted me this trip with a golf invitation through daughter Hiroko—"Roko" for short, a recent college graduate. I warned him my golf was terrible, but he insisted. Mr. Nishioka, who is 54, and his wife were to form a threesome with me, with Roko going along as interpreter.

Tokyo was gloomy with heavy rain as the four of us took off in the family's tiny four-door Nissan Skyline. I sat up front where the seat was adjusted to Mr. Nishioka's legs, and he is a little guy. I felt as if it would take me all winter to straighten up, once I was delivered.

Papa-san fought the buses and trucks and cars and narrow bridges and roads and we finally made it to the countryside. Ibaraki is two courses, a beautiful layout. The rain had ceased and it was warmish, but the weather had limited the day's players to a very few and for this the Americano hatchet was glad.

The caddies were on hand to lift equipment from the truck when we drove up. Mr. Nishioka had supplied my gear, and off we went.

I watched the women with great interest. Each attached a bag to a cart she pushed like a baby carriage. From the handle swung a canvas knapsack, containing dirt and a trowel. This was fertilizer, to fill up divots. As the caddies went down the fairways, they would repair any scraped shots they encountered. Each cart also contained an old Asahi beer can that swung on a wire, the golfer's ash tray.

Well, I had fun. I can't be serious about golf, not the way I play, so I decided to have a relaxing time while not disturbing Mr. Nishioka's game. He is a 14-handicapper at this club and he hits the ball far and straight, with good form. Every time he unleashed a strong drive, which was frequently, I would say "Babe Ruth" or "Ben Hogan" and his gold-filled smile indicated he understood.

My infrequent golf game never was anything to cable home about, but I was not embarrassed with my 103. I led off with a blazing 49 and tired badly in the stretch. Mr. Nishioka laid an 85 on me, and his pleasant wife, bless her, bunted around in 124.

I had Roko talk to the caddies and mine was identified as Mrs. Yoshie Fuhashi, 36. The others were Mrs. Shige Hirone, 37, and Mrs. Ine Ichimura, 51. I hate to doubt Mrs. Ichimura, but she looked 65.

Their wide bonnets were completely covered with white bandanas tied under the chin. Their smocks bore the club monogram, and they wore slacks and bowling shoes. Their headgear made them look like wraiths this gray day as they would cut through a section of woods from green to tee.

Mine turned out to be a million giggles. She seemed to get a kick out of my calling her Yoshie, and I would have little tugs of war with her when she tried to retrieve a club. Ain't I a devil?

I had been told these caddies applaud good shots and shake their heads in sympathy at bad ones. I earned some applause and coaxed some more out of them after my version of a good shot. They knew two English expressions: "Nice shot" and "nice up." Their nice came out "nize."

Yoshie wasn't exactly sympathetic. Once I drove a ball to the adjacent fairway, then caromed the next shot off a tree, and she broke up. I was in a huge scalloped sand trap for four shots, and when I handed the wedge back to her she pointed to all the sand on it and giggled.

I found out Yoshie has been caddying seven years. She is married to a carpenter and has a 12-year-old daughter. Yoshie bicycles to work, a 20-minute ride, and is on duty 7:30 a.m. to 4:30 p.m. For each single round she is paid 700 yen, less than $2. Holidays and weekends, one caddy will work a foursome, pushing a wide cart with all four bags on it.

There are caddy shortages, I learned, at rice-planting time in the spring and harvest time in the fall.

I don't know how Mr. Nishioka felt about them, but I found the gal caddies most competent and a great embellishment. However, I would not want to see them working something like the back nine at Hercules. Ibaraki has no hills.

Warning to the serious golfers: The caddies here do not observe the "silence" rule when a player is addressing the ball. They keep chattering. Back home, they would be attacked with the nearest samurai sword.

Pock-Pock-Pock

Do they have a Backgammon Writers Association of America? If so, this might qualify me, unless they find out I don't know a thing about the game. The very rich enter these big tournaments, and throw money around like dice.

LAS VEGAS—The jet-setters of the backgammon circus play their expensive parlor game as a force of 250 here, and the pock-pock-pock of the dice rattling in the leather cups in the Tropicana's Blue Room does not sound unlike hoofbeats.

And through it all rides—and also plays—their leader, his royal highness, Prince Alexis Obolensky.

"Never mind that royal highness stuff," he booms. "Just call me Obie."

I was prepared to detour the prince as a phony. True, the title is self-applied but on him it looks good, especially on the cover of his book, "Backgammon, the Action Game", and the affectation does not run deep. No accent, for one thing. And the prince talks like a corporal.

He was 7 years old when he had to flee the Russian revolution. His family, he says, was part of the aristocracy, his father a prince and a member of the Czar's guard. They came to America in 1929. I personally will not argue that he is not a prince.

He is a striking-looking man, tall and slender. His 6 feet 4 are topped by a big-nosed, leafy-browed, wrinkled face that could be a photograph torn from a history of the American Indian. His hair is a magnificent mane. Sitting Bull, in casual clothes.

He said he was 58 years old.

"Some girl called me a dirty old man the other day," he laughed. "I said no, I'm just a sexy senior citizen."

Obolensky was director of the world championships that brought his squad of swingers and the staid to Las Vegas. Everybody says he is the one responsible for the resurgence of the old Babylonian pastime. He makes his living organizing the competition and seeing that the right people get to them. There are some 5,000 of these well-endowed right people in his files.

Obie does not only break all the rules of exiled princedom by working for a living—he admits it.

"Listen," he said, "I used to work in a factory in New Orleans, making Celotex. Now most of my income comes from resorts. I arrange a tournament for the resort and bring in nice people, and the place pays me a fee. My staff and I take care of all the details.

"10 years ago, I set up the first backgammon tournament. It was at Freeport in the Bahamas, more or less as a lark. We drew 30 players, all from Florida and all men. Now we get hundreds, men and women, and it's an international group. In 1966, I got a call from Las Vegas and we've had the world tournament here ever since. The game has ballooned; it's an explosion."

One of the things I like about Obie is that he does not attempt to pass off his tournaments as clubroom super bowls.

"It is a nice four-day party, is what this amounts to," he said of the world championships. "And it is a fascinating action game and the money these people play for makes it more exciting. It is an exciting game, that is, if you like it. If you don't like it, forget it. Play something else."

Some of Obie's major productions now are sponsored by Seagram's, which uses them to help push a scotch. He even has an office in their New York building.

"They send out the invitations for me and pick the charity that shares in the proceeds," he explained. "I do everything else. I developed a circuit. The game used to be confined to the big exclusive clubs. I've got plans for things like a tournament in a castle in Vienna. We've had an event in Fort Lauderdale right along, but this year I'm going to hold the finals on a yacht, at sea."

While talking over lunch, we were interrupted by one of the top-rated backgammon sharks. He said a player in the tournament had written a check, and he wanted to know if the guy was kosher. The check was for $65,000.

"He's ok," Obie said without hesitation. "No problem. He'd be good for a hundred thousand."

Turning to me Obie observed that "they must have had a little side bet. I can tell you things about every one of my people. We used to go looking for them to play—now people are trying to get invitations. We check them out. We keep it on a high basis."

Obie has a stable of eight. His chief aides are a son, Obie Junior, and a daughter, Mary. There is another daughter in Birmingham, Ala., the wife of a concert pianist. Obie Junior had been playing all night. "It's taking a hold on the young people, too. I put on my first college tournament at Harvard, and 65 kids entered it. I would say stockbrokers are here in the biggest proportion, of the professions. We've got a couple of bank presidents, too."

It is no coincidence, I suggested, that the big tournaments always seem to be held in rooms next to casinos.

"Well, these people like to gamble," Obie shrugged. "I personally think they're crazy. Me, I might play a little $5 blackjack. Nothing else."

He told me stories of high stakes and sore losers, of the one loser who threw the whole board into a fireplace, like a frustrated golfer throwing his clubs into a lake.

"One of our old regulars—he's dead now—was a guy in London who was hopelessly hooked on gambling," Obie said. "He'd go at it 48 hours in a row, poker, backgammon, and any game in town. His wife finally talked him into going to a shrink, to break the habit. This he did for two weeks, three sessions a week.

"The next week, his wife needed money to pay the maid, so she consulted his change on the bureau. She spied a check for $12,000 made out by the psychiatrist. Here her husband had talked the shrink, who was supposed to cure him, into playing him backgammon."

Obie excused himself. It was time for his match. His royal highness—a former University of Virginia football player, of all things—strode into the pock-pock of the arena and hunched over the game he learned to play as a kid in Istanbul. Obie was with his kind of people, trying to beat their brains out with a pair of dice and 15 checkers.

Le Amazzoni

The harness-racing business never looked better.
We all had dreams of going to Italy to cover a big
return match. Nothing happened.

They all donned cute black hats, black jackets with brass buttons and velvet collars and white riding pants.

They looked good, these lady harness drivers from Padova and Florence and Milano and assorted other towns in Italy. Over there, they are called "le amazzoni." The semipro linguists in the group at Brandywine Raceway at noon yesterday were translating this into "the amazons," which in English means tall, strong, masculine broads like Tamara Press and The Great Moolah.

But then the eight signoras and one signorina showed up on the bus from New York and you could forget Tamara and amazons. These were feminine femmes, dad. They had been taking it easy on the pasta.

They are going to drive a double-header Friday night at Brandywine against a team of North American women. There will be two more races at Monticello, N.Y., and two more in Montreal. This is for the world's ladies harness championship, and if you don't think so just ask Joey Goldstein, who thought up the whole bit, or Dixie Dave Herman, the whole bit's Brandywine echo.

The nine women and several guys came in on the bus for the press conference and to stay through the week. Goldstein is with Harness Tracks of America and he had all the information. He used to be a publicity internationalist for Roosevelt Raceway, scouting foreign countries for harness attractions like Ed Sullivan searches them for animals who can open a show.

Joey Goldstein first met the Italian girls in his Roosevelt capacity and knows them well, and you'd think the least he could do during the promotion would be to change his name to Luigi Goldstein.

Frankie Gennari was along. He is the interpreter, a wee, dapper paison who manages a restaurant called The Hopples, near Roosevelt. He, too, has traveled for the Roosevelt track. He has taken three weeks off from work to relay questions and answers to and from his lovely posse. Phil Spitalny, in a checked coat.

Publicity men, interpreters, you can always get. Back to the girls.

The one with the four rings on her right hand, even on her thumb, was Franca Guintini, an ash blonde, or something. Pearls dangled, almost clanged, from each ring. You could pull off one of the great jewel robberies in harness-racing history just by shaking hands with her.

Signora Guintini speaks adequate English, so you don't need Gennari. She is the only amazzoni whose husband made the trip. These girls are well off. The eight wives are married to prominent Italian horsemen.

Mrs. Guintini was explaining that they were going to have "two games each day" in this country. She meant races.

The unmarried one is Mariana Mescalchin, the signorina. It came out in the translation that she is 20, the youngest. You would guess that the oldest is like 35.

It is a fun group.

"Yes, I am about ready to get married," said Marina, "but don't send that to Europe, will you? I don't want my parents to know, or they will break it up."

Cesira Castellini is striking, her black hair pixie-cut. She owns a 10-horse stable. What do all the husbands say about their women being way over here, driving horses?

"They say go ahead, maybe some day you won't come back," says Cesira, laughing. "They say go to the moon and get lost, if you want."

Yes, there is the Italian equivalent of the old lame claim: A woman's place is in the home.

"It is something like women should be home and making soup," said Luciani Cacciari, breaking up.

Franca Borelli is brunette, and something about her jacket reminds you of Sophia Loren's. She and her husband have this Marisilvia Stable named after their daughters, Marino and Silvia. Luigi Goldstein said something to her in his best wine-label Italian and she smiled and replied.

"I told her she looked beautiful," Goldstein explained. "And she thanked me and said it is hard to look beautiful with all this mud on her."

The ladies, at this point, were mud-speckled, for the scene had shifted to the track. It was the color and substance of runny scrapple, because of rain. Publicist Herman, clinging relentlessly to a hand microphone, had managed to scrape up seven trotters for the Italians to drive for the benefit of cameramen and the press. There are only trotters in Italian harness racing.

There was a slight foul-up. The girls and their borrowed horses took their places behind the mobile starting gate in the backstretch and came around nicely. But the automobile accelerated in the stretch, as per custom, and drove off the track and the girls looked a little over-matched as the horses came thundering into the first turn. A couple of the trotters broke; it turned out one, indeed, was a pacer.

The girls were in control, though, and drove a rather stampeding mile, each time scattering the cowardly press group gathered off the first turn.

"We did not know the starting gate was going to speed up and pull off like that," said Loredana Moretti. "We thought we were going to have a nice ride around just for news film. We did not expect this tempo."

Anxious trainers were a little shook, too.

"This is a $100,000 horse," one growled—and exaggerated—as he reclaimed his sweaty animal. "Herman told me they were just going to jog. He already had a tough workout today."

These nine charmers are the best women drivers of sulkies, but maybe not Fiats, in all of Italy—the best of a field of 17 that drives professionally, in betting races. They race at 53 different European tracks each season, but do not compete against men. Luciani Cacciari was the "championessa Italiana" last year.

You can bet on these Ben Her races at Brandywine, too. Bring lira.

Bow Ties Are In

Baggies were being introduced at this men's fashion show. Till then, I always thought they were something that kept my lunch fresh. Let me know what you think of Dr. Joyce Brothers' outlook on neckties.

CHICAGO—The bow ties, they look like something you'd chase with a net and some bait and hope you wouldn't succeed. Big as man-eating butterflies.

The huge plaids on the suits. Soon as I saw 'em, I thought of Spike Jones.

The white suits. They're also back. This is the best news the dry-cleaning industry has received since the invention of gravy.

The clunky shoes, with the high heels and the platform soles, have toes as bulbous as the safety shoes that guys wear in factories. Maybe that's what they had in mind. Your toes are protected in case you drop your bow tie.

The heels and soles are made of wood. Some soles are cork. You get a hole in your shoe, you just take it to your friendly while-you-wait carpenter.

The baggies. These are pants that are high-waisted and so wide at the bottom, the young studs modeling them looked as if they were wearing long, inverted ice-cream cones. I swear I saw one model take three steps before his pants began to move.

The bottoms can run as wide as 26 inches, which is a lot wider than this newspaper page I hope you are reading. They are cuffed. You can carry your lunch in the cuffs.

This is some of the stuff I learned at the Men's Fashion Association of America spring-summer preview for the press. I don't think I'm ready for the new, or revived, fashions. It may take a while, I just can't see myself coming to the office with one of those giant moths attached to my throat. Or wearing a Great Gatsby white suit to Tessie's Tavern. And the colored shoes with the platforms would get me arrested, or at least embraced.

Max Evans did stress, though, that the baggies primarily are for the young man up through college. So are the weird shoes. I felt better. Evans is the new fashion director of the association. He used to be with Esquire, and looks it. This day he was featuring a blue and white plaid suit with a polka-dot tie. Bow, of course. Even though they were big polka dots, there must have been several hundred of them.

I found myself next to Evans at a party in the Drake—the grandest hotel I've ever been in, by the way. I groped for something to say.

"What are the chances of the narrow necktie coming back?" I finally asked. "I've got a roomful of them."

Evans shuddered. "The narrow necktie does not fit into the new silhouette of men's clothing. I cannot see it returning very soon."

So much for my roomful of bad silhouettes. I pressed on.

"The only reason I feel relaxed in this setting," I said, "is because of my underwear. Nobody can see it so they don't know whether or not it's in style, which I'm sure it isn't."

So Max Evans told me about the latest thing in drawers. It is a one-piecer, body shirt and brief combined. I asked him how in the world you would get in 'em, and he said you step in and zip it up. I immediately began worrying about stuck zippers. A man might never get out of his underwear. But then I know a few guys I suspect are in that rut even with two-piecers.

Speaking of men's lingerie, I was walking around the retailers' exhibit in the vast McCormick Place, as they were setting it up. Martha Espedahl was with me, and we came across a display of underwear on dummies that made me blush. Bikinis, in wild colors, not much bigger than sleeve garters. If you were a peacock, you would wear them. I rushed Martha out of there and we went to look at belts.

Let's see—what else did I learn? Oh, yes, the unstructured look in suits and sportcoats. Unstructured means unlined and unpadded. Now what am I going to do for shoulders? One seersucker suit, in big yellow and black plaids, was described as almost as light as a hankie. An unstructured hankie, I take it.

Lots of seersucker and corduroy. They call this the puckered look, but I've had that for years. And pastels, the Easter egg colors. And sweaters. I was told the layered look is going to be very important. You put on a shirt and a sweater, you're layered. Thus, I will be in style the next time I rake leaves.

I came across one piece of news that shook me: White socks will be important, too. A fellow from Hart Schaffner and Marx told me this. I think he was Marx.

"White trousers and white shoes are a faultless combination," said Marx, or was it Hart? "So don't destroy it. Do wear solid white hose, or white with a colored pattern. Promise me you won't wear black hose, or strongly contrasting hose. This definitely would destroy the desired image."

I promised.

I moved on to people like Dr. Joyce Brothers, the psychologist-author who was commentator at the Hoecsht Fibers presentation. You are not going to believe what she thinks some people think when they look at a man's necktie. Neckties turn them on. Ready?

"There is a theory," said Dr. Brothers, "that while men modestly cover their genitals, they symbolically display them by wearing neckties. Neckties are phallic symbols. Verification of this theory lies in the fact that as societies become more sexually oriented, and less repressed, neckties become bigger and bolder. Perhaps it indicates a satiation with rampant public sexuality, pornography and liberality and a desire to return to a more Victorian attitude."

I got Martha out of there too, and went looking for an overcoat presentation or something. But the psychologist had made me think. I wondered what kind of action I'd get if I were to wear a bow tie shaped like two large fig leaves.

Rookie Umpire

This was the Harry Wendelstedt of 1966. The rookie has gone on to become an established umpire, with World Series and All-Star Game experience. If I ever get to host a talk show, I'll feature umpires and old fighters. I can't miss with them.

Harry Wendelstedt is an umpire, but don't send him any sympathy cards.

A rookie umpire in the National League, at that; right out there, big and burly and new, where Gene Mauch and Leo Durocher and Bobby Bragan and wolves from Chavez Ravine to Shea Stadium can see him and dare him.

But umpiring in the big leagues is ecstacy for Wendelstedt. He talks of his craft and he almost gets emotional—"terrific . . . I love it . . . the greatest thing that could happen to a fellow."

He is only 27 years old, so you figure he must be pretty good. There have been younger umps in the majors, but not many. This 6-foot-2, 230-pound, curly haired Baltimorean has survived the dreary nickel-nursing, the dungeon-like facilities, the dyspepsia and the endurance contests of the road in the minors to qualify for the big-league minimum salary of $9,500, plus $24 a day expenses. He talks as if he should give it back and work just for kicks.

This ruddy oak of German stock, bachelor son of a truck driver, sat on his bed in the Benjamin Franklin Hotel in Philadelphia and admitted it wasn't Brunswick, Ga.

That was where he worked his first professional game four years ago and they haven't stopped laughing. The first time he bent over home plate in his mail-order uniform, the seat of his pants split gloriously open at the seams and stayed split for nine interminable innings.

"There I was, with only my Long Johns between me and the crowd," he recalls. "They howled, and the ball players let me have it, too. It wasn't bad enough I was excited, working my first game. I was ready to call it a career right there. The next day, the papers wrote about my 'southern exposure.' "

That was opening day of 1962 in the Georgia-Florida League. Opening day of 1966 found him in St. Louis, working third base as the Cardinals took on the Phillies.

Wendelstedt came fast, never staying in the same league or classification, always climbing. He advanced to the Northwest League, the Texas, the International and finally the National. He handled all-star games and playoffs and he made it a year-around job by working the Arizona Winter League.

"The National League scouted me and bought me after my second year," he explained. "They took me to spring training two years ago. It was like a dream world, on the same fields with people I had read about all my life. My first game behind the plate, I had the feeling I wasn't doing anything right. It was in West Palm Beach, Braves against the Yankees. I called a third strike on Mickey Mantle. He just looked away."

A thousand games after he broke in, Wendelstedt is learning angles he never knew—"Maybe 10 things a day." He is the junior member of a crew. that also includes Shag Crawford, Doug Harvey and Ed Vargo, and he idolizes them. He cannot understand why a newspaperman would be interviewing him instead of somebody like Vargo—"he had a great World Series last year". The crew chief is Philadelphian Crawford, the professor as Wendelstedt learns to move "not as an individual, but as part of a four man system." They know all the tricks; they have every possibility covered. And they're a happy crew—they keep you loose, don't let you get nervous.

"The managers, the players try you in their little ways. Generally speaking, they've let me alone. I am with a well-respected crew; I have a lot going for me."

Umpires, like ball players, admittedly have their good and bad days.

"I've got to say I had a good day the first time I worked the plate this year," Wendelstedt said. "It was in Philadelphia, the time Jim Maloney of the Reds shut out the Phils. You don't realize how good pitchers like Maloney, Marichal, Koufax really are. That's the big difference in the minors and majors—everybody up here has something on the ball, and it makes me want to bear down even more. Anyhow, I was pleased with my day. But in the umpires' room, the other guys didn't say anything for five minutes. The old silent treatment. I finally got up and sighed and reached for a beer and that's when they all came over and congratulated me."

At the time of the interview, Wendelstedt had yet to banish his first big leaguer. "I'm waiting—it has to happen," he said. It happened a week later in Atlanta, where Harry joined an old club. He threw out Durocher.

A Baltimore friend who umpired in Class D had suggested that Wendelstedt, who had done some high school and sandlot catching, enroll in the Al

Somers Umpiring School in Daytona Beach, Fla. "I was just out of the Marines, doing some part-time school teaching. I was searching, unhappy, restless. I had no idea of becoming an umpire. I went to the Somers school like I was going on a vacation. I was no bug on rules. But I fell in love with umpiring, and here I am."

Here he is, and Owen Friend could have told you. Wendelstedt had his first "real argument" when his career was two innings old. There was a play at the plate in Brunswick, and Friend, the home manager, charged Wendelstedt and his Somers diploma and his airconditioned britches.

"His parting shot was that I wouldn't last two weeks in this business," Wendelstedt said. "This season, after the opening game in St. Louis, some guy runs out of the stands and shakes my hands and tells me he knew I'd make it all the time. It was friend Friend."

Motsy's Yoks

I got a tip from Delaware Park's Bob Kelley about the ad in Variety and ran it down and it led to the surfacing of Lammot du Pont Copeland Jr. from his zillion-dollar bankruptcy filing. If not an Odd Couple, then an odd coupling: Motsy and a gag writer.

I have to give Lammot du Pont Copeland Jr. credit, and there are not many guys who would risk that. They would lock the vaults.

ME give credit to Lammot du Pont Copeland Jr.? Surely I jest.

And I do. I don't mean that kind of credit. I mean credit-as-in-praise.

Motsey Copeland is the 42-year-old aristocrat who is involved in one of history's biggest personal bankruptcy cases.

Four years ago, he said he was broke. It was an inconceivable break, an earthquake. He filed assets of $25.6 million vs. estimated liabilities of $59.1 million.

That came out to an attack of the shorts amounting to $33.4 million.

And this fellow is true-blueblood du Pont. Son of a former president and chairman of the board of The Company. Great-great-great-grandson of the founder. Harvard '54. Bankrupt '70.

He was an absentee dabbler in newspapers, toys, a car wash, a cattle ranch, a junior college. He borrowed a ton from the barbers' union. "Built one of the untidiest corporate empires in history," the Wall Street Journal reported. "A confusing welter of financing and refinancing," said the New York Times review.

I must confess I got a feeling of assurance from reading of his plight, although I wish nobody an attack of the shorts, especially of such magnitude. I have trouble balancing what is hysterically called my bank account, and here was a first-string du Pont going me millions better, or worse.

Now, why I must give him credit:

There was this ad in Variety. It was headlined "Humor by the Pound", and it offered jokes for sale. "Anecdotes, quips, one liners."

You were supposed to write Bob Orben, The Comedy Center, Inc., 801 Wilmington Trust Building, Wilmington, Del.

I checked out 801 Wilmington Trust and Bob Orben wasn't there. He rarely is.

But the president of the corporation was— Lammot du Pont Copeland Jr. The same. He sat in his office with a half-dozen big old fire-fighting prints on the wall, and talked about the business. Pleasantly, but nervously, I thought.

I was happy for him. Here is a guy who is under a bombardment of 109 creditors in a case so complex it still hasn't been settled, and what is he doing?

He is rebounding by selling jokes. I think that is funny in itself.

Copeland might not have been the greatest financier of our time—and he must have gone through hell, along with the money—but you have to admire his style. Selling humor, indeed, while preparing to reluctantly star in an all-time bankruptcy proceeding. It is gorgeous.

First of all, who is Bob Orben?

"One of the top gag writers in the country," Copeland explained. "He had this Comedy Center for 17 years and it's moved around a bit with him. Some years it was in Los Angeles, when he was writing for Red Skeleton. The last several years, the publishing office was in Brooklyn.

"We met through mutual acquaintances and worked out a fairly involved contractual arrangement. His title is editor. He writes the stuff. We print it, mail it, bill, advertise. I'm the president, succeeding Bob, and the lady in the outer office, Ruth Mahaffey, we're the whole operation here.

More on Orben: He writes out of his home in Flushing, N.Y., and lashes himself into composing 25 jokes a day. He used to supply Jack Paar and Dick Gregory. He has written books.

Copeland said the ad in Variety was meant to rid the shelves of Orben's old material. You get a pound of it for $2.

The Comedy Center, Inc., has two backbone products. One is "Current Comedy", 24 issues a year for $42. Four pages of topical Orben zingers. The other is "Comedy Fillers", four more pages, $50 a year for 12 issues. They are directed at oral and printed use, respectively.

Orben started out writing for entertainers. He made a big switch to the business market. A brochure says The Comedy Center has more than 1,000 corporate clients, including Anaconda, Dow, Goodrich, NCR, U.S. Steel. I couldn't find Du Pont.

"Business is quite good," Copeland said. "We reach a full spectrum of people, unlike other services that cater to entertainers. The biggest portion of our clientele is business people. They use Orben's jokes in formal speeches, in various sales pitches. It breaks the ice."

He gave me Orben's latest issues. "Current Comedy" was about streakers. Samples:

—Do you know why streaking will never last as a college sport? Where do you sew your letter?

—Confucius say: Naked student who runs into naked coed, having lucky streak.

—Have you noticed newspaper photographers always take pictures of streakers from the back? I saw one picture of 300 streakers. Looked like sale on Parker House rolls.

I had to mention the bankruptcy.

"Don't you think it ironic," I said, "that some one in your situation would be hustling humor, trying to make people laugh? Is there therapy in this for you?"

Copeland smiled. "There could be a little, but that's really not what led me into this activity. I've always been interested in publishing, in one form or another. And it happened I could handle this, both financially and in terms of time. Any more elaborate venture would have been impossible, under the circumstances."

Lammont du Pont Copeland Jr. said, yes, he thinks he has a pretty good sense of humor. His presiding over a joke factory would indicate it is bigger than he thinks. Under other circumstances, I might suggest the firm's name be changed to "A Million Laughs".

I can picture this: Copeland, under heavy fire from the bill collectors in court, breaks out Orben's latest paper and says, "Did you hear the one about . . ."

Talk about tough audiences.

Horse And Buggy

Hey, Hollywood, here I am just when you need me.

No, not as an actor—you'll have to see my agent—but with a story idea.

You take this horse, see.

An Amish family's horse. They hitch him to their hard-top buggy, seven kids pile in and he pulls the family around town.

They drive him from the farm to the store. Or to church. To visit. Go for rides with him. They even hitch him to a plow.

The scene changes. The horse is at the race track.

No, not pulling a pizza wagon. He's IN the races.

And he stays in them. What's more he wins. In less than a year's time, he wins $27,000.

I know—it would be better if he won the Kentucky Derby, but he isn't that kind of a horse. Besides, you can always change it. And you probably would.

How's that for a scenario? Stinks, you say?

Well, let me tell you something, dad. It really happened, and is happening.

And a Delaware horse, too. If you make the movie, I will insist on the Delaware angle.

Don't have him pulling the buggy in Tatum, S.C., or Tucumcari, N.M. or some such adventurous place.

Make it the hinterlands of Dover, Del.

I drove up to Liberty Bell Park in Philadelphia to check out the story on the horse. He is owned by Bill Kinsey and trained and driven by Preston Burris Jr., 40-ish guys from Clayton.

The horse was scratching his head on the stall door in Barn S. Half of the Kinsey stable, he is a harness horse, of course. In Clayton, they don't admit there is any other kind that races.

Kinsey, new in the horse business—he also was farming, attaching fenders in the GM assembly line and subbing as a mailman—bought a mare named Little Bomber and introduced her to a mercenary stallion named Honor Rodney. Along came a foal, christened Bayview's Billy Bob. Bayview for the road and schoolhouse, Billy and Bob for Kinsey's sons.

Two years later, Kinsey decided to sell out. He unloaded this colt for $700. Another year later, he saw Bayview's listing in a catalog and ordered an agent to buy him.

"I didn't know if he had three legs or two or what," Kinsey said. "I just wanted him back, because he was my first horse, he was named for my boys, and all that. Bayview was 3 at the time. Cost me $700, same price I had got for him."

But Bayview couldn't get to the races. His legs were bad. He was big and clumsy. His knees kept banging. He couldn't pace or trot. The horse stumbled around workouts in 18, which is stable talk for 2 minutes, 18 seconds, for the mile. Such a time probably could nose out a glacier. Then he bowed a tendon. The glacier passed him.

That's when Bayview's Billy Bob was farmed out, literally. Kinsey loaned him to a family named Byler, of near Pearson's Corner west of Dover.

"A friend told me these Amish people could use a road horse, for errands, little trips," Kinsey chattered. "I said they could borrow him for the keep— feed and caring. They had one road horse, but the wife couldn't handle it.

"That was late in the summer of '72. I told them to keep him till the first of the year, but it wasn't till April that I took him back. They had even used him to cultivate their garden. I felt a little bad taking him away, because the kids loved him; the oldest boy offered to buy him. But I turned over Bayview's half sister to them as a replacement."

The plot brightens. Bayview was much the sounder horse for his eight-month domestic interlude.

"The Amish take good care of their horses," Kinsey said. "All that jogging with the buggy had strengthened his legs. I guess they'd drive him 12, 15 miles a day.

"I could see Bayview was jogged up right good. He wasn't puffin' or blowin'. He had his wind built up. He was ready to train."

Kinsey worked with the horse for a week, then turned him over to Burris, a pro. The horse was now 5, an oldish rookie.

I interrupted. "But wasn't it risky, having your horse pull a loaded buggy on hard roadways for seven, eight months? You obviously expected to try and bring him back to the races."

Kinsey shrugged dustily. "I had nothing to lose. The horse had showed nothing. If I sold him, the best I could do was a few hundred dollars. And I'm not the first to put out a horse that way. If it works right, it settles the horse down. The durn horse was bred to trot. I was determined to stick with him if I had to wait till he was 10."

Burris took Bayview to Liberty Bell and qualified him in 8-and-3 (2:08.3) as a trotter and he started winning claiming races there and at Dover and Brandywine. But the horse was very sore. Three different veterinarians advised Kinsey to get rid of him. A fourth vet and Kinsey decided on a course of above-the-knee treatment that worked.

Bayview wound up paying his own way last year with $9,100 in purses. (You can make that $90,000, Hollywood). This year he already has earned $18,300, much of that in a recent big trot at Liberty Bell, the night he won by five lengths and paid $10.20. His time of 2:03.3 is the fastest of the season for an aged trotter. Burris calls him the best trotter, the gamest horse he's ever driven.

Kinsey is a pleased man. "We've done pretty good, with a home-raised horse. Not too bad, for my first one. Somebody like Stanley Dancer, he goes through 100 horses a year, lots of them $50-100,000 buys, and half don't make it."

Take it away, Hollywood. I'll hustle down to Dover and rent the exact buggy. Get Regis Toomey to play Kinsey. I'll be Burris. Get a double for the driving scenes. Paul Newman is suggested.

"Who, Me?"

George Raft: Almost 80, a loser, and saying that wasn't the real Raft playing all those bad guys on the late shows. There are old newspaper clippings that make you skeptical about his new halo.

PHILADELPHIA—The name of the book is plainly "George Raft".

After listening to Raft, I suggest a better title would be "Who, Me?".

The cordial old movie menace—and how can he be 79 already?—talked in his dressing room after co-hosting a Mike Douglas Show.

The patent-leather hair is gone. In its day, you could have lubricated your car by driving through it. He is bald but for a few white wisps on the side. The cold eyes of countless film confrontations now seem to plead for understanding. The big ears, the long narrow nose, are undeniably George Raft. He still is a dapper man.

He was a dancer who made it rich as a gangster in the Bogart-Cagney-Robinson era. A wooden but somehow intriguing actor, he always looked as if he belonged in a tailor's window. Poured into a double-breasted suit. Hat brim with just the right snap. Cuban heels. Not a thread out of place. George Raft looked at a guy, you knew the guy was dead. Sometimes they looked back, which is why George died in a lot of his pictures.

Off the lot, George also had a reputation as a tough guy and a heavy gambler with playmates in Murder, Inc. Cards, dice, horses, an occasional fistfight, were his alleged bag.

Which brings us to the "Who, Me?".

"That image I had—where did it come from?" Raft frowned as he changed into his street clothes. "I was never a gambler. Except on my own horses.

You own horses, you bet on them. But I never bet big. Somebody wrote I once won $100,000 betting on baseball. I never bet a nickel on a ball game in my life. I never bet with a bookie in my life. Never took a drink. Never was locked up.

"How did I get this reputation? Maybe it was my background."

His background was the Hell's Kitchen neighborhood of New York and a contemporary was Bugsy Siegel, the doomed hood.

"They say I lost bundles at Las Vegas," he continued. "Never. That Saturday Evening Post series on my supposed life—they murdered me.

"I was a working guy. I worked four places in one day and night in New York—walked to them in my dancing shoes. If shady guys owned the clubs, what was I supposed to do? When I got into the movies, they told me to be nice to people. A guy would come up to me at a fight or a ball game and say he saw my latest movie—how did I know who he was? Next thing I know, the FBI is questioning me. Was I supposed to ask the guy what he does for a living?

"I'm super-sensitive. What they wrote about me, it hurt. I'm not the guy I was on the screen. I hope to prove it in this book. If it makes any money, the government can have it all."

Raft owes Uncle Sam. In 1965, they charged him with six counts of income tax evasion involving some $85,000, found him guilty of one. The judge declined to sentence him to prison and fined him $2,500. The clippings say Raft broke down and sobbed.

A couple of years later, he fronted for a London gambling casino and they put his name on it, George Raft's Colony Club. While he was on a vacation trip to Hollywood, the British government revoked his working permit.

"And I still don't know why," Raft said. "I was a host. I never fooled with anybody's wife or girl, never gambled myself. I appreciated the job—I couldn't get work in the movies because I have emphysema; my voice breaks down."

In 1941, Raft was getting $200,000 a picture, the season's record in Hollywood. Now he's broke, pushing the book and good-willing for a Las Vegas hotel.

"Where did the money go?" he echoed the question. "I had three vices: clothing, girls, nice living. No regrets. I'd double my life if I had the chance.

"My late wife and I were separated, never divorced. She got 10 percent of everything. We were both Catholic, she more than me—she didn't believe in divorce. That hurt: I had to play the field.

"I fell in love with a girl named Virginia Pine. She was in Gertrude Lawrence's hit, 'Lady in the Dark'. I would have married her, but couldn't. She said she was getting older, and how long could she wait? She eventually married Quentin Reynolds.

"The money—well, I spent $50,000 of my own putting on sports shows for the servicemen in World War 2. The judge said he took this into account at my tax case. Later I got mixed up with somebody promoting a chain of discount stores—I was supposed to be the vice-president—and I signed some things I shouldn't have. I wound up losing my house—to an ice-cream company."

Raoul Walsh said in that moviemakers' series on TV that Raft turned down the High Sierra role that eventually went to Humphrey Bogart, because he didn't want to get killed in the end.

"Not so," Raft said. "It was never offered to me. I did better than that. I turned down Maltese Falcon, the picture that made Bogart. I had it in my contract that I was to do no remakes. Falcon had been done before, by Ricardo Cortez and Bette Davis. Another thing I didn't like. They had a brand-new director. Fellow named John Huston. Oh, well, you can't call 'em all right."

Raft—who called Bolero the best picture he ever did—mentioned he made movies with several eventual Oscar winners.

"But never me," he laughed. "I think I came close to a nomination with Souls at Sea. But I must have ran fourth. Out of the money."

Raft said to say hello to Mario DiFonza, the Wilmington sport and an old friend. I know Raft once came here to visit Mario at a Tatnall Street spot where night people would toss those square things with the spots on them. I've got to feel he didn't come down to give Mario a bolero lesson.

Boom Boom

My friend Boom Boom Felsburg is by Damon Runyon, out of the nearest race track. This really is a merger of a couple of columns on Boom, and it was published in Turf and Sport Digest.

You could call Boom Boom Felsburg the four-wheeled horse player.

Racing day after racing day, January through December, my friend Boom Boom drives to the track with four or five fellow sports, hoping at least one member of the group—perhaps even himself—will make even a small score and thus be in position to up with a tank of gas on the way home.

Boom Boom Felsburg is a lugger. A lugger is a fellow who uses his car to transport players to and from the action.

Harry Felsburg Jr., is his Social Security name. He is 57 years old. He has been lugging for two decades. It is his career; that, and playing the horses himself.

If the luggees do good at the track, then Boom Boom does good, too. They take care of him. If they do not do good—well, Boom Boom guffaws it off and reaches for tomorrow's entries.

Whenever Laurel opens the fall-winter eastern Thoroughbred season, it means that the season opens for Boom Boom. His season never ends. He has the finance company for proof. His racing neighborhood reaches five states— Delaware, Maryland, Pennsylvania, New Jersey, West Virginia.

Sometimes he plays the horses so badly that it even is funny to him.

"When I was a kid," he once told me, "I saw an old guy trying to beat the horses at Havre de Grace. He needed a shave, bad; he had a little stump of a cigar stuck in his teeth, holes in his elbows, run-down heels. I pitied the guy and I said to myself, 'I'll never get that way.' Well, this summer I walked past a full-length mirror at Delaware Park and I saw the old guy again. It was me!"

He has been known as Boom Boom since he was a boy. He would sit on the backs of those careening old *Philadelphia Ledger* delivery trucks in Wilmington, Del., and make like he was shooting at bad guys. If nothing else, he has outlasted the *Philadelphia Ledger*. Now he aims at winners. "I bet a lot of show bets, though. I call it bettin' in the Blue Room, because of the color of the ticket."

Felsburg's current steed is a two-door Dart. He has maybe 100 in his stable of horse-playing friends, and he will squeeze five of them into the Dart each day. He picks them up at the railroad station in Wilmington.

"It is a lot more comfortable comin' back," Boom Boom discloses. "More room. Everybody's pockets are empty."

"I go a distance—Charles Town is 166 miles one way—or a sprint, to Delaware Park." He really talks that way.

He has survived the famed Bowie Blizzard and at least 15 cars. Naturally, he got caught in the big snow at Bowie some years ago and lingered there overnight. The car had to stay a week, until the thaws came.

Lugging can be dangerous. There was the time Boom Boom borrowed a car to drive to Charles Town "because my tires were smooth," and he had an accident at Newmarket, Va.

"I was passing a guy when the left front tire went out. I had the car under control and was huntin' a nice place to land on the inside when a Cadillac hits me in the rear and we land on the inside, all right—out of action. One of my clients had his neck snapped and spent the next two weeks in a hospital in Frederick. We all had to take him there and everybody was moanin', even him, because we got knocked out of the double."

There was the time Boom Boom and his party came out of Pimlico and found themselves without a mount.

"I was goin' good then—used valet parkin," Boom Boom recalled. "Some guy took the car by mistake, I guess, because it was found three days later, two blocks from the track. Meantime, we all had come out broke and had to borrow money to get home."

I saw Boom Boom most recently at Liberty Bell. It had been a long time between encounters. He looked great. The last time I had seen him, I worried. He was shaggy and baggy then, and terribly overweight. Now he was trimmed and trim and he was wearing a suit. I commended him for getting rid of the belly and at least two chins and wondered how he had done it.

"The hard way," B. B. Felsburg said, sonorously. He has a magnificent nose, sort of like George C. Scott's at half-staff. "I had a heart attack. Two years ago. It nearly killed me. No, not the heart attack. It nearly killed me because it happened right in the middle of the Delaware Park meet, and I had to spend 30 days in the hospital. But I did lose 50 pounds."

I offered him my sympathies.

"Thanks, but it was my own fault," he said. "I went back to work, and I should have known better. I wasn't used to it. That's what brought on the heart trouble. I went back to drivin' a cab, after 15 years. Six months later, I'm a heart case. Could have been worse, though. Medicaid took care of the hospital bill. It was like hittin' the double."

Boom Boom can get a chuckle out of anything, even a heart attack. And while he was hospitalized, they discovered he was mildly diabetic. "Not enough to require the needle, though, which is another break. Could you imagine me walkin in a track with a needle? What I do is take pills."

And with that, Felsburg showed me a vial of pills of various sizes and colors. He shook some into his hand, and made with the nomenclature. "These white ones are for when I get tired. The blue ones are for the diabetes. The little ones are for headaches."

I pointed to the red-and-green capsules.

"Oh, those," Boom Boom said. "I take those when my horse is involved in an Inquiry, or a Photo."

He snorts at players who fancy themselves as handicappers. "One time I clocked a guy at Delaware Park who was usin' a slide rule on the entries. It took him 25 minutes to dope a race. He went up to the $10 window and I sidled up in back of him and saw him bet $20 on a 2 to 5 shot. I coulda' figured that out in 25 seconds."

Boom Boom has his own system. One is The Repeat. He will watch for the winning daily-double combinations, then play those two numbers in each race thereafter—one number to win, the other to show, depending on the odds. He also had a hunch system in which he parleys matching names. He remembers a $233 double score that was the result of Oh Happy Days and Gladahad. Once he bet Slow Motion and Diamond Back, but he did not reveal who won, the hares or his tortoises.

Boy and man, he has been playing the horses for a living, of sorts. I remembered he had four children and asked about the family.

"I blew the second marriage since I saw you last," he said. "I'm a lousy handicapper with wives, too. I live with my daughter and her husband."

There are no regrets.

"If I had it to do all over again," he said, "I'd play the same horses. I get by. I never worry about money. I loaned a guy $5 once; the other day he sees me and he was goin' good and he pays me $50. Pretty good interest, right?

"I go into a store for a jar of peanut butter and the clerk recognizes me and he says he owes me a dollar he once stroked me for at a track. I don't even remember the transaction, but I wind up with a free jar of peanut butter. Friends. You can't beat 'em. They all know me at the tracks. I take doubles down for guys and if they hit, they take care of me. My best live one was a guy that hit a $1,200 double. He gave me $200. I run bets at the track, too, and the tips mount up. Biggest winner I ever had personally was $678 at Atlantic City. Horse called Panacea, which means medicine, a cure-all. I know he made me well that day."

No regrets at all, Harry? How about the boyhood friends that now have security going for them, as opposed to your lugging career?

"I don't envy them," Boom Boom said. "I run into old buddies who are supposed to be secure, with nice houses, but they're henpecked and alcoholic and they make me nervous. I could have gone that way. I could have lived with ulcers, like they're doin', but I took the right road. Playin' the horses, it's good therapy. Besides, I don't lose that much. One good Exacta, and I'm in the Cadillac class."

It is always a pleasure to run into Boom Boom. I told him to be sure and take care of himself.

"Don't worry," he assured me. "I do. Since the heart attack, I don't run to the windows. I walk."

Tokyo Rush

A pusher in Tokyo is a guy paid to shove you into the subway cars so the doors can be closed. What you hear about the rush hour over there—it's true.

TOKYO—They say to get the real taste of Tokyo, you should ride the subway system during rush hours.

I did, and it tasted like jam. But Mr. Smucker never filled up a jar like the Japanese fill up their underground trains. Man, there wasn't room for a bamboo shoot.

"Don't do it," a friendly piano player warned when I told him of my plans to hit the 8 a.m. line the next day. "You'll get killed in the crush."

He seemed sincerely concerned, but I already had made my appointment with a young tour guide name of Tsuneo Ikeda. The piano player just shook his head solemnly and in my honor, ripped off a chorus of "I'll See You in My Dreams".

The world's most populated city has a network of seven lines which carry 3.1 million a DAY and here you all thought Almart's on a Sunday was a crowd!

It seemed as if all 3.1 million were marching in the tunnels of the Shinjuku Station, to which we had taxied, as Tsuneo and I went underground. This is the Marunouchi-Ogikubo line, the one with the red cars. They converged, a mute army of trimly attired commuters and students. It was as if they had groomed their lush black hair, wound themselves up with a key and aimed their quick footsteps toward the trains that would take them to the schools, offices, banks and shops of Tokyo.

I commanded a safe spot near a low-slung water fountain and watched in fascinated awe until Tsuneo suggested we go off-tackle.

The start was orderly. Unlike American passengers, the Japanese do not wait in helter-skelter blobs parallel to the tracks. They queue up two-abreast at designated points, knowing automation will stop the cars precisely where doors will meet their columns.

White-gloved pushers are the marshals. What they push are the last boarders as the doors close, and one of them got me good. The train arrived on what was its third stop. They run every two minutes. It already looked full—to a foreigner. But the doors slid open and my column charged—pushing, shoving, elbowing those ahead and inside. Nobody spoke, nobody grunted. Unbelievably, there was space for what seemed like an addition of 30 people.

I was the last aboard through this middle door, propelled by a push from a marshal who must have trained in the Eastern Basketball League. With this help, I barely fit inside as the door closed across my back.

As I was pushed, I had to raise my right arm overhead to avoid bumping a stolid little woman, and I couldn't lower it until the next stop. There wasn't room. I did manage to rest it on a baggage rack. My morning shot of Right Guard apparently did its duty, because I did not see any rider becoming groggy. They would have had to faint standing up, anyway.

People took little naps standing and sitting. Looking over this enormous concentration of heads, I noticed only two hats, one a beret, on what was a cold morning. All faces bore the worldwide resignation of the subway rider. The air was close.

There was a passenger turnover at the next stop. The doors glided open and I popped out like a grape from its skin, then was rushed back aboard. At the next stop the car discharged all but a few passengers and Tsuneo and I could sit down. There was another jam session when we transferred to the orange cars of the Ginza line, via which we visited the transit authority offices.

Tokyo subway cars and depots are clean. The litter, the vandalism, the graffiti, the violence of Philadelphia do not exist here. There is a pickpocket problem, Tsuneo said. The 7:30 to 9 a.m. peak, and its evening counterpart, have to be the happiest of hunting grounds.

We paid 30 yen (about a dime) into the ticket machine and another 20 yen at the transfer deals in this extremely expensive metropolis.

I was to learn that Tokyo subway cars, which are built to carry from 98 to 144 people, depending on the engineering, operate at an impossible 300 per cent of capacity at rush time. Yet, the system is among the world's safest and most efficient.

There are no subway police. They just aren't needed.

The man at the government authority said any new subway line takes 10 years to make a profit, and the cost to build them is 7 billion yen for one kilometer of track, including rolling stock. There are 9,000 employes.

"Profit is a problem," he said as he poured tea for his visitors, "which is why we are asking for a fare raise. The last one was four years ago. We want a 25-per cent increase. You see a lot of passengers, but the expense is great. And we discount ticket plans a great deal for students and commuters."

Tokyo got a late start (1927) in the subway business. London's tube goes back to 1863. One line here was built for the 1964 Olympics traffic, and two more were installed after that.

You are looking at an overnight expert on Tokyo subways. I have the sore ribs to prove it.

Catered Affair

Theo Brans got the Quick Thinking Award for this, and retired from the catering field undefeated. Now he is food manager at Newark, Del., Country Club. No pets allowed.

The luncheon was elegant. Take Theo Brans' word. He catered it.

A birthday luncheon in a Greenville chateau. Let us say the guest of honor's and host's name was Perth Steele.

"Very dignified guy," said Theo Brans. "Walks like a general. This luncheon was for his family and close friends. Very big shots. 30 people, all told."

Theo is from Amsterdam, Holland. He is young and has a continental style and an accent that must be worth at least 12 per cent of what he charges. He manages the CK Ranch for the equally flaired Tom Ballard. On the side, from his house in Northcrest, he has this food service.

"Theo Caterers" appears in the Yellow Pages inside a fancy oval border. The ad mentions excellent service and cuisine with the European touch. It also says "By Preference", and I took Preference to be the name of the chef till I found out his name is George.

"None of this industrial stuff for me—none of those 400-500 crowds," Theo sniffed. "The small intimate party in the home, that is my specialty. I did $12,000 business last year, only my second year. Not too bad, eh?"

I agreed. But back to the birthday party.

Mrs. Steele, with her husband sitting in, had made the arrangements. He wanted to make sure they booked his favorite dessert. Vanilla ice cream with chocolate sauce. To be served with a big sheet cake with blue icing. The icing had to be blue. A simple "Happy Birthday" decoration.

Theo reported in good time with his food truck, plus his crew of three waitresses and George the chef. George the chef is Greek, from the old country, and he doesn't speak much English.

Theo's brown eyes sparkled as he checked the scene. Big, bright, practical kitchen. Easy access to the dining room and its three round tables. Mr. and Mrs. Steele, lovely people to work for. Even the two big dogs greeted him warmly.

"Don't ask me what kind of dogs," Theo said. "Brown dogs. Nice dogs. Retrievers, you say? Who knows?"

Appetizers were to be served by 12:30, to go with the cocktails. Theo hit them with the shrimp on ice with two kinds of sauce, the quiche lorraine and the stuffed celery. He laid an Amsterdam bow on them, for good measure.

Luncheon at 1:30. Caviar, tossed salad, then Chicken Vol Au Vent, with French peas. I asked him what's with the Vol Au Vent.

"Creamed chicken in patty shells," he replied. "But it sells better in French."

Theo was pleased, because the guests seemed pleased as they dined. He told George the chef it was time to fetch the cake. They had left the cake in the truck so it would not wilt in the warmth of the house.

Theo made a final check of the dining room. Coming back, he was greeted by an excited, arm-waving George the chef, who voiced a strangled "Come, come, come!"

George the chef rushed out the back door and Theo followed him into the back of the truck. What he saw almost stopped his Holland heart; his socks did, indeed, fall. The birthday cake, specially requested, the one with the beautiful blue icing, was a mess. A disaster. It also was two-thirds gone.

"The dogs had got to it," Theo said. "One of the girls had left the truck doors open and the dogs walked in and ate up almost all the cake."

Theo did not sag for long. He rallied magnificently. His mind raced and he called for action.

"You, George," he snapped. "See what you can do to patch up what's left of the cake. Smooth the icing over it."

He called to a waitress. "You, Brenda, jump in your car and go buy me two or three birthday cakes, any kind, enough for these people. I don't care where you get them. Seven-Eleven, Wawa, Gaylords, anywhere. But get them fast."

George was already trowling the cake as Brenda squealed her car out of the driveway.

"I had to stall till the girl got back, hopefully with some cake," Theo recalls. "I delayed picking up the luncheon plates, till Mrs. Steele told me it was time. Then we made a production of clearing away the dishes and brushing the crumbs. I personally annoyed the same crumb for two minutes."

The ice cream was served, also laboriously. Still no Brenda.

George the chef had done a masterful job on the almost-totaled cake.

Theo could stall no longer. He put 20 candles on the cake and lighted them and, carrying the plate high above his head on one palm like Veloz used to carry Yolanda, he made his entrance. The party applauded.

"The candles overpowered the cake" is the way Theo put it.

His guests sang as Mr. Steele blew out the candles. Theo quickly retrieved the cake and retreated, apparently to slice it.

"I wasn't about to serve that cake," Theo said, "not after the dogs had been in it. Besides, they didn't leave enough. But if Brenda didn't show up soon, I would have had to make a confession and scratch the cake course.

But here comes Brenda, her car skidding to a stop. The pastry cavalry. She had three round, birthday-type cakes in a brown bag. White icing.

"Got 'em at the A&P," she whispered breathlessly.

The cakes were swiftly undressed and sliced in the kitchen and served.

"And you know what?" Theo said. "Nobody said nothing about the blue icing suddenly becoming white."

The luncheon over, Mrs. Steele came in to congratulate the caterer.

"I'm behind schedule," she added. "It's long since been time to feed the dogs."

Three waitresses turned their backs and smothered laughs.

"I had to tell Mrs. Steele the dogs already had eaten, she was so nice," Theo said. "Anyway, there was a housekeeper there who had seen the whole thing. I had to break the news before she did. So we had a little talk in the living room and I apologized and told the whole story."

You know what the aristocratic Mrs. Steele did? She broke up.

"I thought something was wrong," she laughed. "I looked at that cake with the candles and I was sure we had ordered another type, but I didn't want to say anything."

She couldn't wait to tell her husband and their guests, and the party disbanded on that merry note. For days, it was the joke of the season in Greenville and at the Wilmington Club, where, I understand, they can use one.

"They loffed their heads off," said Theo.

He was proud of the way he and his troops had reacted. I must say I was mildly impressed. But I cannot help but wonder what the action would have been had the dogs gotten into the Chicken Vol Au Vent. I believe they still would be throwing cold water on Theo. And also on George the chef.

Otto at Ragan's

Otto Dekom didn't speak to me for weeks after this fantasy was published. We since have become good friends; some people say it serves me right.

Casimer Ragan called.

"I see in your paper where Otto Dee-kom is going around reviewing restaurants," he said. "Could you talk him into putting my place in his act?"

The name is Dekom, I corrected. Dekom, as in Wreck 'em, which is what his critiques do to the souls of many theatrical and musical groups.

But Otto Dekom in Ragan's Tavern? I just couldn't picture it. But I didn't want to hurt my friend's feelings. I said I would ask.

An hour later, Otto came swirling into the office. He never arrives. He alights. He is from the Loretta Young school of entrances.

I went into my game plan. First, congratulations for the series of dining-out box scores, which thus far has covered the Hotel du Pont, Leounes' and Winklers.

I mentioned the call from Ragan's and when Otto said he never heard of it and didn't intend to hear of it, I said the restaurateur was an ardent fan of his. This made points, because Otto doesn't know I lie a lot.

Next, on schedule, I reminded Dekom he owed me a favor. It was only last week that he tore the hem of his opera cloak, and I showed him how to fix it temporarily with a paper clip.

Then I guaranteed him he would find Ragan's delightfully different.

It worked. He said he would do it for me, but his program had to be respected. Our critic-at-large would show up unannounced, so the place could not put on any special airs. Agreed.

I gave him the address. 1000 block Chestnut St., the section known as Hedgeville. No, you won't need travelers checks.

I had a spy there to report the scene. He said it happened this way:

Enter Otto. He stood at the door, a study in tolerance, until he was greeted. The greeter was the proprietor, Cas, in apron and with cigar stump and big smile.

"I do not have a reservation, captain," Dekom said, "but I would be most pleased if you would sit me near the string ensemble."

Cas, who was just about to tell the stranger to take any seat in the joint, shrugged and led him to the back of the crowded barroom and sat him at a table next to the jukebox.

"On account of we don't have strings," he said, "the music's on me. We did have a record by a mummer's band, but the guys played it to death."

Ragan sat down with Otto. He always sits down with the customers. You cannot say that about the uptown maitres d.

"Can I help you, buddy" he asked, pad and pencil in hand. Ashes from his cigar spilled on the table and he blew them off, right on Otto's lap.

"Menu, my good man," Dekom said.

"We don't have any," Ragan said. "Our menu is in Helen's head. Helen is the waitress. How about something to drink first?"

"May I see the wine list?" Dekom said.

Ragan said sorry, just shots and beer. Dekom ordered a glass of beer. Cas fetched it, and Otto blanched. At Ragan's, they serve the beer in glasses so big you could get an echo out of them.

Cas withdrew and Helen came over and just stood at Otto's table. You could see this was a day her feet were giving her trouble.

Otto wanted to know the soup of the day.

"What day is it?" Helen countered.

"Wednesday."

"We don't have soup on Wednesdays," she said. "Now that you mention it, we never have soup."

"Then what are your entrees?"

"Well," said Helen, "you came in the front door, and we also have one in the back. I bet you thought I didn't know any French, dad."

Otto bridled, just a bit. "You must have something to eat, or you wouldn't be working here."

Helen put a hand on his shoulder. "Don't get upset, doll. We have ham, cheese, ham and cheese, cheese and ham, roast beef, liverwurst, liverwurst with onion, liverwurst without onion, hot dogs with sauerkraut and without, the ham special, the roast-beef special."

"You mean sandwiches?" Otto said. He looked as if he had just dipped into a bowl of bouillabaisse and come up with a fin, or a hook.

Helen shrieked. "Good boy! the customers are getting smarter every day."

At the bar, Ray the Cab Driver, Frankie the Fighter, Dick the Filterer and

Bum the Pensioner turned around to check the shriek. Disinterested, they returned to their beer.

Otto didn't even seem to notice them. The man has style.

"What kind of bread do you have?" he asked.

"Sliced," said Helen, breaking up again.

Otto ordered the roast-beef special, on white. Its dimensions were as formidable as the schooner of beer that still was at high tide.

Otto stood up, directly over the sandwich, and took a picture of it with his trusty Instamatic.

"Must be some sort of a CIA guy," muttered Ray the Cab Driver to Dick the Filterer.

Dekom made notes as he ate and sipped. When he researches a dish, it stays researched. Then he suavely summoned the waitress and asked for the pastry cart.

Helen stared at him. "Oh, yes, the pastry cart. It's not your day, doll. We sent it to John's Body Shop. A guy fell on it, pastry and all. The best I can do, I can show you his sweater. It's hanging in the kitchen, with the whipped cream still on it."

I do not have a report on the finish of the scene, because my spy became overmatched by the beer and had to leave. But, back in the office, I did manage to get a peek at the outline of Dekom's upcoming review.

"Food: A rather limited menu but surprisingly tasty and plentiful, considering the many responsibilities of the chef, who also waited on me and proved a delightful conversationalist. The bread was fresh and as the chef pointed out, sliced."

"Atmosphere: Charmingly saloon. A very intimate room in which you rub elbows with the colorful natives.

"Condiments: Salt and pepper are available in salt and pepper shakers. The horseradish comes in its original jar. There is a jar on each table, thus eliminating that international but rather annoying request, 'Please pass the horseradish'.

"Men's room: Yes.

"Services: Very snappy. I suspect the folk humor of the neighborhood runs deep among the staff.

"Prices: For a robust roast-beef special and a remarkably sized flagon of beer, my bill was $1.15. This was most reasonable, even with sliced bread. In fact, my visit was profitable. On the way out, six natives asked me if they could order wallet-sized prints of the picture I took of my sandwich. They could."

The Deep Comic

Red Buttons was a marvelous interview. He gave a classic description, I thought, of the ups and downs of show business.

The deep little comedian had reminisced and philosophised. Now he softly counterattacked as his reply to an unasked question.

"My comment—is that what you want?" he said.

I nodded. I had mentioned Carol Lynley. She said, right there in the wire story, that Red Buttons was bad news to work with in "The Poseidon Adventure". ("Red didn't like me very much. He made my life miserable because he thought I had a much better part than he did. Of course I did.")

Red Buttons, lounging in a dressing room at The Playhouse, twirling a Brandywine Room toothpick, paused.

"I know about the quotes," he said. "You don't have to repeat them. She blasted everybody in the picture, not only me.

"I don't want to dignify her remarks. Carol's reputation in the business speaks for itself. This time, it was a case of 'Hell hath no fury like a woman scorned.' "

I was about to ask if he was the guy who did the scorning, but I didn't have to.

"She wanted to get romantic," he continued. "I wanted nothing to do with it. It was embarrassing to me and the producer and to the people at Fox—everybody. It was bloody awful stuff. I can't understand how she could go out on a promotion tour and malign the cast. She was supposed to make points for the picture, but she completely rejected it.

"This is the most I have spoken on this subject. It is really very embarrassing, and I don't think about her. As far as my being jealous of her part, make up your own mind. See the picture."

Red Buttons is almost jockey-sized, and he admittedly has had more ups and downs than the steeplechase variety. He was in town Friday night to head the firefighter's annual benefit show. For $2.50 you could see Red Buttons and Frankie Fontaine and Pat Suzuki, among others. Fontaine was pinch-hitting for Louis Nye. These vaudeville stands are more of a down than an up in Buttons' career, but he is dropping out late this month to play the Palladium in London.

"They're a pain in the fanny," he said of the one-nighters, "not recommended for guys who are huffing and puffing. You've got to be in shape. I am. I can still do my pirouettes."

He wanted to tell me the story of the last time he played Wilmington.

"32 years ago," he said. "I'll never forget it. I came here with a play, a farce, called 'The Admiral Had a Wife'. As good a cast as you could ever put on a stage. Jose Ferrer, Uta Hagan, Mildred Dunnock, Alfred Drake.

"We rehearsed in New York, and opened in Wilmington. A week or two here, and we whipped it into shape. Then we went to Baltimore, from there to New York. We were to open Dec. 8, 1941. You know what happened the day before. We were the first theatrical casualty of the war. My first Broadway show, and we never opened."

Red Buttons, nee Aaron Chwatt, now 54, wound up in the Army. He also was to wind up with an Oscar, an Emmy, a Golden Globe—and a sinking spell that was years ahead of the good ship Poseidon. The Oscar was for best supporting male actor—to Brando—in his very first movie, "Sayonara".

Red Buttons, for his Academy Awards upset, for a hit show on early TV, was a sensation. It seemed as if every kid in the country was imitating him 20 years ago, cupping an ear, hopping around chanting "ho-ho".

"As thrilling as it was for me to win an Oscar with my background—Catskills, burlesque," he said, "it didn't match the first year on TV. Everything that you can imagine that happened to Frank Sinatra happened to me. Fans ripped off my clothes. Parades in the streets. Bands meeting me at airports. Thousands of kids with signs with my name on it. It was overwhelming. I swear to God I was punchy with success. Maybe if I hadn't been punchy, I wouldn't have made the mistakes I made.

"The horror of the whole thing is that you think it is going to last forever. It doesn't. That one great sustained year, the first of three, I was knocking out opponents like Joe Louis. I thought I was going to be enshrined. Then came the problems, too many for me to enumerate.

"Things start going the other way, and fright sets in. I'm an emotional animal. I felt I was losing it all, and my behavior left a lot to be desired. There were people encouraging this behavior, compounding the felony. I went up quickly and I went down quickly. I thought the problems were indigenous to me, but my situation became a cliche. I had writing problems, and I wasn't mature enough to handle them, and I didn't have the organization to handle them. My memories of TV are bittersweet."

Buttons now was walking around the room as he talked, but the emotional animal was not emotional.

"Don't knock three years with your own show," I said. "That still would be pretty good durability on TV."

"Thanks," he said with a smile. "But I thought I was set for 140 years. You take three from 140, it leaves you desolate."

But you can look it up that Red Buttons was big, and he likes that.

"Like Babe Ruth and his home runs," he said, "I'll be in the books as long as there are books, because of the Oscar. It was a fantastic boost for my ego—it made me think I could be a serious actor. I hoped others would feel that way and, 20 pictures later, it seems to be working out. Working with Brando, though, made me realize how little I knew about acting. And I did something about it. Seeing Marlon work encouraged me to go to an acting school in New York, Wynn Handman's, for six months. As they say in my trade, I learned to press the button."

The tiny redhead turned back some more pages.

"It's funny that Japan has been such a strange touch on my life," he said. "Not only did I get the Oscar for 'Sayonara', but the actor I had to beat out, in my mind, was Sessue Hayakawa for 'River Kwai'. And then there was Pearl Harbor, knocking me off Broadway before I even got on it. It's almost as if Japan felt sorry for me for that, the way things turned out later."

He was a 16-year-old bellhop, entertaining in an Irish joint in City Island, N.Y., when the owner dubbed him Red Buttons.

"Those early years, people kept after me to change that name," he said. "One of them was Billy Rose. He said I'd never go anywhere with a handle like that. Even the producer of 'Sayonara' suggested I drop the 'Red' and get a real first name. That would have been ludicrous, me being Hildebrand Buttons, or something like that. I decided to be myself, even though Red Buttons wasn't really me. But it had been for a long time. Understand how I felt?"

There is a Mrs. Buttons and two little Buttons. He has an album of poetry out, dedicated to his daughter. They live in Bel Air, Calif. "We send care packages to Beverly Hills."

The Button future book, he says, includes a sequel to "The Poseidon Adventure". That won't be a sequel if Carol Lynley is in it. It will be a return match.

Porky Oliver

What a folk hero the Porkchop would be today, the way pro golf has exploded—and how the game could use his color. As the purses might indicate, this was written in 1961. Professional Golfer Magazine re-printed it.

Porky Oliver always insisted that his biggest thrill was the third round of the 1953 Masters.

Paired with Ben Hogan, he shot a 67 and Hogan a 66 and between them their best ball was a 59.

It was described as the greatest two-man competitive round in golf history.

Hogan was to win the tournament with a 274—still the Masters record. Oliver finished second with a 279.

Besides that twosome, only three others ever have broken 280 in all the years of the distinguished Masters.

It was a telephone call you never wanted to get, but it had to happen. There was no escape.

"You don't know me," said the voice, "but my name is Yost. I'm a patient at The Memorial Hospital and I wanted you to know that Porky Oliver just died. I have a room near him."

Everybody wanted to be Oliver's partner.

"We always like to play with Porky," Jack Burke Jr. said. "Let me tell you, the Tour would be more attractive to everyone if there were more guys like Oliver.

"I don't think he ever awoke in the morning but that it was a beautiful day to him."

At 2 p.m. Wednesday, September 20, 1961, the gray, perspiring, cancerous shadow of a remarkable athlete had taken a little orange juice.

With a wave of his hand, he indicated he wanted his bed cranked down. The nurse was lowering the bed when her patient gasped once, twice. His head slumped to one side. Porky Oliver was dead.

On the Tour, they called him the all-American runnerup because he had more than 20 second places.

But the runnerup checks included the PGA Championship, the Masters, the All-American Open and the USGA Open.

There was a phone call from Oliver himself a month ago.

"C'mon over to the hospital and see the letter I got from the Ryder Cuppers. They've made me Honorary Captain and invited me to England."

There was the 1956 Colonial National Invitation at Fort Worth, when Oliver was playing with Tommy Bolt.

Bolt was complaining about his putting all day, and threatening to throw the club away. On the 18th green, before 15,000 people, Bolt blew another putt.

Porky went over to him, quietly took the putter out of Blot's hands and threw it right into the middle of a nearby pond.

Everybody broke up—Bolt included.

"The pain is sharp sometimes," Oliver said in the hospital, shaking his right fist, clenching his teeth.

"Look at my thighs, my legs—so thin. Good thing I've got this belly going for me."

The Army drafted Oliver in 1942, and the fat boy with the immovable grin was drafted into some good luck.

They put him in Special Services, and he and Joe Louis entertained thousands of GIs.

But he had even better fortune. In Tilton General Hospital at Fort Dix, N.J., to have his tonsils removed, Ed met the Army nurse with the funny name who was to become his wife, Clara E. Hee.

Being a former nurse didn't make it any easier for Clare Oliver. She must have known of the inevitable from that first lung operation in May of 1960.

For what was probably the thousandth time, she tried to console her husband. "It's inactivity that's doing that to your legs, dear—it deteriorates the muscles."

Porky, spirits momentarily low, argued defeatedly: "No, no. It's this thing running around inside of me."

When Oliver first wrapped his fists around a golf club, he swung it crosshanded. Even so, he sent the ball a mile with the tremendous power of his arms and back.

He was a natural athlete—maybe Delaware's all-timer.

Ironically, he never won the Wilmington Sportswriters' "Outstanding Athlete" award, started 10 years ago, because he didn't qualify under the residential rule. In that span, he worked out of Seattle, Boston and Denver.

Porky and family moved back to Wilmington from Denver the day after last Christmas—his very last Christmas.

A' La Carte

Oliver knew the medical score, but he insisted: "Miracles happen. You just hope for the best. You start praying to The Man."

Easy come, easy go. That was Edward Stewart Oliver Jr., who went away as "Snowball" and soon became "Porky" to his delighted new companions.

In 1947, he was fourth leading money winner in the country with an official $17,941.15.

The next spring, the PGA had to send him five letters before he remembered his dues. As happy as a horseplayer—which he was.

Clare wiped Porky's perspiring brow, again and again. You tried not to notice tears being dried, too.

But the Porkchop reverted to form. "I get a kick out of watching the Saturday races on that thing," he said, pointing to the television set.

"Somebody will bring in a scratch sheet and we sit here and dope 'em out and I figure that television man owes me $97."

At 43, the one-time Boy Bunyan of the Brandywine scored what was his biggest victory ever in the 1958 Houston Open, $4,300 worth. You saw him tie for fourth in the televised Bing Crosby National in early 1960.

Only weeks after the Crosby, driving from a Texas tournament to Denver, Oliver complained of dizziness and decided on a check-up.

Within a month, there was that first operation. "Make sure you aren't over the limit of 14 knives," he cracked to the surgeon.

Porky Oliver, internationalist. Three Ryder Cup playing appearances. Second in the Ampol Tournament in Australia. Winner of the Jamaica Open, second in the Puerto Rico Open, first in the Philippine Open.

They should have turned him loose in Russia, too—with or without the golf clubs.

"It's almost a year since that operation," Porky was saying as he paced his living room last April, "and I'm tired of sitting around the house.

"I asked the doctor if I could get out and hit a few balls. He said I'd better not count on it."

Show and Bark

I'm glad my old locker-room friends didn't see me on the way to covering a dog show in a grade school. Turned out to be a cute event, though. This is when I was making the transition from sports to general columning. What a test!

It might not have been the Westminister Kennel Club classic, but then Madison Square Garden never had Toby.

Toby is a dog, a she, and she was an entrant in the show at Shipley Elementary School yesterday.

The children did the judging, the exhibiting and the announcing as their contribution to National Dog Week. The custodians did the cleaning up, a requirement that developed when the show had to be held in the gymnasium instead of outdoors because of rain.

But back to Toby:

They had this category "Most Unique". The judge here was a sixth-grader, Barbara Miller.

When announcer Mark Clemens of the fifth grade asked Barbara for her decision, she awarded the badge to the Irish setter named Toby.

Toby was owned and handled, as they say in the field-trial results, by fifth grader Robert Siley.

A pretty dog, with the friendliness characteristic of her breed, but what made her unique? A news hound asked the question of Robert.

"Well," the boy exhibitor replied, "she used to be a cocker spaniel."

Could this be the canine Christine Jorgensen? You mean, son, she changed from a cocker spaniel into an Irish setter?

"Something like that," Robert replied, as he continued his tug-of-war with the straining Toby's leash. "When we got her we thought she was a spaniel; now she's a setter."

The news hound, rather dazed at this point, looked for another badge-winner. The "Smallest" prize was in the clutches of Brian Marolf, a sixth-grader, and his miniature poodle with the well-fitting name of Tiny.

Brian was congratulated, and was asked the age of his curly little winner.

"I don't know yet," he replied. "I haven't been keeping track. But he's full-grown."

Also full-grown, and then some, was the "Biggest" winner. Brock is an Irish wolfhound, all 168 pounds of him, a dog show in himself. Around the AKC he is known as Bracknagh of Eagle.

Brock had the "Biggest" badge wrapped up as soon as he appeared. His appearance was somewhat reluctant. He was the official entry of first-grader Maureen Lundy but because of his size he was shown by her mother, Mrs. Thomas Lundy.

Mrs. Lundy, who is very small, had trouble getting Brock into the building and had to get him to cooperate on a running start while someone held the door open.

Itch, a miniature dachshund, came dressed to kill and took the "Funniest" badge with a Santa Claus costume that included a peaked hat. His owner was Alan Ladd of the second grade. ("That's right," he said. "Just like the movie actor.")

Alan explained that Itch's outfit was made by an aunt and that while it might be a little early for a Christmas costume, "We just got it."

Sisters Lisa and Laurie McKernan, of the fifth and fourth grade, respectively, had the "Furriest" winner in their collie, Baron. He won by a hair — several thousand of them. If there had been a "Noisiest" division, Baron would have won that, too. He featured a very bass and consistent bark.

The "Prettiest" was fourth-grader Eileen Joukainen's Jackou. He was identified by his sign as a "Maltise" as the spelling teacher winced. Asked if she thought her dog would take the beauty prize, Eileen replied "Yes . . . sort of."

There were about 25 assorted dogs in the contest and all the kids from the 200 Wing of the school came over to watch. The six judges, holding signs identifying their categories, were stationed around the gym floor and were surrounded by contestants. Then the judges retired to a set of bleachers to announce their decisions.

Mary Grace Stanis, a third-grade teacher and 200 Wing leader, and fellow teachers of the wing in the Alfred I. du Pont District organized the show with the encouragement of the principal, John Gray.

"I'm a great one to be running this," said Miss Stanis as she awaited the arrival of the entries. "I like dogs—but I'm a little afraid of them."

Other judges were Stephen Larson, David Williams, Elizabeth Ryan, Steven Brown and Stephen Stier. Martin Markiewitz helped with the announcing, and Maria Donley gave a talk about National Dog Week.

A lot of dogs got to meet each other. The custodians, Donald Cox and Jack

Green, mopped up the show—literally. And where they mopped was in the area of the "Funniest" sign.

A black French poodie named Noel showed up just as the show was breaking up. She was to have been the candidate of Billy, Suzanne and Richie Bartz, but all had dental appointments and arrived too late for the competition.

"Noel might have won one of two prizes," said their mother, Mrs. Nancy Bartz. "If not Prettiest, then Most Unique. She's pregnant."

The Hard Loser

More than two years later, they still haven't found who murdered Horace Dyer. A ball field in Claymont, Del., now bears his name.

I used to kid Horace Dyer on the sports pages by referring to him as Harvard Horace Dyer.

An Ivy Leaguer he so obviously wasn't. I hope that doesn't sound stuffy. Horace never took it that way; I think he got a kick out of it.

He was a large, argumentative guy with a beer belly. He worked for the State Highway Department. Year after year he organized and managed semi-pro baseball teams, and it takes a special breed to stay with this. Little income, great outgo, hours and hours and weeks and weeks of getting sponsors and players and fields; of sweating out victories and defeats and rain and darkness and umpires; of getting booed by the other team's partisans.

He was a throwback, the classic sandlot manager. A near-extinct breed. Wilmington is one of the few towns that still has a baseball league for adult players. A few martyrs like Dyer kept it glued together, and it is going to be even tougher without him. A semi-pro baseball league may not be on your list of things worth saving, but Horace Dyer would have given you a debate on this.

He was the only guy I ever knew who was named Horace. The man and the name were an incongruous match. I have a vague picture of a Horace-type, but he wasn't it.

Beneath that sometimes truculent exterior, though, lived a loyal man. He would do anything for the athletic community in Claymont, even to sticking his nose into school-board business. When he championed something, he wouldn't budge. He managed American Legion teams and he administered a whole Babe Ruth League and he organized a boosters club for the high school football team and so on into the realm of the thankless avocations.

The loyal man lives no more. They found Horace Dyer murdered behind a railroad station at 2 o'clock in the morning.

A violent end to an aggressive man. With a bullet in his head and two in his back, he had managed to get into his car and start it and drive it before the life went out of him and the car crashed into a building. You can't die much harder than that.

I didn't know about the slaying until the paper came out on that afternoon. I saw it on Page 1 and I felt as if somebody had shot me, too. Horace had his weaknesses and he had encounters with the law, but I admired his almost masochistic devotion to his sports hobby. I liked the guy.

He had called me up not long ago. It was a day or so after the Academy Awards, the Oscar presentations, on TV.

"This fellow who came on as president of the movies, this Taradash, I think he used to live in Claymont," Horace said.

He was referring to Daniel Taradash, president of the Academy of Motion Pictures Arts and Sciences and a topflight scenario writer.

I was interested and asked Horace if there was any way of checking it. Horace thought the family had lived on Commonwealth Avenue and that they moved away when Taradash was about 14. He said he knew a woman in Claymont who corresponded with the family, but couldn't recall her name.

"I'll think of it in a day or two and I'll call you back," said Dyer.

He never did. He never will.

Horace was a great needler and if you couldn't take it and wanted to get physical about it, I imagine Dyer would oblige you. He was from the we-may-lose-the-game-but-we'll-win-the-fight school. They say the best action in the history of the semi-pro league never happened on the ball field; it happened at league meetings, during the winter, when Horace and a strategist from another team would get to discussing a problem. If you can discuss a problem through a headlock, they discussed it.

Dyer always was whipping up a banquet for some Claymont sports team or other. His last one was the Boosters Club dinner for the high school football squad in December. He had asked me to m.c. it and because I had been forced to turn him down several years running, I thought it about time I accepted. I'm glad I did.

And as we walked into the hall I gave Horace my annual rib about one of the all-time banquets he had thrown. This was about 15 years ago. He was managing this Legion team in Claymont, and he arranged for a dinner in the Legion hall.

He had me on the bill, and Danny Murtaugh and Benny Bengough from the big leagues were to speak, also. Maybe 10 of us.

We took our places at the head table and the room was nicely set up. There was one small flaw. There were only about six people in the place. Horace had forgotten to invite his baseball team. Honest. It was the only banquet in history where the speakers outnumbered the patrons. As I recall, Horace scrambled to a phone and got some show of strength to report, and we even had the help come out of the kitchen to hear the program and help fill up the room. Murtaugh still likes to tell this story.

I guess I'll stop writing about Horace Dyer on that light note. He will be buried tomorrow. There must be hundreds and hundreds of kids and men who played ball for him, and they have to be sick about his terrible death.

Horace Dyer worked hard for his teams and his athletes and his community and sought no credit for it. What ever he got into, he got into to win and most of the time he did. When he didn't, he lost hard. Right till the very end. So long, Harvard.

Ernie Borgnine

The Mike Douglas Show in Philadelphia is a great source of interviews, and Douglas' staffers are most helpful in setting them up. I love Borgnine's wives-and-shoes analogy.

Ernest Borgnine in a musical? Next they'll be putting tap shoes on Telly Savalas.

I assumed my look of incredulity, the one I usually wear at meat counters, as I brought up the subject.

Borgnine cut loose with the hearty hunk of laughter that is a trademark.

"Hey, I don't do anything too musical in this, but I wouldn't be a stranger to it," he said. "I did a musical for 20th Century Fox called 'The Best Things in Life Are Free'. Story of Da Sylva, Brown and Henderson, the song writers. I played Lou Brown, and Dan Dailey and Gordon Macrae were the other two. I carried on like a fool."

He must have carried on very well, as usual. I checked it in those marvelous old New York Times film reviews our library stocks. The year was 1956, and the critic said the best thing in that particular life was the actress, Sheree North, but "running her a close second, and bellowing like a jovial bull, is the portly Mr. Borgnine".

The versatile Mr. Borgnine, who runs the gamut from menace to Marty to McHale's Navy, soon will be with us at The Playhouse in a show called "Untamed Land". It also features the American Dance Theatre, Jimmie Rodgers, a full orchestra and a barnful of banjos, fiddles and guitars.

Borgnine will be the narrator of this story of the pioneers, which means we won't get to see the burly bully of the movies sing and soft shoe.

"I could hold my own at that, I think," he said. "They asked me if I also wanted to do bits and pieces in the show. It seems they've had narrators who also got into the acts. But I told them I had enough to do as narrator. They seemed relieved, because they always preferred to leave this to the specialists and didn't really want my predecessors cluttering up the place."

He unleashed another laugh.

"I give myself a 4 as a singer, maybe a 5 as a dancer," he calculated. "When I was going to drama school for 4-1/2 months, the curriculum included modern dance, and there I was doing the splits and all the other maneuvers with Martha Graham's proteges. I looked like a 248-pound bear in tights."

We were talking in a Mike Douglas Show conference room in Philadelphia, and it was a little disconcerting to me. Borgnine, who was to be the mystery guest on the show, was in heavy clown makeup. Rubber nose, red wig, shiny grease paint, baggy costume, suitcase shoes, the works. If it hadn't been for his laugh and the spaces in his teeth—he'd make a great Vince Lombardi—I never would have guessed.

He has a thing about clowns.

"I love anything to do with them," he said. "Matter of fact, my clown life comes third, after my private life, then my screen life. I go to Milwaukee every Fourth of July to narrate a marvelous circus parade, and I'm crazy about that opportunity. I'd like to make a movie about a clown, but I'm afraid it wouldn't be box-office. There aren't many that share my great respect for them, the way they devote their lives to making other people happy."

Borgnine figures to enjoy himself with "Untamed Land", but the 55-year-old actor has no lofty stage ambitions, like to be in a winner on Broadway.

"I couldn't stand the monotony of doing the same play weeks on end," he said. "A repertory company, that's okay. But a long-running play would be too mechanical. I'd be an automaton. It would drive me whacky, which the stage has done in much less time. Don Rickles and I did four weeks of 'The Odd Couple' in California. I was the sloppy guy, the sports writer. It was fun to hear the audience respond, and Neil Simon told us we did a fine job, but the repetition was a drag. Eight performances of the same thing each week would drive anybody cuckoo."

Borgnine said he has a clause in his "Untamed Land" contract that will permit him to drop out, should a movie opportunity unfold. Specifically, the lead in an untitled story about an unknown who discovered he has six months to live. He is revered at the time of his death.

Having free-styled his way to safety in "The Poseidon Adventure", Borgnine now has one out called "Emperor of the North Pole", in which he and Lee Marvin—according to the commercials—wage the screen's most brutal fight.

Borgnine grinned through the paint. "Cue Magazine said that in this picture I am the meanest, most villainous SOB that ever hit the screen. It is a good role, one of my best. I've done some fair to middlin' work since 'Marty' and the Oscar, maybe better. Like 'Bad Day at Flat Rock' and 'Pay or Die.' The worst one I ever made? When they first brought me to Hollywood, I did one in seven days with Jon Hall, 'China Corsair'. I played a Chinaman. I never have seen the picture, but I had the feeling while I was making it that my Chinaman wasn't going to win any award."

There is a Du Pont angle to the Borgnine background. Our clippings show that in 1964 he went to court in Los Angeles to try and collect $25,000 from Ricki du Pont, the widow of Francis V. du Pont, son of the fifth president of The Company. I wondered what ever happened.

"Nothing," Borgnine said. "I signed a note for $25,000 for Ricki du Pont. She was in cahoots with someone making a motion picture, and she said she needed this loan on Friday to meet a payroll. She was to pay me back Monday. I'm still looking for that Monday. She fell out of sight. When I find her, we'll come to terms. The interest should be pretty good, eh?"

I had to bring up the marriages. He has had five of them. I suggested this could be viewed as a sign Borgnine is tough to get along with.

"All I can say is that I wasn't the ONLY one married," he said. "It takes two to tango. Let me tell you a story."

He did. About the famous man who was told his wife was an absolute gem as a housekeeper. He agreed. His wife also impressed people as an outstanding hostess and mother, too. He agreed. Then the man pointed to his feet.

"See these shoes?" he said. "Genuine alligator. Made by Ben of Hollywood. $200 a pair. They look nice, don't they? Well, let me tell you something—they hurt, and I'm the only one who knows it."

Maybe that's why they didn't insist that Ernest Borgnine dance in "Untamed Land". His feet must be killing him.

Foul-Ball View

They wouldn't be interested in me today as a foul-ball chaser.
Now they use girls. Wonder why?

BALTIMORE—it might have been a first.

First sports writer to be on the field while a major-league baseball game was being played. No fair counting Jim Brosnan.

The sports writer had to pose as a foul-ball chaser—a title for which he was at least 50 per cent qualified—one of those two innocuous guys who sit in foul territory right next to the stands. This is an operation designed to (1) speed up the game and (2) keep the customers from grabbing all the baseballs.

Innocuous? A rookie felt like the most conspicuous person in the park. Conspicuous and scared—a sitting duck, he thought, for a decapitating line drive.

The bit had been proposed to the Orioles and they said sure, come on down. Bob Brown, the traveling secretary and public relation, took it up with whoever he takes things up with, and it was no problem.

The Phillies had first shot at this virtually brilliant idea. They wanted no parts of it.

"It's a league matter," said John Quinn, who hadn't listened to Ford Frick all those years for nothing.

And even if the league okayed it, Quinn said, it would make the Phillies vulnerable "to a lot of other requests".

Quinn really is a most cooperative man, and he wasn't fooling anybody. He just didn't want a maimed sports writer, with dependents, on his conscience.

The resident foul-ball chaser on the left-field line in Memorial Stadium is

Ken Norris, 23. By day, he works for the city Water Department. He moonlights at the ball park for $4 a night. He will break into a Chandlerish "I love baseball" commentary at the drop of a rosin bag.

The Orioles were playing Cleveland this night. The ball boys work for the head groundskeeper, Joe Brown. Brown turned us over to Norris for coaching and to Skeets Bittner, his assistant, for outfitting.

Bittner came up with a spotless uniform in the proper sizes—well, almost proper. Orange cap, heavily starched whites with "Orioles" in pale orange on the front and back of the shirt. The shirt even had a number. It was No. 5, and it didn't seem a fair thing to do to the fans. Brooks Robinson is No. 5, too, and think of the confusion.

Joe Brown, an old baseball hand from Buffalo who has been at this job since 1955, made it all sound suspiciously simple. You changed clothes in his office under the stands.

"Just get the balls and throw 'em back," he said, breaking up. You pressed for particulars.

"If the Orioles are at bat, throw the ball to the third base coach, Billy Hunter. If the visiting club is up, throw it to the ball boy who sits by the stands in back of the plate. Don't get the throw too close to the stands, or somebody will reach out and grab it, And don't skull anybody. One time one of our guys winged the plate umpire.

"Don't touch any balls in play. If there's a foul fly hit near you, get out of the way fast, and take the stool with you."

Norris was sympathetic. "You won't get much action. One, two, balls at the most. I do this because I love—"

He was right. Not much action. But the responsibility felt heavier than six Boog Powells.

The squat, orange stool was surprisingly heavy. I lugged it to the gate along the box-seat fence beyond third base, maybe 160 feet from home plate. You sit by the gate because that's the end of an aisle, and you obstruct fewer views.

There were 19,000 people in the big horseshoe. A jittery flunky stood with them for the National Anthem, hat over heart.

Well, the game lasted 2 hours, 51 minutes—the Indians won 10-4—and one ball was bounced to my territory. Pedro Gonzalez of the Indians hit it. It hopped past Coach Reggie Otero and, at a nice, comfortable speed, headed right for the stool. I got up, bent over gracefully and, as the baseball writers say, booted it. People booed. However, the throw to the ball boy was rather magnificent. He had to come up only about 15 feet to meet its dying gasp.

The possibilities, though, were frightening, especially when right-handed smashers like Rocky Colavito and Frank Robinson came up. "Pitch 'em outside, baby!" we found ourselves whispering to the pitchers. A background of white shirts was no help. And you had to keep reminding yourself to stay clear of any ball in play. Man, you're sitting for nine innings, but it's exhausting.

A' La Carte

The view is marvelous. It's a new angle on the beauties of baseball—the base-running of Russ Snyder, the fielding of Brooks Robinson, a soaring home run just inside the left field foul pole by Frank Robinson.

To nearby spectators, the foul-ball guy is both a conversation piece and an information booth. These seats were full of Little Leaguers and their chaperones from Galena, Md. The kids literally begged for a ball.

"If you get three of them, will you give me the fourth?" pleaded one wisp of a boy with a voice like Tallulah Bankhead's.

"Grab his hat," another boy urged, "and when a ball comes, scoop it up."

"Next time I come," the first boy said, "I'm gonna bring a rope. Then I'll tie you to this fence and keep all the balls."

The youngsters, restless after less than an inning, kept up a steady chatter as they slurped sodas and ate peanuts. They grew to love me.

The Orioles relieved Eddie Watt with Moe Drabowsky in the fourth inning, and I took advantage of the lull to walk to the end of stands, out of sight, and stretch. I returned to find a symbol of the kids' affection. There, glistening on the stool, was a hunk of ice—nice and melting and sloppy.

It might have been a first. It definitely was a last.

Sale Day

A guy could get hurt in the rush on a sale day at Wilmington Dry Goods. Photographer Pat Crowe produced some great art of the lady shoppers in action, to go with this column.

The last note of the National Anthem still was on the recording when the gates were opened.

In they came, silently, swiftly, and there was no indecision. They deployed, knowingly. And at 7 o'clock in the morning, it's not easy to be so resolute.

This was a sale day at Wilmington Dry Goods.

I was there with the floor force as it braced for this attack.

I tingled as the crowd formed outside. Had Sergeant York felt this way? Does Dick Butkus experience this thrill each time he goes into battle? Does Mannix? Emily Womach?

They play the Star Spangled Banner every day just before the kickoff. This was at the Tri-State Mall, now the headquarters store. Len Zimmerman and his managers, his buyers, his clerks, his cashiers stood at attention, facing the flag near the doors.

I had the silly feeling that Zimmerman, who is the president, next should throw out the first bra (3 for $2.50, Adjustable Strap, Perfect Quality) or the first panty hose (2 for $1, Clings With Your Every Move, Slight Irregulars). After all, it WAS opening day, of Founder's Days.

7 a.m. and there must have been a hundred people patiently staring at us through the glass of the main entrance. They looked as though they were on a large elevator. One of the few men was wearing a hat, and he removed it when he heard the music. I suppose the other entrances were similarly populated.

"Nowhere else in the country . . . " said Zimmerman, more to himself than to me as the first wave of customers strode in. "Other store owners are still in bed."

Tables were piled high and neat. Mountains of goods. Racks were fat with garments.

"600 dozen panties will be on that table alone," pointed out Zimmerman. He has great pride in his store and his staff and he says that is what makes the place run. Pride.

I was prepared for Bernard Gimbel and I got Len Zimmerman. He is 49, and I will label him The Swinging Merchant and mean it as a compliment. Mod of dress and mind. 23 years ago, he came out of Penneys in Lancaster, Pa., to join Wilmington Dry Goods as an assistant in its only store. Now he bosses all four stores—there is one in West Virginia—and is overseeing the building of another in Vineland, N.J. He is a member of the State Commission on Drug Abuse; he works at this, too.

I had shown up with the sun at 6:15, and there were Zimmerman and two-dozen-some managers and buyers having coffee at the lunch counter. Joe Simmons, Sportswear, was breakfasting on a grilled-cheese sandwich. I was surprised by the youth of the group. Doug Shatley, Shipping and Receiving, is 22. And if you are wondering what ever happened to Harold Trotter, the phenomenal Claymont High athlete, wonder no longer. He manages Children's Wear.

There were no cars on the main lot, no waiting line at 6:15. 30 minutes later, there were.

"Hey, boss," a manager called to Zimmerman, "don't let that crowd fool you. They're really lining up to see 'The Godfather' next door."

I asked Zimmerman how many customers he expected.

"It is tough to project them in numbers," he said. "Put it this way: We will have about 50,000 transactions. One customer may make one purchase, another five, but there will be 50,000 total sales. A couple hundred thousand dollars' worth. And 65 per cent of our action will be from Pennsylvania."

Seconds after the opening, the Knit Tops $1 and Coordinates $3.99 tables were surrounded. The mountains slowly toppled. These were right inside the door. The shoppers were orderly. There were only a few men. One had headed immediately for the cigarette bargain. The others caddied for their wives, holding pocketbooks, merchandise.

Not for nothing does Zimmerman refer to a customer generally speaking, as "she" or "her". Dozens of hers had marched immediately to the left for Women's Fashions. Hangers squeaked on racks. They tried on dresses over their own dresses. There are no fitting rooms on sale days. A young housewife-type wearing slacks tried on a long dress in an aisle, and she wriggled into the dress she allowed her slacks to drop down to her ankles, the better to check the fit. I did a double-take, and she caught me.

Within 15 minutes, there was a line at the dress cashier. One woman bought $330 worth. I saw a lady write a check—left handed—for a $207 purchase.

Richard Hershoin, 30, Ladies' Ready-To-Wear manager manned the cash register. He kept up a running comment as he fielded each item. "5 dollars for a polyester dress—this is really your day! . . . Ladies, if you get the opportunity to remove the hangers as you wait in line, I would really appreciate it, and there will be no extra charge. I love ya . . . Be sure to remember the big sale at the end of the month."

The recorded music switched to marches, starting with "Stars and Stripes Forever". Between numbers, there were commercials from the buyers in various departments, even a plug for "two eggs any style, our breakfast special, 39 cents." A Mrs. Wickersham was notified that her party would meet her at the car.

At 9 o'clock, Hershoin still was playing a tune on the cash register.

"This department is one of the first the customer goes to," he reminded me. He seemed like a guy who would dare other departments to match his action. "We'll go strong till mid-afternoon. Then we'll pick up again around 6 o'clock."

Guys and girls came around to take readings on the 75 cash registers. They do this four times a day, on sale days. Regular days, the readings are at 12 and 5. This way, they can see how they're doing vs. the pace of a year ago.

By this time, the shoppers had spilled over into most all departments, as Zimmerman had predicted. They kept coming.

I wandered around. I heard one lady say "I don't know whether to take the elephant or the lamb." I thought I had evaded a rather exotic pet department until I discovered she was looking at what I would call throw rugs (Broadloom Cuts) with figures on them. I stuck around to see who would win, elephant or lamb. Neither. She bought one with a train on it. "That'll look good in Kenny's room."

Jack Ber, the general merchandise manager, came up with a news flash. He had just called the Midway store, and reported the very first customer there had purchased $300 worth of summer furniture. I wondered if he would follow this announcement with hockey scores.

Richard Scarlott, the store manager, said the crowd would peak between 10 and noon. "We'll have traffic backed up to I-95 by then." When he was managing the Market Street store, he said, the staff called him out of the office one sale day with a "you gotta-see this lure". And what he had to see was a "willowy" blonde, peeled down to bikini underwear, trying on jump suits in an aisle.

Zimmerman nodded to a security guard.

"Ten years ago," he said, "you didn't need any—now we have 15, our own force. Sale days, we figure to attract more shoplifters, but we also apprehend and prosecute more. And we prosecute every case. Just this week our men picked up a woman schoolteacher who stuffed a pack of men's briefs into her coat. It would have cost her a dollar-fifty. She winds up paying $32.50 in court. Why do they do it? You tell me."

He showed me little mirrors near the ceiling. But they are mirrors one-way only. The other way, you can look through and scout possible shoplifters. And there is a telephone behind each "mirror".

I was impressed with the vast, bright store and its crew and its preparation. I thought business was great. But I was deflated to learn that this is only the fifth biggest sale of the year for Wilmington Dry Goods, whose crisp, tremendous discount operation—and they were in it before it became stylish—must drive other merchants giddy. August Dollar Day is the biggie. Last year's grossed a million dollars at the four stores.

"If you think this is busy, come around next August," suggested Ken Nash, who is an operations trainee bucking for assistant manager. In the old days, you call him a floor-walker. "You can't move then. People park on the lot all night, waiting for us to open."

If you can't get near Ladies Acrylic Slacks in April, what must it be like on August dollar Day? I will return and find out—but I will wear a helmet.

The Extravaganza

Life as a sports editor was never dull with Ralph Tribuani around. I looked him up for a reunion after the indestructible old fight promoter and bar man announced he was going to run for governor. His political career opened and closed with one press conference.

I didn't know Ralph Tribuani intended to turn in his bung starter for a possible scepter and declare for governor, so this will have to be a flashback sort of piece.

After his big announcement, everybody knows where Ralph is now, and he will settle for that, believe me. His "campaign" already is a success. But when I returned to circulation here this summer, I wondered whatever happened to the one-time Toots Shor of Fourth Street.

I hadn't seen him for a couple of years. I hadn't even heard him, which is even more dramatic proof that we had drifted out of touch.

Then I saw this ad on the amusement page about a "Hot Pants Extravaganza" at a place called Bomba's on the Du Pont Highway.

Girls were to call "Ralph T. or Pat for further information."

Ralph T.? Could this be Ralph Tribuani, the old boxing promoter and cafe operator, last seen drumming cherry cheesecakes, used cars and calendars?

Ralph Tribuani, promoting a hot pants tournament? Gad, how the flighty have fallen.

"Yeah, it's me," he said, grinning around a long cigar as he emerged from a storeroom off the bar. "The joint drives me crazy, but I love this business. I'm back in the groove."

Give Tribbie a saloon to run and guys to talk fights with, maybe a little event to hustle, and he is livin'. He said he did not own this joint but that he was the "banana". I nodded knowingly, not having the slightest idea what he meant.

I mentioned the ad.

"It shook me at first," said Tribbie. "You know the line that reads 'We Need Contestants For This Show'? Well, the first morning the ad was in, I wasn't focused too good. I thought the line said 'We FEED Contestants', I like to died. I could see hungry broads stampedin' my kitchen."

I guess you would call Ralph a lovable bandit. Some of the prizefights he promoted, featuring his own prizefighters, had finishes that were spellbinding. If you thought the Hindenburg went down fast, you should have seen some of these pros. But Ralph always had the ability to charm any upset citizens out of unspeakable actions such as demanding their money back.

This promotion had to be a challenge. So how do you rig a hot pants contest?

"This is on the up and up," he replied, testily. "Stick around and see for yourself. The shows are a big hit. They have jacked up the bar business. The girls get candy for prizes. We're going to have the finals in November, and the winner gets a trip to Nassau."

He didn't say which Nassau. There is a village in Sussex County named Nassau, hard by romantic Red Mill Pond. Just thought I'd mention that, ladies.

Tribbie thought of something, and busted out laughing.

"I got a call one week from some University of Delaware girls who saw the ad. They said they wanted to enter but were a little leery about the action—thought it might be topless.

"I looked them up and told them it was real easy and nothin' to be ashamed of. One was a southern gal and she asked me what the prize was for the next contest. I said a trip to a beautiful resort and she said which one. I said Marcus Hook. She said do they have a nice beach? I said the best. She showed up, but lucky, she didn't win."

The ad had said the show would begin at 9:30. At 9 the bar was full. Two barmaids were busy. At 10 it was still full. No show yet.

At 10:15 a guy yelled "Show time!" and people headed for a side room. It cost a dollar to get in—what else?

Maybe 30 paid their way. It turned out to be a "talent show", not just hot pants. The house orchestra was there, consisting of a lively piano player with bow tie and white shoes. There was an m.c. whom Tribbie identified rather grumpily as "one of those dry-humored guys from Arden".

Tribbie's sprained English, by the way, remains one of his most priceless assets. It might even be No. 1. He was explaining that one night there weren't enough girls for the contest, so he drafted several lady customers from the bar, including "one who was drinking Alexander Brandies pretty good."

The talent took over. Two young men did guitar singles. The "Pat" in the ad, the one you were to phone for information, sang. She was introduced as "formerly singing with Ricky Nelson, all through the Midwest".

"She's my secretary," Tribuani whispered. "Also a singing waitress. A double threat."

A guy named Joe got up and sang. "Formerly with Tommy Dorsey." He did have a professional manner.

Then came a wild act. They introduced the off-duty cook, a mustachioed fellow who is preparing to go into professional wrestling billed simply as "The Greek". His act, said the m.c., was to do a flip in mid-air and land on his back on the rug-covered concrete floor. The Greek did just that. I winced. He was a little slow getting up, and he staggered into the wings as if he had opened and closed his show-business career in one. One severed spine, that is.

A red-haired boy, all of 9, did a dance. They called him "Strawberry" and the audience pitched coins.

"You are helping to keep this boy out of trouble," coaxed the piano player. They also were helping to keep him out of bed.

Now it's 11 p.m. and finally, getting to be Hot Pants time. Four guys, each armed with a beer at a ringside table, are introduced as the judges.

Here come the contestants. All four of them. It is announced the judges will pick the top three girls, and after this the audience will determine the winner by applause while the fourth girl undoubtedly was committing suicide on the parking lot. Meantime, three gaily wrapped boxes of candy are sitting atop the piano. You just knew they were all cream centers.

The girls are introduced and walk across the stage "just so the people will know you."

Then the m.c. yells "Intermission" and everybody files back into the saloon.

Don't ask me who won. It was close to midnight and I was getting a little bombed, having reported well in advance of the alleged post time. I left. At least, I outlasted two judges. They didn't stick around, either.

Police Patrol

*I don't know how you feel about it, but I'm glad
people who man prowl cars are on my side.*

I had been riding shotgun in the patrol car for maybe 45 minutes.

Some shotgun. Pad, pencil and for a while, trepidation. The captain at the station had started that when he dead-panned "Maybe you'll be lucky and get in on a murder."

Now the car was cruising up Orange Street, between Second and Third.

"I will bet you," said Fred DeCusatis, "you've already been the subject of at least three phone calls. The city grapevine. They're asking each other who you are; they know you're not a cop."

Fred DeCusatis is. A cop. He is a sergeant who rides alone in his supervisory car, the mobile foreman of the city's western district fleet, on the 4-to-midnight shift. In appearance, Matt Zabitka with muscles.

And "they", he explained, are people interested in police activities. Defensively interested.

As if on cue, what is known as a 1036-A came over his radio via Car 14.

"That's confidential stuff," said the sergeant, pushing a switch. "You hear a 1036-A, you switch. Now we're off the regular band—only us cops can hear this. This defeats the people who tune us in with their short-wave radios. You'd be surprised by the number who listen in."

This was a Friday night, and DeCusatis had expected it to be busy. It wasn't, by his standards. The radio squawked incessantly, but nobody called his Car 20.

DeCusatis has the impressive ability to converse while not missing a syllable on the radio. "Normally by this time (it was going on 11) I've had a flock of calls for decisions, advice, maybe assistance. I'd rather it be that way—busy. Makes the time go faster."

Things were busy enough for his passenger. Especially when the sergeant accelerated after getting another 1036-A.

DeCusatis had whistled when he heard Car 140 broadcast it had a suspect wanted for "1-X and 1-F," at 3rd and King.

"That's robbery and murder," he said, heading for the action.

The suspect had fled, but already had been apprehended in the 300 block of Shipley. DeCusatis drove up behind two other patrol cars, one a detectives'. He got out to talk to his men briefly. I saw the suspect handcuffed.

At 9th and Jefferson, DeCusatis saw two boys twirling a BB rifle. He stopped and called them over. After examining the rifle and asking who owned it ("My uncle," said one of the boys, both very scared), DeCusatis told them to take it in the house because without adult supervision of the gun, they were breaking the law.

"You get all kinds of action," he told me. "We acknowledge all calls. The other night, a feeble old lady fell out of bed and we were summoned to help her. You hear a Code-A, and that could be anything from a barking dog to a homicide. It's a catch-all, because the person who called in was vague, or hysterical, and you don't know what's happening until you get there."

He pointed out the prostitutes' favorite corner, and the busiest intersection for dope addicts to make their purchases, both at 7th and Tatnall.

"We bust 'em," he said. "But they come back."

The car drew various reactions. Stony stares. Averted faces. Grins and waves from kids, and happy shouts from guys laughing it up in front of gin mills. Sometimes, the sergeant said, the shouts aren't happy.

Near the northern city line, DeCusatis drove by what he said was the homosexuals' retreat. It was a bosky setting.

Back in town, he called attention to a sallow youth slouching across a street. "He's a pusher-addict. Most addicts are pushers. They have to be, to get the money for drugs for their own use."

At 14th and King, a young man was parking an underslung white sports car.

"I hope it's his," muttered DeCusatis. "That's a Corvette. It's high on the priority list among car thieves."

The sergeant routinely drove up behind cruisers that had responded to calls. The mattress fire on Corbin Court. The hit-and-run truck with the drunk driver, at 5th and Harrison. The two guys who had dropped an undoubtedly hot stereo set and fled into the woods in Southbridge.

I noticed the youth of the patrolmen as they came over to DeCusatis and saluted and filled him in on their situations. I noticed the unstarched rapport between the men and their sergeant, who never got out of the car to throw his weight around nor was officious behind the wheel. You say to yourself, "This is a good man," and eventually you feel very comfortable patrolling the city with him. You also feel very comfortable to see the other cars at work. There is something cozy about the inside of a patrol car—from the front seat, at least.

In the Brandywine Boulevard area, earlier, DeCusatis had called to a big boy who smiled and waved.

"That's my moose of a son," he said, the gruffness not disguising his pleasure. "Goes to Sallies, plays football."

DeCusatis drove by his own house. "Porch lights are on; everything must be okay."

Cops have families, homes, jobs to do. Fred DeCusatis likes his, after 14 years. He has liked it from the unscheduled beginning.

Unscheduled, because he had been laid off a construction job at the Chambers Works and needed work. A friend told him he has just joined the police force, and why don't you give it a try?

So Fred DeCusatis from Hazleton, Pa., who never dreamed he'd turn out to be a policeman and had not the slightest interest in that direction, became one. Now he knows the city like you know your back yard. He has walked and driven every district.

Near midnight, his car finally got a call—to pick up a foot patrolman whose tour of duty at Howland and Lincoln was over.

"It's nice to feel wanted," said the sergeant, changing directions.

The Bull Park

I passed up the 1,500 meters at the Mexico City Olympics to see my first bullfights. I don't want to see any more. I hope you remember Dick Farrell, or that clever bullpen line is wasted.

MEXICO CITY—When you got the ticket for the bullfights, the price on it was 46 pesos. That's $3.68, American money.

But the tour guy at the Hotel Maris Isabel said the tab would be 135 pesos, which is $10.80 American money. For the difference, he threw in a car and a driver and a drop-dead look.

The driver was funny. He was a little vintage Mexican, all dressed up in a bad suit. As he drove, he kept referring to the traffic police as schlemiels. Instant research proved that Alberto formerly lived in Brooklyn and worked in Times Square, making sandwiches for Horn and Hardart. Thus, he knew a schlemiel when he suspected one.

The trip wasn't long, and Alberto filled it in by giving his passengers his standard lecture on the history of bullfighting.

"I've never fought a bull," he announced, "I just throw it at the tourists."

In the neighborhood of the Plaza Mexico, the biggest bullring in the world, the streets are named after United States cities and states. Alberto unloaded his cargo of Americano journalists and said he'd be waiting for them at Baltimore and Atlanta, which sounded like an old Junior World Series playoff.

"Watch your money and your cameras and everything," he warned. "Keep a good grip on your tickets. There will be 50,000 people here today and in addition to the local pickpockets, many international thieves, attracted by the Olympics. They can steal your shorts without disturbing your pants."

The Plaza Mexico is a deep, steep bowl, circle after circle of concrete seats with iron armrests. The ring itself is 150 feet in diameter, with a bright red fence around it. Vendors were selling cushions and beer and other goodies. The beer was Corona and it was good. So was the price: three pesos.

This was a bull park. Like an old ball park, it was tattooed with signs. Tia Maria. Admiral TV. Whisky Suntory. Alka-Seltzer. The dirt floor contained a welcome and the five Olympic rings, made with flowers. There also was a huge Coke bottle which suddenly began to move, around the ring and through an exit. Mexico City's version of the marching-cigaret commercial.

"Toriles" on one gate meant bullpen.

"Don't be surprised," a guy said, "if Dick Farrell comes marching out of there when they blow the trumpets."

At least one member of the crew wasn't feeling up to making funnies. He was at the bullfights gripped by curiosity but prepared to be sickened by the sight of people slaying animals for the entertainment of other people, at the same time risking their own bodies. He had tried to understand that this was a passion that is a part of Latin life, an art, they call it, dating back to B.C.

The rituals were colorful and slightly schmaltzy. The blackclad horsemen galloping in and sweeping off plumed hats before the judge's box and receiving both permission for the fight to begin and a key to the bullpen. Then the parade, or paseo, of the three matadors and supporting cast. The matadors make the sign of the cross as they enter, and they are not hippodroming here because they are about to dance with very possible death, but the bulls always lose.

"The running of the bulls" began with one named Americano. This was "Olympico Sunda". So the animals bore names like Oceanico, Asiatico, Mexicano.

Three peones took turns making passes at the bull with their capes while the show's opening matador scouted its moves from a little shelter. Then it was his turn to meet the bull. When the picadores rode into the ring on padded and blindfolded horses, their own legs encased in armor, the bloodshed started. The bull was induced to charge a horse, and the rider would jab him with his pick to reduce the use of the lump of muscle on the bull's neck. This is so el toro will keep his head lowered, and be killed in the prescribed manner.

Thick blood streamed over the bull's shoulders. Now came the banderilleros, graceful, agile and daring, with a long dart in each hand. They reach over the charge of the deadly horns and, arms held high like a Flamenco dancer, plant their sticks and escape, until the bull has a mane of six darts hanging from the hide of his shoulders.

The matador performs with sword and cape. If the crowd approves of his risk and his style, there are choruses of ole's. If not, they whistle. His aim is to get the bull fixed with its head down and its front feet together through a series of charges at the cape, thus opening its shoulders for the sword thrust.

The first matador's resplendent costume was bloodied. But this was from brushes against the bull. After perhaps 10 minutes, he plunged his sword horizontally over the bull's head and into the shoulders, its red handle macabrely waving like a TV antenna. The bull bled through the mouth. The peones returned to make the bull turn in quick circles, so the sword would "work" and make it bleed more quickly. Americano crumpled ponderously and pitifully to its knees. A puntillero gave the coup-de-grace with a dagger into the brain.

A team of plumed burros dragged the bull from the ring by a chain. By this time, the novice spectator had that I've-had-enough feeling. But he lasted through five of the six fights. Spectacularly inadequate lights now were on.

The opening fight, in shuddering retrospect, was one of the more acceptable ones. There was another in which the matador had to make 11 sword thrusts, either hitting bone or another non-fatal spot, before the beast practically died on its feet. Thousands whistled their criticism and threw cushions into the ring.

One massively built bull turned the ring into a frightening hellzapoppin. A crazy young Mexican came down out of the stands, vaulted the fence and challenged the bull, who bowled him over twice. The espontaneo, as these wild fans are called, was carried off. The same bull jumped the fence twice, picked up and toppled a horse and its rider, gored a peone and flattened the matador. This magnificent fighter—"a good bull," grunted an English-speaking fan in the next seat—finally was dispatched on the fifth thrust. Miraculously, humans and horses missed serious injury.

This visitor to Plaza Mexico didn't leave it. He escaped from it. He found Alberto at Baltimore and Atlanta and he settled back in the old car and he decided he was no art lover, Mexican style.

Herb Lesher

I really wanted only a few specific columns to be included, if they were going to publish this book. This is one of them. I hope I convey the reason.

I went to bed knowing Herb Lesher had died that night, only a few hours before, and I woke up hoping it all had been a bad dream.

It wasn't. It was the bad and incredible truth. There it was on the front page of the newspaper.

Alive one minute at the dinner table. Fatally injured the next, was this hearty, robust, industrious man, by a fall from an apple tree.

The phone call came that he had been badly hurt. An hour later, there was the call that he had died.

Funny thing. First time the phone rang, I was sitting there watching TV and eating a peach. Herb's wife, Lois, had brought us a basket that afternoon. Herb grew them and he also picked them. It was a good peach, of course.

I guess Herb Lesher was one of the very first people I met when I came to Delaware. This was long before they talked him into going into politics, where seemingly everybody was to know him as a state representative from Brandywine Hundred whose country-smart, money-managing skills led him to the chairmanship of the Joint Finance Committee.

He loved people, and the conversations that went with them, and the little things of life were a joy to him. He was a neighbor, the sort who was always around for help. He would fix something for you, or help you build something, or build it for you. He was glad to see you even if you did have this problem. How I would envy the way he used his hands on a motor, or a house, or any mechanical or construction challenge.

He was a white-collar guy with work hands. Strong hands, and stained, a test for any manicurist.

Handsome Herb Lesher, so morally and physically fit. What Gene Mauch said about Alvin Dark, you said about Lesher, the father and husband: "He's the kind of man we'd all like to be, if we had the time." I never even heard him cuss.

He was a friend of the family, and how it hurts to past-tense that. We watched each other's kids grow up. I'll remember him that way. I'll let others tell how much he'll be missed as a legislator.

He never told me; but I must guess he worked his way through college. He was always working. His wife wanted him to give up the peach orchard in Pennsylvania, which amounted to still another job. I guess the Lesher property is the biggest in Claymont, and he and his boys did all the caretaking and the renovating. This besides Herb's Du Pont Co. position and his long hours as a representative. No wonder he lapsed into catnaps in church.

I remember the little things about Herb Lesher that all of a cruel sudden are now so big.

I remember the two of us pushing Herb's antique pump-organ down Harvey Road's old turtle-backed two-lanes, from his house to mine, because a boy wanted to learn how to play it. That was from his first house in Claymont.

I remember the frustrating job he had of registering members for the Brandywine YMCA, 20 years ago. That's when the Y had nothing to offer but a day camp and a dream.

Herb's volunteer door-knocking led him to the Speakman property on the same road. A huge house, scores of acres. I don't know whether Herb ever enrolled Mr. Speakman as a Y member, but his visits did lead to his buying the Speakman property. And then along came I-95's condemners, and Herb became very comfortably fixed. But he was never comfortable unless he was doing something.

You drove by his house, you many times saw him driving a tractor mower or chopping away at wind-blown trees or putting up a corral for horses he began boarding. He was an outdoors guy, and I don't mean a golfer. An out-doors worker. And in the end, this killed him.

I remember his making his land available for a church-benefit. Or bringing a pony to a community event, for rides. I remember his trying to make himself into a speaker as the man they elected president of the PTA.

Herb Lesher, striding along in the Memorial Day parade. Tall and trim and good-looking. Herb Lesher, possibly the world's worst dancer, but he'd dance all night.

Herb got so involved, you had to catch him on the fly unless you wanted to interrupt his groundskeeping. The last time I saw him was three weeks ago at Brandywine Raceway. They had a Legislators' Night and it also happened to be Steve Carlton Night. Herb and Lois did a little tablehopping down in the ball player's corner of the dining room.

A' La Carte

I remember the scene in church this summer. The new minister said he wanted to inaugurate a practice of fellowship.

"Say hello, shake hands, with the person next to you, or in front of you, or in back of you," he requested. "It'll make you feel good."

The congregation did, and while they were greeting each other, something startled the preacher. It was the sight of a big, grinning man striding up the several steps to the pulpit from the second row, and then shaking the preacher's hand.

Herb Lesher had made the minister "feel good", too.

There was a memorial service at the church yesterday. The new minister conducted it, for the man in the second row.

Memories of Ruth

Henry Aaron was closing in on the home-run record, and I was looking to do a Babe Ruth nostalgia column before Henry caught him. It is nice to have Mrs. Herb Pennock in the neighborhood.

KENNETT SQUARE, PA.—It was when Babe Ruth was with the Boston Red Sox.

Herb Pennock was there, too, before both were dealt to the Yankees. They were to be teammates for 17 years.

Maybe the season was 1919. Esther Pennock was watching a doubleheader in Fenway Park with Helen Ruth, the Babe's first wife.

Ruth pitched the first game and won it with a home run. He played the second game in the outfield and won that, too, with a home run.

"My goodness," said Mrs. Pennock to her companion. "What in the world do you feed that man—raw meat?"

Helen Ruth laughed. So did Esther Pennock in her home here as she replayed that long-ago day.

"Helen said I shouldn't tell anybody, but I guess I can now, after all these years," said the bright, stylish widow of the Hall of Fame pitcher.

The night before, the Ruths had driven to a roadhouse for dinner, 60 miles out in the country. They stayed well past midnight—then ran out of gas on the way back to Boston. The Babe got out and walked till he acquired a can of gas. He walked six miles.

By the time the Ruths got home it was 3 a.m. The sleepless Babe wasn't interested in rest. No time. What he wanted was breakfast—steak, eggs, potatoes. Maybe steaks. Then he changed his clothes and went right to the ball park and the doubleheader that was to become his personal possession. An afternoon doubleheader, of course. Whatever night games the Babe played in his career had nothing to do with baseball, because they hadn't been invented.

This is The Year of Ruth, because it is The Year of Aaron. It comes 26 years after the Babe died of cancer.

Mrs. Pennock asked pleasantly to be excused from any discussion of The Record, other than to say she wonders how many home runs the Babe would have hit in the 2,800 more times Aaron has been at bat.

But I was more interested in her memories of Babe Ruth. Like the time he was the Pennocks' house guest one fall.

"We took him fox hunting here," she said, "although he didn't know too much about horses. He had a splint on his left forearm, to protect boils, or something. Anyhow, he broke the splint when he bumped it against the saddle. He just kept on galloping, ripping off the whole bandage along the way."

Herb Pennock, whom the ball players called The Squire, looked around during the hunt and didn't see Ruth. Re-tracking, he found him dismounted in a corn field, chewing on an ear of field corn.

"You'll get indigestion," warned Pennock, even accustomed as he was to the Babe's appetite.

"Waddyamean? It's delicious," Ruth retorted, finishing the ear.

To Esther Pennock, the Babe was a warm, kindhearted man, beautiful with children. And if he was loud and profane, as you read he was, he never was in her company.

"We never socialized with the Babe, simply because nobody could keep up with him. He went a different route. Maybe Leo Durocher could have stayed with him. They couldn't stay with him on the field, either.

The Yankees and Browns were in a scoreless tie after 13 innings in the desert heat of St. Louis.

"Babe, you'll have to hit one," Pennock gasped as the Yankees came to bat. "I'm nearly dead—been taking aromatics since the 11th."

"Why didn't you say so?" Ruth replied. "I never realized it. It's nice and cool out where I am. I'll see what I can do."

What he did, of course, was hit one.

"Hang on to that lead, Keed," the Bambino said to Pennock. "I can't promise you I can do it again."

Pennock, then general manager of the Phillies, was fatally stricken with a cerebral hemorrhage at the baseball convention in January of 1948. The last time Esther saw Babe Ruth was two months later, at the Phillies' spring camp.

"He came to the hotel and he said he wanted to see me," she said. "He looked so bad. He put his arm around me and I guess we both wept a little. He told me not to grieve for Herb. He said I wouldn't have wanted Herb to suffer as he was suffering."

There must have been only one Babe. Everything else is a statistic.

Ring Them Bells

Our Miss Delaware went on to kill 'em in Korea. They voted her USO entertainer of the year, and she went back in the fall as a single to receive the award and do encores.

ATLANTIC CITY, N.J.—This is on the second floor of the Arcade Building, on the Boardwalk at Tennessee Ave.

It is a school room—the old-fashioned kind—of the New Jersey College of Commerce, whatever that may be. The window shades are tattered. Through them you can see the beach scene. A floor fan hums. A tape recorder blares music, a girl soloist belting out something identified as "You Gotta Ring Them Bells".

In the drab, dusty room, six girls are rehearsing a chorus dance number. They are working hard, perspiring, hair askew, practicing fixed smiles as well as footwork. A blonde choreographer plays the song over and over. Each girl makes coy maneuvers with a pair of phony bells.

It is rehearsal time for the Miss America-USO Show, Asian division. The six girls were competitors in last September's pageant in Convention Hall, a few blocks down the Boardwalk. A seventh, Miss America herself, has been excused from this workout to make an appearance.

It is a cram course in show business. When they take off for the Pacific on Sunday, the girls will have rehearsed 10-11 hours a day for two weeks. And they still won't be mistaken for the Rockettes, for this is but a spinoff of the world's biggest amateur show, the Miss America contest. But I have the feeling if I were a serviceman stationed in Korea, or Okinawa, or the Philippines, these cupcakes would look pretty clever to me if they did nothing else but show up.

Miss Delaware '73 is here. She's the shortest one, the one with the red top and the flowered shorts. The others are wearing leotards. The black case in the corner, beneath the table with the three picked-over boxes of cookies on it, contains Miss Delaware's banjo. Cathy Lawton of Claymont also will have a solo spot. The list of the show's number pasted on the wall goes from No. 1, "Overtures", to 20, "Bows", and No. 18 is "Banjo, Lawton".

The choreographer, Marcia Hyland, gives the girls a 10-minute break, and the vivacious, personable Cathy Lawton, a University of Delaware senior, jokes about her dancing ability.

"No doubt about it, I'm the worst one," she laughs, as though she enjoys the distinction, "but Marcia's been very sweet, very patient with all of us. They told me last December I had been picked for the tour, and recommended I take some dancing lessons because I had no experience at all. I went along with that, even though it was to be at my expense. So I took a 30-minute lesson a week, for 12 weeks, at the Louise School.

"As you can see, I'm not ready for Radio City Musical Hall. But I keep plugging along, and smiling."

The return to Atlantic City ended a summer of strumming with the Banjo O's. Her father and Tom Crowley are the other O's. They were big at crabfeasts on the Eastern Shore, and also played at Herman Brown's Republican picnic.

"I never thought I'd get this much out of being an old banjo player," says Cathy, speaking of the upcoming trip. "I'm truly excited about it. You know, there is a European troupe, too; they're already over there. Rehearsed in this very same hall. If I had my choice, I would have picked the Asian company. Nowadays, it's pretty common to go to Europe. There's always the chance I will get there on my own, some day."

Miss America herself, Terry Meeuwsen of Wisconsin, will sing the "Bells" number, although it will be pre-recorded. The toupe's musical accompaniment will be on tape. They all went to New York yesterday for the recording session.

Other soloists will include Miss Indiana. She will do an acrobatic dance to the theme from "Ironsides" and I had a hard time containing myself when I read that. There is something about the association of dance and theme that kills me. But I checked out Miss Indiana in the chorus line and she is indeed a doll—the Ava Gardner type—and I predict she will be a smash in Okinawa and, given the opportunity, would be of tremendous visual therapeutic value to Mr. Ironsides.

And then there are the Misses California, Kansas, Oregon and Maryland, who is Miss Delaware's roommate here.

They told Cathy to pick her own banjo tunes.

"I'll play different things," she says, "so that it won't be monotonous for me. We'll be doing two shows a day for 3-1/2 weeks, and I'll have from 3 to 5 minutes. I'll probably stick to the oldies—you can really sock it to 'em with a banjo. Happy, bouncing stuff, that will get 'em swinging and smiling. I play by ear and can come up with almost anything."

Cathy has one singalong number. It is to the tune of "Jada" but comes out "Sara, Sara, working' in a gravel pit". She played this during her reign as Miss Delaware, she says, until somebody complained that it was "offensive".

It is time to rehearse, again. The girls dance before blackboards that have notes scribbled on them from the European troupers who practiced here: "Good luck (you'll need it!)" . . . "Sweat!" . . . Break a leg (and a toe!)"

The producer, George Cavalier, comes in and announces that some pageant directors and some NBC technicians, in town to organize the next Miss America show, are coming up to watch them. The girls reach for combs and compacts. They do their "Come Rain Or Come Shine" number for the visitors, and Cathy breaks out the banjo and does her bouncy pagent medley of "California Here I Come", "Back Home in Indiana" and "Alabammy Bound". I wonder if the arrangement is by Rand-McNally.

A board member gets the girls aside and says he wants them to do their thing at next month's pageant. The reaction is shrieks, screams, even tears.

Five boys, maybe 9-10 years old, poke their heads in the doorway and Cavalier invites them to come in and watch the rehearsal.

Shortly after the kids leave, there are more tears, from Miss Oregon. She has reached into her pocketbook, and discovered her wallet is missing. She frantically searches the whole room. A director, or maybe he is a technician dashes after the boys and in several minutes comes back with the wallet.

You gotta ring them bells. You also gotta watch them thieves. Hang on to your banjo, Cathy.

The Busted Hero

Jack Sugarman beat the rap, and I must confess I was glad. But his track record indicates there will be other raps.

They busted into the "Wilmington Massage Salon" and they busted the manager.

Police said they found him and two women standing there with no clothes on, and the only other person in the joint was a vice-squadder with his pants down and a transmitter inside his drawers. He said he had been invited to an "orgy" and that women would be brought in for a "swinging party".

Rain apparently held down the audience participation to one guy. Unfortunately for the house, it was the partially uncovered undercover man with the shorts-wave radio.

Sounds hilarious, doesn't it? Just mention "massage parlor" around here lately and you get a laugh.

I agree it paints a funny scene, but I am not laughing because I know of the guy they busted. His name is Jack Sugarman.

I know of him a lot better than I know him, although I met him a couple of widely separated times when he was associated with legitimate joints here. I liked him.

Everybody knew of Jack Sugarman halfway through World War 2. And when I say everybody, I mean just that. The whole country.

Jack Sugarman, you see, was a super war hero like Sergeant York and Audie Murphy were super war heroes.

A kid hero, and weren't they all? He was 19. A Marine.

With a machine gun, he killed 132 Japanese in a battle on the island of

Guadalcanal. That punctuation mark in the South Pacific is a place we learned how to say and spell 30-some years ago. Jack Sugarman learned it the stark way. For one bloody, terrible, unbelievable night, he WAS Guadalcanal.

Sugarman was a big, athletic kid from Media, Pa., a freshman at Temple who suddenly dropped out of the university to join the Marines. What moved him, literally, was a broadcast over a fraternity-house radio about a fight the Marines were putting up on a place called Wake Island. The next day, he was at the recruiting office.

It wasn't long before Sugarman himself was in the South Pacific, on the island called Guadalcanal. The Japanese had seized that, too. Those were the days they had seized everything. Now the Americans were the invaders.

This sticky October evening in 1942, Sugarman's outfit had set up a line of defense for what they thought would be a small attack, a nuisance job. The Japanese main attack was expected elsewhere.

They started coming, just before dark. And this was no nuisance. This was it, the main attack, 3,000 enemies' worth.

Sugarman was operating a watercooled machine gun that became water-hot. He said later he remembered seeing the Japanese trying to get over barbed wire to reach the Americans. They tried to get over the wire and then they tried to get over each other.

Sugarman kept firing throughout the night. Japanese mortar fire made him change positions. Another time he had to move because bodies were in his way. He was to say he didn't recall being being frightened—"I was just a kid. No worries, no responsibilities. I didn't know what fear was."

Dawn came and so did Gen. Alexander Vandergrift, the division commander. He visited Sugarman at his post. Sprawled before the young private were 132 bodies.

He got the Navy Cross. His war ended a few months later when an air-raid shell wounded him. He spent 18 months in hospitals and returned to a reception in Media they still talk about.

Jack Sugarman was a national sensation. The government sent him on a tour promoting War Bonds. Lucille Ball, Henry Fonda, Victor Mature were in his troupe.

He came home to stay and he became night people. A night-club saloonguy. He started the old Hi Top in Chester, with name talent. He went on to a string of joints. One of his modest ventures was a nice little bar in Wilmington, at Ninth and Orange, the Saxony. That's when I first met him. Nice guy. Likeable. Un-phoney. He never talked of his service career.

He went on to clubs in Philadelphia and Baltimore, and they weren't so nice. He had a place in Baltimore called Club Inferno that was bad news even for The Block. They say he now is ruled off The Block, which is a very difficult status to achieve. He is well known to such Baltimore organizations as grand juries. Trouble, and violence, followed Jack Sugarman.

I feel for Jack Sugarman—not for being locked up as the alleged male madame in a sleezy massage put-on—but for what he was. I know he wouldn't appreciate my sympathy. He long has been shrugging his way through trouble. He is that type.

But this is the type he was on the citation that accompanied his Navy Cross:

"For extraordinary heroism during action against the Japanese forces in the Solomon Islands area on Oct. 24-25, 1942. Serving with a Marine division during a mass frontal attack by a numerically superior force, Pfc. Sugarman, with his gun temporarily out of action and his position threatened by hostile troops, removed the weapon and with the aid of a comrade repaired and placed it back in action under heavy fire.

"On four separate occasions, he saved the gun from capture, repaired it under fire and continued to maintain effective resistance against masses of attacking Japanese. By his skill and determination, he inflicted heavy casualties upon the enemy and helped prevent a breakthrough in our line, which, at that time was weakly held by a small group of riflemen."

The charges were obscenity, providing a criminal nuisance and maintaining a disorderly house.

Jackie

*I was a Jackie Robinson fan. When he
died in 1972, I reprinted this as a eulogy.
It originally was written during the 1955
World Series.*

BROOKLYN—This was at Ebbets Field some 10 days ago. A couple of guys were killing time in the stands because Marciano-Moore had been called off that night, so they condescended to watch the Dodgers, long since in as champions of the National League, go through the motions of taking two from the Phillies.

There were sage remarks passed during the doubleheader in the tranquil ball park, like Newcombe slowing up in the late innings, Hoak being a good spare infielder, Bessent fooling the righthanders as much with his delivery as he does his actual pitch.

One of the visitors pointed to Jackie Robinson on third and commented it sure was a shame that the old boy was letting himself get into such condition. Jackie looked pretty scroungy at that—paunchy, one pants-leg drooping, blouse fighting to get out of the belt line and practically succeeding.

"I guess Jackie just doesn't care any more," or something like that was the gist of the observation. "There must be something to those stories you hear about his not getting along with Alston, because he sure looks like he's just finishing out the season."

Yesterday, Jackie Robinson singled and doubled and scored twice and drove the Yankees daffy on the baselines and played third base like a Cooperstown occupant. This was in a world championship game, not in a necessary evil against the Phillies because the schedule had to be completed. This was in a game that was to put the Dodgers back in the World Series, and nobody had any more to do with it than the gray-haired, irrepressible Negro giant. When you are toasting Podres for his pitching and Campanella for his clouting, don't forget Robinson for just being the Robinson of old.

Old-Timers have called him the greatest runner of bases since Cobb. Leo Durocher calls him the greatest pressure player of them all. Yesterday, as it was Dodgers 8 and Yankees 3, Jackie cemented both arguments.

If there was anything typical about the Brooklyn victory—referring to Dodger victories of the Robinson-Snider-Campy-Hodges era, and is there any other one worth citing?—from this seat it was the devoted labor of the trouper on third. He no longer is the physical specimen whom Branch Rickey introduced—as who is. He's slower and there are times when he is running out close ones to first base that there is no other word to use but waddle.

But he remains the very breath of the Dodgers. There were stories in the off-days before the World Series that Manager Walt Alston was considering lineups that would have put Robinson on the bench. The Quiet Man must have been feeling the awful pressure of a World Series. The Dodgers are not yet ready to win without Robinson, no matter what the calendar says. Keeping the amazing leadership that is Robinson's on the shelf would be like pinch-hitting for Ruth in the clutch.

As Alston well knows, you can't hardly get them Robinsons no more, and personalities can play no role in World Series battle plans when there is a Jackie in the barn.

So where was Robinson the first two days, while the Yankees were doing all the winning, you might query? Pretty prominent; as much as any member of the Brooklyn combination that went under. On base three times in the New York games, including a triple. Three runs scored, including a brazen steal. And a vacuum cleaner at third base. By the way, the man has been on base five times in the three games and he has brought home a run on each occasion. The way he operates on the bases, both with his noggin and his feet, he remains the best bet in baseball to go all the way once he's aboard—no matter what the rest of the batting order has to offer in the way of potential.

Ever hear of a fellow both scoring and batting in a run at the same time? There was Robinson on third yesterday with the bases loaded and making those sarcastic feints towards home. Young Bob Turley had no chance in the face of this dare, and everybody in the park knew he wouldn't regain control under this situation. He put over just one strike in walking Gilliam with the bases loaded, and Robinson sauntered home with the run that broke a 2-2 tie and sent the Brooks on their way.

Gilliam is credited with an RBI, under the rules. There must be a way to give Robinson at least half of it.

That was in the bottom of the second, a round that started with everything even on the scoreboard in the wake of the Mantle and Campanella home runs.

The unfortunate Gil Hodges had just made an out for the umpteenth time, but Robinson launched the rally that got rid of Turley, almost doing it himself with a line drive single that whistled past the ear of the Yankee speedballer. He must have been bored by the events that pushed him around to third base—a hit batsman, a bunt single. But then he turned on what is known as the Robinson treatment, deviling Turley with pantomime dares, until the walk and the run were completed.

Part Cobb, part Billy Rose, that's Jackie. He got his next chance on stage in the seventh with a double that went over third base and down the left-field line a mile a minute. Jackie steamed into second and of course made the turn—it is against his religion to park on any base, once he is there. He made the usual large turn, too.

Elston Howard is going to learn all the moves one of these days, and become a truly grand outfielder for the Yanks.

Howard learned one of them right here, in a World Series classroom; i. e., don't throw to the base behind Robinson. But he did this time, fielded the ball cleanly, saw a chance to eradicate the great Robinson and fired the ball to second as quickly as he could, to cut off the Robinson retreat.

There was one small flaw. Robinson didn't retreat. Howard made his move to second, and Jackie was on his way to third. Before Yank infielders could turn Howard's mistake into a play at third, Jackie was there, sliding. Seconds later, Amoros singled him home.

"The way Howard is fielding the ball and setting himself, I know he must go through with his intention to throw to second," Jackie was explaining in front of his locker. "So, I take off. Now if Noren is out there, I would hold up because Noren can pretend to be looking at one base and then make the throw to another, like a clever basketball player. But it is Howard in left field, and I hustle to third. A couple of years ago, no slide would have been necessary.

"That was quite a burst of speed by a gray fat man, wasn't it?" grinned the perpetrator.

With a glove in his hand, Robinson also showed the Yanks no mercy. Seven assists, just two short of Mike Higgins' World Series record, many of them the type that Traynor must have made. By the way, whatever happened to Billy Cox?

"Mr. Chairman..."

Maverick stockholders have to be a pain at these annual meetings, if you're a non-maverick. But for a one-shot visitor, like me, Evelyn Y. Davis was a gas.

Some nice guy with Du Pont steered me to the only vacant seat in the Playhouse. Last row orchestra, on the aisle. A perfect stakeout.

This was my debut at the annual stockholders' meeting of The Company. A turnaway crowd—I was amazed. First, I had been shunted to the balcony with other latecomers, although it was 10 minutes till starting time, and I wound up in the last row there, too. I was so high, I couldn't have heard Ethel Merman.

I figured I could do better, and descended to the main floor. That's when the nice guy noticed my sad face and sat it down.

There was a rather husky lady in the next seat.

"You Security?" she asked.

I was tempted to say no, I'm Cartwright, but the place was full of dignified-looking guys who looked as if they were on leave from Mansure & Prettyman's window and it didn't seem like the setting for yoks. So I said no, I'm Press, and she said she was Security and that was all she said. I felt secure.

C. B. McCoy was at the rostrum between two tables on the stage. The initials stand for Chairman of the Board, and he also is The Company president. He said this was the first annual meeting in the Playhouse.

"We have 1,200 seats here compared to 830 in the Gold Ballroom and adjacent rooms, and it is more comfortable. That is why we have moved here."

But they also could have been thinking of Evelyn Y. Davis when they decided to change halls. What better place for her performance than a theater?

I have come in late on Evelyn Y. Davis. She is old hat with the business regulars around here. Tom Malone, Gene Knoblauch, Frances Beach, John Gates—they hurled their professional sneers at me when I mentioned how this gal had intrigued me. They made me feel like a guy who went about asking how long this guy Willie Mays had been around.

Evelyn Y. Davis is a regular at Du Pont stockholder meetings, among many others. She is a professional participant. You always know she is there. The lady stands up and impatiently beckons for the portable mike. She holds it with one hand and her material with the other and she would go on for a whole sales quarter if they would let her. I guess boards of directors would refer to her as a scorch.

Evelyn Y. Davis holds four shares of Du Pont common. She gives her address as a post office box in Grand Central Station.

For four shares, Evelyn had herself a party. She always does, they tell me. She was wearing like a knitted ski hat and some kind of fur coat. Last year, I hear, she showed up with jodhpurs and a whip. She speaks in a New Yorkese that sounds like Jackie Mason giving an impression of Fred Allen's old neighbor, Mrs. Nussbaum. She has the pallor of a subway token seller, but she is a live one.

Evelyn took on C. B. McCoy one-on-one and they could have charged admission. An ordinary board chairman would have buckled. C. B. McCoy had style. He never lost his poise. He might have left the Playhouse after the meeting, locked a door and wreaked his vengeance by flogging several unsuspecting department heads in Fabrics & Finishes, but on stage he was superb.

Evelyn Y. Davis and a guy named Lewis D. Gilbert, another regular ("What, you never heard of him either?" spat Malone) did all the talking. Well, almost all. There was a women's libber from NOW campaigning for better representation in The Company, and an elderly gent who said he had purchased a pair of Corfam shoes and liked 'em and was there any chance of getting the franchise back from Poland, or something. He also gave the lighting in the Playhouse a knock. From his raps of the visibility and his investment in a pair of Corfam shoes, I deduced he should see an oculist.

Evelyn Y. Davis was on her feet early.

"I vigorously protest, Mr. Chairman, a woman employee grabbing me by the arm when I tried to enter," she said. "Maybe I should sue. Maybe I have blue marks. Who is this woman? I don't mind if a handsome man grabs me. If she doesn't know who I am, she ought not to be an employee of this company."

Evelyn is a big reader of the New York Times. She was armed with pages of it, and she mentioned the paper so much I kept waiting for the subscription rates.

She took off on Bess Myerson and Du Pont, and "Mrs. Lady Spencer Churchill" and Du Pont. She objected to Du Pont's sponsoring Miss

Myerson in a TV series and to The Company's having Mrs. Lady Spencer Churchill's model dresses. She insisted on knowing the fees.

"Bess Myerson's program is to be called 'What Every Woman Wants to Know'. Well, here is one standing who is not interested one bit in what she has to say. Mrs. Lady Spencer Churchill is known in England as No. 1 publicity hound. Now who is this P.R. man in New York who arranged this deal and what was his cut?"

A Du Ponter with an answer said there were no fees. Evelyn demanded some other figures. She learned the advertising budget is $63 million a year, public relations $3 million. McCoy said he would have some information on "the P.R. man" for Evelyn after the meeting. She kept popping up and reminding him.

She bugged McCoy about his directorships, and seemed slightly set back to hear his only other board affiliation was with Diamond State Telephone.

"I never heard of it," she said. "You should be with AT&T, someone of your stature. What happened to the influence of the Du Pont Company?"

Without breaking stride, she asked about contributions and was told there was a $50,000 donation to the Kennedy Center.

"I guess this entitles some company officers to some good seats at the opera," she sniffed.

Evelyn—"it's Mrs. Davis, not Miss," she corrected McCoy—accused Du Pont of sending people to other meetings she attends, to scout her questions. She wanted to know how many Du Ponters spend how much company time promoting political candidates. "And how about retreats for executives, like this excellent article in the New York Times—now what is going on like this here?" She had a proposal on the books for the appointment of more outside directors, and it was overwhelmingly defeated.

Gene Knoblauch clocked Evelyn at 45 minutes, not counting the times the agenda interrupted her. Growls, shouts from the audience just bounced off her. Once the Security gal sighed defeatedly as Evelyn got up for the umpteenth time.

"I shall not be told to sit down by a bunch of jealous old women," Evelyn snapped.

The meeting adjourned at 1:25 and I don't know whether or not Evelyn Y. Davis ever got her answers, but she appeared pleased as she filed out with the big crowd. I picked up some comments on the way out.

"It could have been worse," a man said. "Like, I could be married to her."

I heard a defense. "She was okay. You need somebody like that. You never know about skullduggery."

"Women's lib just received a setback," said another. "I felt sorry for the girl from NOW."

A guy up on his ethnics said he thought he knew what the initial stands for in Evelyn Y. Davis: "Yenta".

Bunny Susie

Mission: Talk to a Bunny at a new Playboy Club-Hotel, and stay a couple of days. Sometimes a guy can't get a break.

M<small>CAFEE</small>, **N. J.**—"The staring doesn't bother me. This is like wearing a one-piece bathing suit. I have a bikini that shows more."

Now that I have your attention, meet Susie Kimsey, who said that. She is a Playboy Bunny who looks just as good at 10 o'clock in the morning as she does at 2 in the morning, which is quite a challenge, indeed.

Susie was encountered during the official launching of the $40-million Playboy Club-Hotel up here in the woods below the New York State line. From what I hear, the area is going to become something of a goyim Catskills.

This ski-golf-booze resort may have the jump, or hop, on the Catskills because the woods are full of Bunnies. It never can be open season on them, however, so you can relax, men. It says so right there in the Playboy Bunny Manual, the girls' handbook. I managed to put the clutch on a copy in a clever move. Pulitzers have been awarded for less.

Page 12: Any Bunny who arranges to meet or be met by a customer either on or off the premises will be dismissed immediately.

Page 35: The rule against mingling prohibits dating, any physical contact, fraternizing or socializing with customers. A Bunny may never divulge personal information about herself such as last names, phone numbers, etc.

In other words, don't mess with the talent. Just bring money.

This is the largest Playboy Club in the world, if that impresses you. If it doesn't, then I give you Susie Kimsey and if she does not impress you, then you are better off staying at the McAfee YMCA.

Susie and her cotton tail were working the oasis called the Living Room late this night. She waited on Chuck McGowen and me, two dubious qualifiers for what was called VIP Holiday Weekend. Unsuspectingly undergoing a thorough scouting test, Susie within 15 minutes had ended our informal search for The Bunny We'd Most Like To Print. We identified ourselves as press, not key-holders, thus beating the rule-book.

She said, sure, she'd meet us in the lobby the next morning. Ooops, the same morning. And Susie was there in casual clothes—blouse, slacks, maxi-coat.

The first thing I thought of was a demitasse Kim Novak. Only 5 feet tall. Blonde, great brown eyes. She said she weighed 110 pounds, "10 too much." Complexion creamy. She insisted she did not know her statistics. You will have to settle for the scouting report: Perfectly proportioned.

All this, and an un-phony personality, too.

Page 2: You can take pride in being selected as a Bunny. We are extremely selective in our Bunny hiring procedures. The Playboy Bunny has become what the Ziegfield (sic) girl was to another generation, ranking with the most glamorous girls in the world.

I would have said she was 19. Wrong. Just turned 23. I asked her if married girls could be Bunnies and she said yes, and she went on to disclose she was a divorcee. Not only that but the mother of a 4-year-old daughter. Married at 17, to a fellow 24. "It didn't work out. Once is enough."

The little girl is with Susie's parents in Kansas City, and Susie wants to bring her East as soon as she can find an apartment.

Susie was a hairdresser in Kansas City. Kansas City has a Playboy Club. She applied, was hired, then was transferred to this posh, swinging, 700-room hotel at her request. She is crazy about New York and besides, there is a boyfriend, a saxophone player, who lives there.

Susie soon found out Bunnying beats hairdressing, especially financially. She works for 90 cents an hour, but hold on. There is a 15-per cent service charge on each bill and the cocktail-waitress Bunny gets that, plus any cash tip the customer might want to part with, plus commissions. Susie gets paid every two weeks. Her smallest check has been $187 and her biggest $651. Her record tip was $75, this on top of the 15 per cent.

Page 26. Certain jobs, like Door and Gift Shop, are salaried. Bunnies are paid a specific hourly rate, receiving regular increases after six months' continuous employment in one of these categories.

She pays $50 for room and board in the dorm.

"It's difficult to estimate what you are going to make," she explained. "Business varies so much, like with the weather. We all have to learn to budget."

The costume, Susie. You all look as if you were engineered right into it.

"It's not uncomfortable—it's built to go with the body," she said. "It pulls in your waist—I guess it makes me a 21. I don't like the shoes, 3-inch spikes. We're going to get new ones. Still 3 inches, but not so outdated. People ask how I can walk around 'half-naked,' but none of us feel that way. I was nervous the first night I worked in K.C., but not about being stared at."

Page 3: Your costume is the world-famous symbol of the glamorous Playboy Bunny. Wear it proudly. Each Bunny is supplied with two costumes and matching ears, collars and cuffs, bow tie, cufflinks, Bunny tail, rosette nameplate, flashlight and lighter. A Bunny purchases her own regulation hose, bikini panties and shoes dyed to match each costume.

I was surprised to discover that Bunny training does not include karate, the better to fend off amorous lushes.

"I feel safe and secure," Bunny Susie said. "There's always a room manager to help us if things get sticky. Some customers can't resist batting at the Bunny tails. Worst thing happened to me was a guest pulling off my name tag. The room manager got it back, tactfully. Something like that happens, we just retreat till it's worked out."

Susie likes this life so much she wants to go the distance. She says the work is tiring "but I like to be active; I'm a worker."

Page 35: Bunnies, specifically, can no longer continue to be employed as Bunnies when they lose their "Bunny Image," meaning, among other things, the physical beauty, attractiveness and youthful appearance of the Bunny established by company policy, as the Bunny was informed as a condition of employment.

The next night, I continued my winning streak; I discovered a Bunny from Wilmington. I was attending a 1 a.m. splash party in the pool, and had just finished a pretty bad free-style in the paper trunks I was issued, when somebody said "Hey, there's a Delaware girl working the party."

Correct. Tall, brownette Michele Voyer is from Gwinhurst. She told me she had been an insurance secretary in Wilmington, but found the work boring. A disc jockey's comment on WAMS got her started in this direction. A "discouraged" Miss Delaware loser in the 1970 pageant, she felt better when she won the Miss Pennsylvania Hemisphere contest. Her modeling work and residency in Philadelphia made her eligible.

Michele and another Mount Pleasant High graduate, Cindy Everett, were hired together. Miss Boyer has done a lot of publicity posing. She participated in a Christmas bit in which she flew with Santa Claus in a helicopter from the nearby Great Gorge ski trails to the hotel.

"I love all this," she told me while balancing a poolside tray. "Maybe it sounds vain, but I like to look nice and have people think I look nice. I can always go back to being a secretary, but I'd sit there thinking 'What am I doing with my youth?' This work is fun, and, it's lucrative. I anticipate averaging $300 a week."

The next morning—oops, the same morning—she was working as lobby greeter as I checked out. You couldn't ask for a better getaway sight.

I drove home thinking I'd like to do something for all the Susies and the Micheles. You could write a pretty good musical comedy around them and their glamorous hutch. I'd call it "Hare". How's that grab you, Hef?

THE *Batboy*

*What great copy the Orioles of '71 were, clear
down to their fingerless batboy. Jay Mazzone's
college plans didn't materialize, but he is
working in an electrical-assembly plant and
might be married by the time you read this.*

BALTIMORE—"He's been good for us and we've been good for
him," said Brooks Robinson. "I know he's done a lot for me."

The greatest of the Baltimore Orioles—in or out of uniform—wasn't referring to his manager, or one of the club's practically unbeatable pitchers, or
the brew-master who owns the franchise.

He was talking about the batboy.

This batboy will call it a career after the World Series.

Jay Mazzone is his name. He is something special, such as magnificent. He
doesn't have any fingers. He is 18 years old and he had to have his fingers
amputated when he was 2 because he was terribly burned in a backyard fire.
He was wearing a snowsuit with a plastic zipper, and the burning zipper ate
its way to a diagonal scar across the boy's body. He also is scarred on the
jaws and chin. Skin grafts have marred his thighs, back, hips.

"All these stories about me say I don't have any hands. That's not true. I
have hands. I don't have any fingers," said Jay Mazzone of the champion
Orioles. It was the only thing he said in a long clubhouse talk that was
anywhere near a complaint.

He showed me those "hands" and explained how the left fingers had been
amputated across the lower knuckles, and the right fingers slightly more
towards the wrist, thumbs included. They are purplish stumps. His fingers
now are what he calls hooks. The correct name is prosthetics appliances.

"If I should suddenly grow fingers," he said, "I wouldn't know what to do
with 'em."

He knows what to do with the hooks so well now that people who go to ball games and don't know the Jay Mazzone story, are amazed to find out later the batboy they had taken for granted was wearing the metal fingers, the cuffs, the straps that are the hooks. Nobody pays attention to batboys, and this one was doing the usual job of fielding fouls off the screen, picking up hats, feeding balls to the umpires, tossing the rosin bag to batters.

If I were Dock Ellis or Jerry Grote or Alex Johnson or any of the other grumpy guys in baseball, I would take a look at the action around the Baltimore dugout and I would forget about being unpleasant. Jay Mazzone makes the alleged problems of grown-up ball players appear mighty unimportant. He even makes his own problems appear insignificant.

Jay is getting ready to retire because he is a Parkville High senior.

"The batboys, they all pack it in when they're finished high school," he said. "I want to go to college and be a teacher, I've only missed about four games in six years, but doing this and going to college would be something else."

He is going to major in mathematics. I could have told him that it's hard to become good in mathematics when you don't have any fingers to count on, and I'm sure he would have gotten a sincere laugh out of it.

The slight young man long ago became one of the boys, or players. They get on him as much as they do each other, and he is capable of giving it back.

Boog Powell recalled the time a bunch of Orioles were discussing the top curve-ball pitchers.

"I don't know about curves," spoke up Jay, "but I know I've got the best hook in the league."

They send Jay for coffee and tell him to be careful and not burn his hands. The Orioles have this clubhouse kangaroo court in which bonehead plays or remarks are liable for a $1 fine. The voting procedure is thumbs up or thumbs down. Jay showed up one day with a big paper thumb attached to his right hook, and thus became a qualified jurist.

"He was the visiting club's batboy in 1966, and came over with us the next season," said Brooks Robinson. "I felt sorry for him, but not for long. Jay can do anything he wants to. He was shy at first—conscious of the hooks, I have to believe. It's been beautiful for this club to see his personality come out."

All Jay knows of the fire and the operation is what his parents tell him, which is one of the blessings of the tragedy. His mind is not scarred. He and brother Gary were playing around a kerosene drum's spigot and drops splashed on Jay. There was this smoldering trash fire nearby and a spark flew on Jay's snowsuit and this happy little boy became a horrible flame.

"I do remember spending my third birthday in the hospital," he said. "My brothers and sister and the neighborhood kids were too small to visit me, so my dad recorded them singing 'Happy Birthday' and played it for me."

Jay laughed as he told about brother Gary.

"We're close in age, and always got along real great, but he never gave up his right to beat up on his little brother just because I had lost my fingers. He'd stick up for me, but he'd fight me himself. He did something that meant an awful lot to me. One time his English class was assigned to write an essay about the person each was most honored to know. Gary wrote the whole thing about me, and got a good grade, too. I still have it."

Jay says he never had a "sudden awareness" he was fingerless. He literally grew into the hooks. "I developed a feel with them. The only time I have trouble is using them in small areas. I used to wear them all the time, but they are bulky and sort of uncomfortable and I do without them a lot of times, like I am doing now. I have a feel without them, too. I can do most things without them, outside of picking up stuff one-handed."

Jay Mazzone drives a car and he won a varsity letter as a springboard diver. He has a steady girl and he shoots pool and well, name it. He was a Little League right fielder—"I led the league in getting hit by the pitcher, walks and striking out. I had a good bunting average and a .190 batting average."

The first time Boog Powell saw the new batboy "I thought, what a tragic thing this is. That wore off quickly. His dad never let Jerry feel sorry for himself, so nobody else does. He carries his own weight around here. We all see to that."

You're not supposed to feel sorry for Jay Mazzone but I am—sorry he is graduating from batboy. I want to see him again. He is what is known as visual therapy.

Blewynn Gold

It was amazing how many readers thought my ancient U. of Delaware football consultant really existed. I concocted him as a Monday morning quarterback. When I left the sports field, I erased him this way. Sorry, Blewynn.

You don't know me," said the man on the phone, "but I thought you'd like to know a friend of yours is in the hospital, in bad shape. Remember Blewynn Gold?"

He had to be kidding. Not with the information, for I had been anticipating this call for 10 years, but with the question.

You just do not forget Blewynn Gold, my old University of Delaware football consultant. And I do mean old.

Blewynn Gold, Class of '90, the only Delaware who saw 'em all.

A wispy little geezer with a cackling laugh, bad jokes and shrewd observations. Never missed a home game, and he always wore the same outfit. Turtleneck sweater, knickers, sneakers.

I had been out of touch with him for a couple of years, and I hated myself for this.

Expecially when I saw him in the men's ward, his tiny, bony body hardly making an impression in the bed. Blewynn Gold was born old, but now he look fossilized.

He was sleeping. I looked with wet eyes at my dear friend. I turned to leave, but that familiar raspy voice called me back.

"Hey, dad, don't go," he croaked laboriously. "I was just lyin' here thinkin' about old times. About when I had my bad knee operated on after my freshman season. Busted kneecap, bursitis, fluid, torn tendons. Know what I told that surgeon during the operation?"

I feigned interest.

"I asked him," said Mr. Gold, "what a nice guy like him was doing in a joint like that."

Blewynn laughed, or tried to. His laugh was big on gums, short on sound. He just shook. He always was his own best audience.

I told him I'd see him at the first game.

"Don't con me, daddy," he said. "I ain't goin' nowhere but into the ground. I'm just agein' away. Tubby and the boys will have to play without me, from here on in. Hey, did you check the wheels on the head nurse?"

Blewynn then said a strange thing. "You know, I'm fadin' out at a good time. I felt myself losin' interest last season."

Blewynn Gold losing interest in Delaware football? I looked at him suspiciously. But the way he said it, I knew he was serious.

"The scene has gotten too big," he said, soberly. "Them two huge cement stands, Mount Nelson and the newer one. A real major park now, but I just don't feel at ease in it. They draw more people for one game than we used to get all season."

Blewynn said it had been lots more fun going to the stadium in the days when it had bleachers for stands. Cornfields to the left and right, even some Ag School cows, a gorgeous piece of woods for a drape.

"Those so-called big teams would come in," recalled Blewynn, "and they'd look at the cornfields and the cattle and they'd die laughin'. Then they started the game and ended the laughs. The way Delaware beat on 'em they wished they were out with the cows."

Blewynn said he hated the traffic his now widely beloved Blue Hens generate each home Saturday.

"Fellow offered me a ride home after the Villanova game last year. Took an hour just to get away from the parking lots.

"I guess it just ain't as personal any more. Like the Boardwalk Bowl. I got to buy a ticket here, but they didn't even put me on the Delaware side. I was stuck upstairs on the 3-yard line. The game was in Atlantic City. I felt like I was watchin' it from Asbury Park. That athletic department has a short memory.

"And I've missed seein' Davey Nelson around the stadium when he was workin' some other game as a TV commentator. Nice prestige for Delaware but—well, I always looked forward to talkin' with Davey."

Blewynn was running out of gas. He asked me to give the coaches and troops his best—"I'll never see them again." I ached for him.

He died minutes later. I saw him die. He had said there was no way he could make the Gettysburg opener Saturday.

Then he feebly motioned for the glass of water on his bedside table, and sucked some through a straw. His pink claw of a hand motioned me to come closer.

"Tell 'em" he said, barely audible, the water dribbling down his chin, "to win this one for The Sipper."

I couldn't bear it any longer. I sobbed. I picked up a bedpan and I bashed Blewynn over the head with it. Twice. I swore at him. The old cornball had set me up for a line for the last time.

The only Delaware who had seen 'em all is dead. Just like when he was playing guard in '89, he never knew what hit him.

The New Flyers

This was in 1967. Seven years later, the Flyers won the Stanley Cup and Philadelphia flipped. I knew 'em when— when they had to paper the house to get spectators.

A fellow just back from his first big-league hockey camp heard as much talk about salary checks as he did about body checks.

The Philadelphia Flyers are not alone in their contract arguments. This is the year of fresh money in the National Hockey League. There are six new clubs, and they are having trouble signing the players they chose in the expansion draft, without whom they would not have much of an act.

Joe Watson is only 23 years old and a little young to be saying things like "Look, if I don't make it this year I never will." He is considered an outstanding prospect at his defense position.

But that's what he said up in the Flyers' Quebec City Camp. Drafted from the Boston Bruins, the youngest and worst club in the league last year, he explained why he won't accept the Flyer offer:

"I've got a year's experience in the NHL. That should be worth a lot of money on this club. A year from now, a lot of guys will have NHL experience. I won't have this bargaining point."

The Flyers will have their act, of course. Watson and the others will sign. They always do, but they will sign for more than is now offered. The Flyers and the five other newly minted clubs paid $2 million for franchises and 20 players apiece, but now come the salaries.

"I've been signing hockey players for 17 years," growled Bud Poile, the Flyers' general manager, "but this is too much. Where do they think the money is coming from—a pump?"

The Defense Rests

Poile's frustration reached its peak—he hopes—in the just-resolved case of Bernie Parent.

Parent is a goalie and probably will be the highest-paid of all Flyers when the smoke settles, for goalies are a special breed in this game. Same as quarterbacks.

Shortly after the Flyers' made Parent their very first draft pick, Poile visited him at a Canadian summer hockey camp and offered him a three-year deal. Parent accepted. He shook hands and said "I am very happ-ee," and the mimicry is Poile's. Poile said he would mail the contract the next day.

The Flyers announced they had "signed" Parent, having every right to believe that the actual signature was just a formality. But it came out in Quebec the other day, when Parent didn't suit up for an exhibition game, that the goalie had not signed and what's more, wasn't about to for the original offer. Parent said he wasn't worried about what the public might think about his reneging, but he looked most uncomfortable as he tried to explain his stand.

"I have been talking to other players," Parent said, "and I think I am worth more."

The "other players" had to include Watson and Ed Van Impe, another drafted defenseman. So the three big unsigned Flyers were the goalie and the two guys who play right in front of him. Poile suspected a plot. He wouldn't even let Parent on the ice for practice until he signed. Watson and Van Impe were fined $500 apiece for reporting late.

The Toughest of Games

The Flyers took off on a four-game exhibition swing and left the three golden boys behind. A lot of players on the trip aren't signed, either, but this is the way hockey operates. The contracts run from opening day to opening day, and thus the players are obligated to report to camp and train.

The NHL Players Association counsel is in the middle of all this. Alan Eagleson—great name for a lawyer—has most of the other camps shook up, too, as financial adviser for many players. Eagleson has been in the Flyer camp and talked to Poile, but the Philadelphia g.m. refuses to make any deals with any agent.

Despite the financial fussing, you were impressed with Poile and his coach, Keith Allen, as organizers. They started with 80 players, and there were no lost motions as four shifts a day labored—and we do mean labored. Up until now, I always thought sculling was the toughest of all athletic endeavors. After watching the Flyers get into shape, step by step, bruise by bruise, I'll take hockey.

"Oh, it isn't as bad as it looks," Watson said. "We slam each other into the boards and the noise fools you. Sounds like we're getting killed."

Maybe so. But this is the same Watson who got hit in the mouth with a puck two seasons ago. Result: Six fewer teeth, 15 stitches.

A' La Carte

And so we bid farewell to French-speaking Quebec City, where communication was both a problem and a delight. Like the time I stopped in a village and, using mostly sign language, asked an old inhabitant the directions to the Royal Quebec Country Club, where the Flyers were having a day-off golf tournament.

The villager understood and groped through what little English he knew trying to explain the way.

"Merci," I said in appreciation, exhausting half my command of French.

And you know what he said then? "You're welcome."

The Busy Cart

I was kind of proud of this subject. Everybody else headed for the clubhouses, as per custom, after the World Series game. Best Sports Stories 1968 selected this for the book.

He did not know he had participated in a World Series record.

What's more, he didn't seem to care. It had been one of the ancient Boston organization's most splendid hours, this victory over the Cardinals that condensed the tournament into one big showdown, but he said he was not impressed with his performance.

"After six seasons," he said, intercepted on the ball field as the giddy crowd reluctantly left Fenway Park, "you learn to take these things in stride."

Maybe time will melt his indifferent approach to standards. Maybe in seasons to come, maybe next season, he will be glad to mention that he was in on it.

He was in on it along with Gary Waslewski, John Wyatt, Gary Bell, Dick Hughes, Ron Willis, Nelson Briles, Jack Lamabe, Joe Hoerner, Larry Jaster, Ray Washburn and Hal Woodeshick. One by one, they climbed the pitching pinnacle in the snake pit that is Fenway Park, with its monster fence in left field.

Eleven pitchers in one game, breaking the Series record. The Cards, using eight for the day and four in one inning, tied two more records.

And yet the man who had driven pitchers to try and do their best attempted to get away with saying only that he had tried to do HIS best. Al Forester is the guy who drives the cart that brought 11 pitchers into history.

Newspaper types jammed the Red Sox clubhouse, analyzing the day's heroes. On the diamond, policemen and ushers protected the turf until the park was empty. By the Red Sox dugout, Dick Williams was being interviewed on TV by Joe Garagiola through what looked like four miles of cables.

You had to squeeze past Joe Cronin, the well-fed president of the American League, to get down the box-seat aisle to the field. You were looking for the gent in the brown uniform with the overseas cap and the sunglasses and there he was working—pulling a drag over the basepaths with the same red buggy he had used for his record-shattering trips.

Al Forester and his "caht", as he calls it, had shuttled between the bullpens—they stretch from right to center fields, in front of the bleachers—and the first-base line so many times you feared he'd run out of gas and strand a reliefer in short right, or somewhere.

"Not gas," corrected Forester, a tanned little man in his 40's. "Electric—six batteries. I charge it every night. Tonight it might need a pretty good charge.

"I knew I was busy, but I never gave it a thought this might be a record. Seems to me I had to fetch 10 pitchers one day this season when we played the Angels—it was the Game of the Week on NBC-TV—but I could be wrong."

Hoerner did not lose his lunch on the way into the arena. Jaster did not perspire all over the front seat. Bell did not grimly swear to avenge the Jim Murray rips at the Red Sox as he got into the cart. No scoops, blast it.

"Nobody said much—they never do," commented the star pilot of Fenway's automotive pool. "Lamabe said hello—he used to be with the Red Sox, you know. Woodeshick mentioned that I've been around here a long time—I've been a member of the ground crew for 11 years. I knew Woodeshick when he played in our league with Cleveland and Washington.

"But there wasn't any comment about the way the game was going, or what they were getting into. I just picked 'em up, took 'em to the game. I park this thing in a little runway beyond first base. We call it Canvas Alley. That's where we keep the tarpaulins, too."

What Forester was driving the pitching queue to—and specially the Cardinal troop movement—was a tremendously exciting spectacle. For the customers, that is. For the pitchers—well, just check the line score and the home runs.

Forester has been at the wheel since August, 1960.

"That's when we installed the cart," he said. "My first customer was Luis Arroyo of the Yankees. He was the first and last Yankee pitcher I drove. Casey Stengel said he wanted his pitchers walking—not riding. Yogi Berra and Ralph Houk kept the rule going. Makes no difference to me.

"I give the boys a safe ride. I have to make a sharp right turn to get in foul territory from the bullpens, and once Sparky Lyle of our club almost fell out, but it wasn't anything serious. They've kidded me about it ever since."

Al Forester drove into millions of homes yesterday on TV. Little did he realize that he would finish the game as a member of the "Haul of Fame".

Richie Allen

*He's Dick Allen now, three trades later, but he
remains one of the most exciting athletes I've
ever seen. And, at times, one of the most unap-
proachable. We had this talk at the Phillies'
training camp in 1968.*

CLEARWATER, FLA.—Richie Allen was switching from street
clothes to baseball clothes in the Jack Russell Stadium clubhouse.

Over the weekend, he had told the persistent Ralph Bernstein of the
Associated Press—Ralph is Pennsylvania sports editor, and he is covering the
Phillies for a week—that he would not discuss his leaving the Phils and the
subsequent fine. The word was out—Allen's not talking.

"Can't I ask you some questions?" I said.

"What about?" Allen replied, not unpleasantly.

"About the business of your going home, what you think of the disciplinary
action, things like that."

Allen pulled his baseball undershirt over his head and over those unbelievable shoulders.

"I'm not going to say anything," he said, talking rapidly. "I'm not even
going to talk about baseball, or about the club, and that goes for the whole
season."

I've always gotten along well with Allen—I think—as an undisguised
admirer of his skills. And it never has been a problem getting along with him.

"You don't want me to print something like that, do you, honestly?"

"A couple of sports writers have written bad stories about me in
Philadelphia," Allen said. He seemed upset. "I read quotes about me I never
said. One of them called up my mother and called her a liar. I have to punch a
man like that."

Allen continued dressing.

"I'm not a bad man," he said. "I want to keep my friendships with everybody. I just want to be treated like a ball player. I don't see why they should ask about personal things, and write about them."

Remember, this is the Allen who only minutes back had announced he wasn't going to say anything, about anything. But unless I read him entirely wrong, he couldn't be that type. In a troubled sort of way, he seemed to welcome the opportunity to talk.

The great young hitter of the Phillies was dead wrong in just picking up and leaving the camp to go to Philadelphia to have his hand checked, or for any other reasons. He still does not realize this, however. He left camp without permission. Unfortunately, he is the only person who sees nothing wrong in this.

"I would have gone home even if I had asked the man and they told me no," he said.

"I pick up the paper in Philadelphia and the headline says 'Allen Quits Phillies'. That's ridiculous. I had my car here and I had my clothes here—is that quitting? And I had my wife call the ball park to tell them where I was. I didn't quit anything.

"I had come to Florida in the middle of February, long before I was supposed to, at my own expense. My hand bothered me and it worried me, so I went home to have it looked at. Bobby Wine went home to have his back checked. Why didn't everybody write about that?"

Bobby Wine was given clearance to consult his specialist, for his own peace of mind. There was no reasons to believe Allen wouldn't have been given the same right. He didn't ask, though. He doesn't think he should have had to ask, apparently, but there was no use pressing the point.

Richie Allen does not think he is news. He is the highest paid Phillie, a superstar, and the best is yet to come out of him. In this book, the Philadelphia franchise never has had a ball player of his equal. He does things and he gets written about. Things like holding out until mid-March last year, for a record contract for a three-year man. Things like the terrible accident of last August, when he butchered his throwing hand while pushing a third-hand car.

"Bobby Wine is not Richie Allen, and forget everything else about his going home," I suggested. "You're the big man on this club. Things you do are news, are interesting to people. Take your friends with the Philadelphia 76ers. If Matt Goukas should up and leave, it wouldn't be the same as Wilt Chamberlain leaving."

Allen was not buying. He shook his head.

"I don't see why I have to be used to sell a few papers," he said. "It all started with the Frank Thomas thing. They wrote those stories and people started booing me. That's when all the booing began."

Allen finished dressing. He had to be going.

"I'll be around," he said with a little smile. "Maybe we'll talk about fishing, or hunting, or something."

Bill White was in Wilmington for a banquet in January and he got up and said that neither Mantle nor Mays nor Aaron nor anybody in his time had the natural ability that is Richie Allen's. From this seat, he could be an athlete of truly heroic proportions. He also is a complex young man who has alienated people and appears to have been wounded by his own little storms. You would have to say he is an unpopular baseball star, and that is too bad.

"Richie Allen is mixed up, but he is a good guy," observed Jim Bunning. "We talked the other day. I just told him not to let things get him down."

Somehow, it doesn't seem that simple.

There She Is

The Miss America contest—I don't think I'd like to do an encore, but I got a kick out of covering my first one. This despite the world's worst press-box arrangement. At least, it was in 1971.

ATLANTIC CITY—Maybe it was the waitress, who said as she served the flounder, "You won't believe this, but I was Miss America once."

I looked at her and decided the words must have come from the flounder. If there is a town in South Dakota named America, then she might have been Miss America. Otherwise, her best shot had to be Miss Low Tide of 1940. But she was fun.

Maybe it was the housewife from Georgia sitting up in the balcony waiting to applaud her cousin, Miss Georgia, during Friday night's preliminaries. She had a daughter with her. Another daughter, a baby, was back in the motel being minded by the husband. They had started driving from Smyrna, Ga., at 5 that morning.

Maybe it was all the rooting sections around the Boardwalk. People wearing badges that said "Miss New York—We Love Liz". Straw hats with "Miss Connecticut" bands. Badges picturing a horse's head (a filly, no doubt) over "Kentucky". The "Sheila—Everybody's Choice" badges were from Minnesota.

It could have been the bellman in the motel.

"You want me to give you three of the 10 semifinalists?" he offered with race-track eyes.

They all helped because I was determined not to like the Miss America Pageant. All these years on television, it had been an unfinished bit of toleration: unfinshed because I invariably tapped out before the midnight coronation and went to bed announcing the sure winner, who never seemed to win. And who needed Bert Parks?

But on the scene, it is difficult not to get snared in the fun, speculation, excitement and the whole tinsel bag, if the pageant committee will overlook the ill-fitting noun.

The 50-girls-50, Misses Alabama through Wyoming, are real. On TV, they come over with a frightening sameness, right out of the Max Factor-y. See 'em live and they are, well, 50 different young ladies and as many nice kids, similar only in radiance, wholesomeness and enthusiasm. See 'em in their street clothes, going to and from rehearsals, and you see 'em as the individuals they are, not the look-alikes, act-alikes that home viewing implies.

Seeing 'em live, though, can be discouraging for those tucked away in the eerie reaches of Convention Hall, the Astrodome of the Atlantic. First-timers get their message right inside the door: "Opera glasses $3."

Still, everybody seemed to be on a fun thing. So how can you knock 20,000 live fans and zillions of TV watchers, annually? The Miss America joust must have something, and it does. It is an escapist dessert to a long, hot summer. It is a folksy, straight-arrow show certainly worth the $3.50—if you bring your own opera glasses.

This is tough to write, but Bert Parks does the job. He is admirably fitted to the shallow role of m.c., and just when you think he might be a little too neighborly, he comes out with a change of dinner jacket to prove you really are on Broadway. You don't want Shelly Berman in this spot. The family audience, for want of a better description of the crowd, soaks up Bert Parks. He comes out in that flared tux and purple shirt and flashes his great bulkhead of musical teeth and if you could box this charm, you'd murder the salt-water taffy business. Friday night, he introduced "my own personal Miss America, my wife of 28 years," and there were ah's all over the hall.

He was introduced as "America's own Bert Parks" and after his 17 years in the pageant, you can't deny that. His nickname should be "National".

On the world's most famous runway, as they put it, the girls paraded in swimsuits and evening gowns and they did their small talents on stage and it all wound up as Miss Ohio, which is all right with me. Incidentally, I see nothing evil in the swimsuit event, as do some critics. These one-piece suits are overcoats, compared to what is worn on the beach, and how else are we going to avoid picking a bow-legged Miss America? And how else would I discover that Miss Pennsylvania has a long scar on the back of her right shoulder?

Friday night, for want of a seat in the peopled earthquake known as the press row, I sat with the overflow across an aisle from the very end of the runaway. Its floor was at eye level, and I felt like a headpin. Had the girls been bowling balls, I would have been destroyed.

The luxury of an assigned press seat Saturday did wonders for my handicapping record. Midway through the program, I penciled my Top 3, strictly on looks: 1. Massachusetts ("dainty" was my note of identification), 2. Pennsylvania ("stacked"), 3. Idaho ("dimples"). They finished 2-3-1 as runners-up behind Ohio. I would have picked Miss Ohio, but didn't like the short price.

I also came here prepared to snub Miss Delaware because she lives in Pennsylvania. But that feeling began melting on sight, and her Miss Congeniality success wiped out the last traces of my sulk. So I'm a front-runner. So who can't use congeniality, imported or not?

Mrs. Tubby

*Sue and Tubby Raymond always did stand
tall with me. Even more so, when I heard the
story of the football coach's wife's long-time
adjustment to sudden total deafness.*

Sue Raymond dialed a number but did not wait for an answer. She
put the phone in a cradle on a table.

Within seconds, a bulky, repainted machine beside the phone was acti-
vated. It typed out a greeting.

"HELLO GA" appeared on the yellow paper.

Mrs. Raymond pecked at the keyboard and replied "Who is speaking
GA."

"THIS IS SANDI GA."

"THIS IS SUE HOW ARE YOU? GA."

"I'M FINE HOW ARE YOU? GA."

The GA stands for Go Ahead, meaning end of message and it's your turn
to send.

This is how Sue Raymond helps herself "hear." She is the wife of the
University of Delaware football coach. She is totally deaf or legally deaf or
whatever the term is for people who cannot hear naturally. She has been that
way since the winter of 1959-60, when she was stricken either with a virus or a
"vascular accident."

The reconditioned teletype machine was Tubby Raymond's Christmas
present to his wife—"the best one I ever received." There are only six in the
state. You can make local and out-of-state calls to deaf friends, who are
alerted by a flashing light.

Sue Raymond could hear as well as anybody until that day 14 years ago. It was another routine morning around the house. She was dusting. She straightened up, and felt extremely dizzy—"weird, like the whole world was going around."

It wasn't long before her world became terrifyingly silent. Now she can hear you with an aid, but you must raise your voice and she must be looking directly at you. As her husband says, "she does great one-on-one."

I am writing this to inform you that Tubby isn't the only winner in the Raymond house. He wins insignificant things like games and championships. Sue has won back living itself, something she thought she had lost along with her hearing.

They can laugh now, this wholesome couple with the three handsome children. I remember when they first came to the campus, Tubby as Dave Nelson's backfield coach and straight man. They looked as if they should be carrying books themselves.

"She'd be nothing without the deafness," Tubby cracked to me with that crooked smile, loud enough so that Sue would hear him. "What I mean is, she had developed a great deal of character through this. She has completely licked it."

She is her old smiling Sweet Sue.

"It is silly to say anything good about it, to glamorize it," she said. "If I had a choice, of course, I wouldn't be deaf. But it comes to a question of what are you going to do about it? I guess I wasn't doing much about it till I met adults who were born deaf, and realized what they had to go through. They don't just exist. They live. They enjoy life."

Sue Raymond said she went through four stages.

"I was upset, depressed. Then I told myself this couldn't be true, that my hearing would return and everything would be okay. Next, I realized this wasn't going to happen, and I grieved over a valuable something I had lost. Fourth, I faced reality, I was deaf. It took me 10 years to accept this."

They took midnight walks around the block, to settle her down. Name a top hearing specialist, and they saw him. The kids, then ages 3, 5 and 7, were wondering what was going on.

Five years ago, she went to work as a teachers' aide at Sterck School for the Hearing Impaired. "I forgot all about myself. It was the first time I had met anyone deaf from birth. I thought I knew everything about being deaf, but I knew nothing. The administration then did not believe in teaching the sign language, but the kids knew it and taught me and I got to be pretty fluent with it later working with Lou Ann Simpson as a State Vocational Rehabilitation counselor. It is a beautiful language."

I asked Tubby if he could sign.

"Slowly," he laughed, rubbing the back of his left hand with two fingers to illustrate the word. "I know it is easier to send then to receive."

Sue did rehabilitation work with people with various handicaps, for 18 months.

"The telephone made me decide to leave," said Sue, who places its receiving end on what Tubby irreverently calls her electronic bosom. "Two, three calls I could handle, but spending all day on the phone, I was out of it. That's the big hangup of most deaf people. That's why the teletype machine is so great."

She is back at Sterck School as part of a requirement for the master's degree in psychology she is pursuing. She was deaf when she resumed her marriage-interrupted education and got her bachelor's degree at Delaware.

She now has, in her husband's words, "total communication. She reads lips, gets some sound with the aid. If we have trouble with a particular word, I clue her with the first letter."

Sue says she practices reading lips. "But if I'm talking to a man with a bushy mustache, or a beard, or smoking a pipe, forget it. I can't do it with the TV. I can only enjoy the sports events, where no sound is needed, but I do miss Howard Cosell and his gang. I can't discriminate radio sounds. Words or music, it's just noise. My poor kids—it bothers me because they can't turn up the record player."

Sue Raymond goes to Coach Raymond's football games, and being deaf at the stadium isn't all bad, she claims, "It's marvelous—I can't hear the people hollering at Tubby."

The Jersey Veldt

I love to watch animals. I even could spend hours looking at ostriches, or is it ostri? It must be a great summer job, working with the livestock at one of these wildlife parks.

PROSPERTOWN, N.J.—It is Disneyland with giraffes.

They are building one of those "safari" parks in the Pine Barrens of Jersey, in Ocean County, as part of a $100 million entertainment center called Great Adventure. It is scheduled to open for all you adventurers on July 1. Bring pith helmet, bwana.

Safari, amusement-park style. Drive your car through, don't get out, keep the windows up, go 5 miles an hour and see the animals roaming or snoozing right out in the open. You could have a lion or a gnu or a llama staring back at you, or a baboon on your hood.

You run out of gas, you honk your horn and a zebra-striped truck will respond. Get out of your car, and you could run out of limbs.

There will be 2,000 animals here by opening day, and about half of them have checked in. I got a preview drive through safariland's 500 acres and 13 different sections, all beautifully landscaped, and it seemed funny to see one of those absurdly built ostriches—three hoses sticking out of a feathered football—walking faster than the vehicle.

They have this great flock of ostriches in with a herd of 30 baby elephants, who seem to like having them around. Not that it makes much difference, because I am told in a match race the elephant never would catch the big bird.

They brought the elephants over from Africa on, of course, a jumbo jet. All the other animals are being shipped in by train from other parks on this continent. A lot of them and the head animal man, Rodney Dring, are transplants from Parc Safari Africain in Montreal, which the parent company also owns.

Rodney Dring prefers to be called Butch Dring, and I acquiesce. Nobody named Rodney Dring should be supervising beasts. Butch is much better.

Everything about Great Adventure is big, and I just don't mean the elephants and giraffes. It is the largest drive-through safari park outside of Africa. The park, tastefully carved out of the pinelands and landscaped by one Basil Francis Hanger, will be ready to go when the rest of the wildlife boarders appear. Basil Francis Hanger—now that fits—has simulated "the actual environments of the exotic animals", according to the publicity.

All I know is, if they must have animals in captivity, then this is the way to do it. I get unhappy in zoos.

Not that they have not taken steps to see that the animals do not wander or leap their way to Trenton, or Mt. Holly. There are great wire fences, and fences within fences. Some have green metal panels to discourage the climbers.

If you don't recognize the stars as you drive from section to section, there will be help. Turn on the car radio to a certain number, and you will be tuned in to tape recordings that are signaled by underground wiring.

The animals are only half the show at the park, which now has 1,000 construction workers putting in six and seven-day weeks. The other half is the entertainment center.

I was reminded of movie mob scenes of guys throwing up instant towns during the gold rush. Only those towns didn't have the world's largest merry-go-round, built in the 19th Century and imported from England. Or a 3,500-seat aquatic stadium in which high divers from Mexico and dolphins will perform. Or the 6,000-seat Great Arena, where there will be a wild bag of circus acts, rodeo stuff, sky divers, chariot races.

If you like Ferris wheels, you'll flip. This one also is the world's biggest— 15 stories high, fetched from Europe. Remind me not to get on it.

Plus cable rides and restaurants and shops and, naturally, an Enchanted Village. I watched them working on a tepee made of Douglas fir logs eight stories high. The company had to take over a paper plant in Oregon just to have them peeled.

A "runaway" train, a flume ride, street entertainment by jugglers, minstrels.

All this is not Walt Disney, but Hardwick Companies Inc. Its president is Warner LeRoy, son of Mervyn LeRoy, the movies man. They are going with a one-price policy of $7.50 adults and $6.50 children for the whole works, safari and entertainment, or $2.50 and $2 for safari alone and $6.50 and $5.50 for entertainment alone.

Cleverly located on the veldt between New York and Phildelphia, the park expects to draw 2 million people this first summer and I don't see how they can miss. I was grumpy when I got here, and still was awed by the size and the class of the project. Great Adventure's brochure tells you to get off the New Jersey Turnpike at 7-A and proceed East. But there ain't no 7-A, Charley, not just yet. So I went to 8 and wound up in Freehold and groped my way down from there. If they had needed anybody to answer a lion's roar, I was ripe. My Great Adventure was finding the joint.

What do the neighbors think? There was early opposition, but it has disappeared, thanks to a public relations campaign and, more importantly and shockingly, the decrease of the township folk's property tax by 23 cents on the hundred. What Great Adventure, which bought 1,500 idle, woodsy acres, will mine for the tax collector will more than make up for that. The park also will mean 1,300 jobs, the greater part of them for college ages.

There's plenty of room to expand. On the drawing board are golf, tennis, boating, swimming and riding facilities and hotels.

Now if they can teach a Dromedary camel to get on the Ferris wheel . . .

The Prison Game

Delaware has since erected a new "correctional center" and torn this one down. I wonder how many players moved with the franchise?

The outfield walls are brownish gray.

No signs. No scoreboard.

The diamond is skin, wall-to-wall dirt. A few blades of crabgrass significantly defy all the laws of agriculture along the two low concrete tiers that serve as the stands.

It is a good place to play ball, though. The field is well-kept, well-lined, devoid of pebbles, nice and level. The bounces are true.

It is a good place to play ball if you are with the visiting team.

If you are with the home team—well, you are a convict.

They call it the New Castle Correctional Institution, but no matter how you spell it, it is a prison, a penitentiary, and there is a sign on the lobby wall in "The Center" that says it was opened on Nov. 4, 1901. They don't make prisons like they used to, fortunately.

The field is in the "V" formed by the East Wing and the equally bleak and weary brick building that houses the laundry, kitchen and dining hall. The concrete fences are 40 feet high, and not just to keep the ball in play.

This is where the team known as NCCI plays softball, and plays it extremely well. It has just finished winning both the pennant and playoffs in the Major League, the strongest of the Wilmington Park Recreation leagues. It wanted to play in last month's Delaware State Championships, but there is a house rule against traveling—"We couldn't leave the premises," explained C. Vernon Cline, superintendent of education and recreation—and also, it could not supply any gate receipts for any games played at home. If they passed the hat, there was no guarantee the hat would come back.

This was the evening NCCI was about to play Delaware City in the second game of the playoff finals. It had won the first.

Dr. Louis M. Partnow is director of rehabilitative services at the institution. He doesn't know much about technical softball. Ask him a certain player's position and he'll say "Oh, he plays in back of the first base," meaning right field.

But he recognizes competitive softball, and its contacts with the "outside", as rehabilitative potential for the entire institution. Along with Cline, a tall, soft-spoken Tennesseean, Dr. Partnow was instrumental in reviving the "varsity" after a lapse of three years with the blessings of the warden, Raymond W. Anderson.

"These are tough guys, no getting away from it," commented Dr. Partnow. "We've got seven long-termers on the squad, men who have been sentenced from five years to life. Two are lifers. They couldn't get along on the outside. But it is amazing, almost miraculous, to see them subjugate their feelings and pull together to win games. Their desire to win is tremendously strong, but it is a harnessed desire. Umpires tell us this is the best-behaved team in the league."

One of the night's umpires, Phil Stewart, was to concur. He is a little fellow who a couple of months ago had his forehead laid open by a berserk, bat-wielding Industrial League player in a game on the "outside".

"None of us have any qualms about coming here," Stewart said. "They give us arguments on close calls, like any other club, but not even as prolonged. There's never been any rough stuff, no threats. I like to work here, I know, because their team is so strong. You like to work the good ones."

Only the players' nicknames will be used here, to protect the guilty.

The pitcher was a 48-year-old who calls himself "Old Folks", but who doesn't throw like same. This is a fast-pitch, by the way. Old Folks is a lifer, for second-degree murder. You had great difficulty identifying these fellows with crime, after meeting and talking with them. Old Folks, for one, looks like a kindly bus driver.

Or take the inmate manager, Jim, age 36. He is a wispy fellow, gentle in voice and appearance, who left the third-base coaching box for an inning to come behind the backstop and chat with a visitor.

"Everybody gets a little something out of this," he said. "We win, the guys who root for us feel good. We lose, the ones who hope we lose got to feel okay. I was glad to see us get back in an outside league. The competition breaks up the monotony. I've been here 14½ years, and I've been playing ball all but two years. That was when I was in the padlock. The original charge was armed robbery and while I was doing five, they indicted me for murder and I missed a couple of seasons and then I got life. Yes, I read the papers and follow the big leagues. I'm a Yankee man, and I been dyin' with them until the last couple of weeks."

NCCI has a whippet of a shortstop called Chick, who wins all the house track meets, the handball tournaments, stars in touch football. The third baseman is Floogie. The catcher is a big, strong guy called Mel. They wear regular softball uniforms, blue, with "NCCI" on the jerseys, and they put on golf gloves when they bat. All of them play hard, and so did Delaware City. It was about as hard a softball game as you'll see.

There were maybe 200 inmates watching, half the enrollment. One guard was in the stands that stretched along the left-side foul-line. A few others watched from the barred porch of The Center. The fans seemed to enjoy the action, but did not cheer. Once Chick was bowled over by a base-runner and hurt his leg and a white-suited guy from the medical staff emged from The Center as several inmates made noises like sirens. Others yelled: "Don't talk to him—take his pulse!" . . . "Get out your aspirins!"

Delaware City won 3-2 in a game halted by darkness. The spectators took over the yard and started throwing footballs around, for it still was their recreation period.

They played the deciding game the next night. It was sort of nice to hear— and we hope Delaware City will understand—that the bad guys ended their season with a trophy-earning victory. Only the season closed. The years immediately resumed their endlessness.

Sammy's Bad News

Big Nose Sammy, a downtown landmark, eventually was locked out of his gamey pad. But he's still selling papers on the sidewalk, and who knows where he sleeps?

The voice on the phone sounded sad, and a little indignant.

"They are throwing out my friend Big Nose Sammy," he said. "The Board of Health. They nailed a sign on his door that says he's gotta get out this month. The city can't afford to lose this landmark."

The lament was worth looking into, because Big Nose Sammy indeed is a landmark. He has been noisily pushing newspapers from a dark, mysterious "store" at Eighth and Orange for years.

Big Nose Sammy always needs a shave and he wears a sweater and no socks, summer and winter, and he usually is surrounded by characters that make the place look like a breakfast mission.

Characters, and dogs. Sometimes a pedestrian has to slalom when the dogs are sunning themselves on the sidewalk. Or when there is what there is on the sidewalk when the dogs aren't sunning themselves.

Sammy lives with the dogs, and feeds pigeons. He does not ask much out of life. A belt or a beer at Mom's, a game of knock rummy in the horse parlor. I was going to say both are within talking distance, but in Sammy's case, when he talks, this could mean Harrisburg. The volume is always up.

Sell a few papers, a little produce, play a number, play a horse, shout around, that's Big Nose Sammy.

I investigated. And you can relax, landmark lovers.

True, there is a sign on the door at 201 West Eighth that says it is unfit for human habitation and nobody can live there after Aug. 20. But this is "upstairs," next to what the city directory identifies, quaintly, as "Samuel's Newspaper Stand".

"That don't mean my business has to leave," Sammy said hoarsely. "It just means I can't live upstairs no more. It's the landlord's fault. He won't fix it up.

"Me, I've been livin' in here, with the papers, even before they put up the sign. Or I could move in with my brother on Harrison Street."

I gathered that Sammy had a roommate. The roommate persuaded him to move out, and the roommate is still up there. He persuaded Sammy by hitting him on the head.

"With a mason jar," Sammy said matter-of-factly, as though the roomie had done it before. "28 stitches."

There was another guy on the sidewalk with Sammy while we were talking. He kept chattering pleasantly to us even though we weren't paying attention. He wore a polo shirt that said Miami, Florida. Every now and then Sammy would yell "Aw, shut up" but Miami, Florida wouldn't, for long.

"I been upstairs 10-15 years, and in business here 25 years," Big Nose Sammy said. "I gotta story for you. Next September, I'll be the only paperman in the state of Delaware to be a 50-year man, sellin' papers and magazines on the street. Started when I was 4½ years old."

Miami, Florida: "Sammy and me were in the paratroops together. And he don't get no welfare, either."

Sammy: "Aw, shut up! The man can't hear me!"

Sammy says business is terrible. "The Morning News, I sell mostly. They don't care for the Journal no more, not since Market Street died. I used to sell the Journal in the old days on every corner on Market Street. I can tell you the names of all the old stores. Lippincott's, Snellenburg's."

Miami, Florida: "Sammy, he's the only hippy around sellin' papers. We ain't partners, just buddies."

Sammy told him to shut up, then said the scratch sheets aren't moving. "Armstrongs are nothin' any more—you can't give 'em away. I used to sell 250 Armstrongs a day at Fourth and Shipley. Now I get 50 delivered and I'm lucky to sell 20. Magazines, they're dead too."

Miami, Florida: "They don't let us hang at Sixth and Market no more, since the Family Court moved in there. They chase you off."

There were several boxes of potatoes and some completely relaxed celery next to the newspapers. There should have been a condemnation sign on the celery.

"The produce, I sell that just to keep in beer money," Sammy said.

Miami, Florida: "Yeah, beer money. I can still see the stitches in Sammy's head. He don't get no welfare, either."

"If business is that lousy," I said, "how do you get by?"

Big Nose shrugged. He really doesn't have a big nose, a schnoz. He said he got the name because he's always telling people to keep their big noses out of other people's business. "I play a few hands of cards to keep goin'. I cut down on my beer. If I drink 6, 8 glasses a day, that's a lot, anymore. And no more than a fifth a day. I been sick many a day, but never close. All my 25 years, I never closed up."

I asked about the dogs. Sammy smiled toothlessly. He likes dogs.

"Used to have a dozen here," he said. "Now there are five, and three belong to the guy that hit me with the jar. He don't buy nothin'. I feed 'em, and they eat better than you do. You know what they call this street? They call it Dog Street. And they call it Sammy's Beach, too, on account of me."

Miami, Florida: "Sammy, he's been all over Florida. He used to have eight cats, too. Eight cats and 56 dogs."

Sammy asked me to wait a minute. He opened the posted door, hustled up the stairs and returned with a piece of paper with seven typewritten verses on it. The title was "Come On, You Customers, Come On". It read like a Wilmington shopkeeper's lament. Sammy said it was a song, and he wrote it. No music, just words.

"I copyrighted this in 1968," Sammy sputtered. "Tony Bennett, he's gonna sing it. All I gotta do is get a band. This is gonna sell a million copies—in one day."

Sammy sang the first verse, to the tune of what must be a thousand country-western tunes. He has a pretty good voice. He started on the second verse, but I told him I now had an idea of how it went.

Miami, Florida: "The Sunday papers, they don't sell good because nobody is going to church any more. Sammy, he sells fruit, too."

Sammy: "Aw, shut up!"

Never fear. Big Nose Sammy's still here.

Earthquake!

*A recordable quake in the flatlands of Wil-
mington, Del.? It really happened, and it really
scared people. I am delighted it was the kind a
writer could have fun with—the next day.*

My ever-alert wife was the first to be awakened by The Earthquake. She won't admit it, but I'm sure she thought it was me coming home again, until she remembered this was one of my health nights.

She shook me. Seconds later, that would have been unnecessary. Then both of us were shook. So was the entire estate.

"I think somebody's trying to break into the house," she whispered.

I couldn't hear her over the din. She repeated her suspicion, shouting it.

"Who do you think it is?" I asked.

"Godzilla," she said.

By this time, it seemed as if the whole room, the neighborhood and the county were rocking and rolling and roaring.

"I think you're wrong," I yelled. "If somebody is trying to break into the joint, from the sound and the motion of it it has to be Dick Butkus. Why don't you go down and see?"

My favorite spouse had another explanation. "Maybe it's the gas station again."

We have an Arco station at the head of our street that is open all night and features noise from the time the neighbors go to bed till they get up. Unless you have had experience playing first cannon in the Warsaw Concerto, you can't get a job there on the night shift. They attract the loudest motors in the east. And you should hear the din the Coca-Cola man makes when he refills the cases at dawn. Hard drinks aren't that noisy.

But I ruled out the gas station. I had to be fair.

"It's not loud enough to be the gas station," I said.

The scientists were to call it a minor earthquake, this one, that struck—or whatever it is that quakes do—at 3:21 in the morning. Lord save us from the major leagues.

I was sound asleep, and was experiencing a rather nice dream. Lee Remick and Miss America of 1952 were fighting over me, and it was a draw. We decided to make it a triangle.

But the intensity of The Earthquake quickly dispelled thoughts even of Lee Remick and Miss America '52. The scientists said it was most severe for a period of only seven seconds. Seven scary ones.

You can do a lot of guessing in that time. None of our speculation mentioned an earthquake. What, in the flatlands of Delaware? Earthquakes are for California, or Nicaragua, or Chile, or somewhere.

So we cringed in the thundering darkness and wondered what was happening.

"I've got it," I said. "Tyler McConnell just dropped his wallet, and it is tumbling down the stairs."

"Either that," my partner said, "or Delaware Trust just dropped Tyler McConnell."

I tried to remember what had been on the afternoon's entertainment page.

"Could be Cass Elliot is appearing at The Sulky, and fell off the stage," I said, almost hopefully.

Impossible, she parried. "Mama Cass isn't in town, but maybe she fell off the stage in Detroit. We'd feel that, wouldn't we?"

"Well, then," I said. "Perhaps Manny Klein and His Orchestra have installed a tuba section, and are staying up late rehearsing a new arrangement, and that rumbling is their sock finish."

But I withdrew that one. I decided Manny Klein and His Orchestra are still trying to master the old arrangements, and also the old instruments.

An especially potent blast rattled the windows. I couldn't see in the darkness, but I'm sure it also tilted my prized oil painting of Dean Steele's birthplace.

"This is getting serious," I said, brilliantly, trembling beneath the blankets. "It must be something really big. Maybe he did it at last. Russ Peterson, I mean. Maybe he snuck back into the state and blew up the Gaither Committee."

We were only conversing to keep up our morale, but the guesses were beginning to make sense.

"I've got it," my roommate said, triumphantly. "The Summit Bridge just ran into another ship."

Heaven forbid, I thought. Now they'll have to close Virginia, the Carolinas and South America to Delaware trade. If this keeps up, they'll have to lower the canal.

"Could be we have a new paper boy," she shouted. "A large one, throwing the Morning News against the door. Were they expecting a big edition today?"

"Not that I know of," I said. "But even so, that would bring us back to Godzilla. Nobody else could throw that hard."

The terrifying rumbling subsided. I stayed awake wondering what really had happened, and how other people had been affected.

Everybody had a story. Like Phil Crosland, the critic. He was just about to leave the house (Phil types very slowly, and has to get to the office early) when the tremors hit.

"I knew it was a miracle, or a phenomenon, or something like that," he said, "because my support socks fell down. And here, the guy at Woolco told me they were earthquake-proof."

Like Harry Pappas, the Greek Victor Mature who coaches at Brandywine College.

"I've got a basement full of basketballs," he said. "And the force of the earthquake started 'em all bouncing. They kept it up for an hour. I climbed out of bed to see what was going on and it was the darndest game you ever saw. The Spaldings beat the McGregors 30 to 28."

I got back to Crosland, the critic, I wondered if it were possible to review an earthquake.

"Sure," he said. "You just say it was a moving experience."

"I'd Kill Myself"

Bob Cherrix didn't make it. He died within weeks. At his request, he was buried at the finish line of the training track on his property.

SNOW HILL, MD.—Bob Cherrix lounged on the front porch and idly waved a fly swatter. The porch was screened, but this is a bad time for flies, he explained; a few had gotten by the defense.

A long stretch of lawn led to the sun-baked highway out front. In a field to the right, a black young horse exercised friskily. The new corn crop was to the left. Two big shepherd dogs rested in the shade. You could hear kitchen noises. The white barn and a half-mile track and great pastures were behind us.

The scene, 75 acres of farm and horse land, was peaceful. Bucolically beautiful. The horses, including a number of babies, made it look like a picture torn from the Kentucky countryside. Strangers driving by must have envied the occupants.

But they could not hear Bob Cherrix speak.

"I always said I'd kill myself if I ever got cancer," he said with a smile. "But when I got it, I changed my mind in a hurry. Goddammit, I didn't want to die. When I found out about this, that's when I really wanted to live."

Cherrix owns, trains and drives harness horses, and he is one of the country's better hands in a sulky. The books show he has won a thousand races and $3.5 million in purses in 19 years.

He will tell you life has been good to him. A fine school-sweetheart, very pretty wife, Peggy. Three devoted children. A nice business.

Cherrix is 43. A year ago, he found out he had a malignancy in his chest.

Since then, he has had six operations. On his chest, both lungs, a kidney, his left armpit, a shoulder blade. August into May.

Now the treatment is what they call Chemotherapy. It is an injection that he gives himself, once a week. It is powerful stuff, and it makes him nauseous for an hour afterward and it takes away any appetite he might have had.

But he has returned to the races. In fact, with doctors' permission, he drove a race between the time he lost a kidney and part of a lung, last October.

He drives at Rosecroft Raceway in southern Maryland, as much as five times a night. Last week, he was at Brandywine Raceway for a qualifying race, and he won it. I saw him do that. I noticed he wasn't the same size Bob Cherrix I had seen before, and that's when he first told me about what he calls "this cancer business."

"I'm not setting the world on fire at Rosecroft," he said. I longed to tell him he was indeed, just by being there. "I'm trying to get the stable together after being out so long. It's a good place to start the 2-year-olds and race the green 3-year-olds. And I feel better when I'm doing something."

He also has horses in New York, "And would you believe it that the other drivers in New York have been handling my horses, and they won't take a cent for it, even though I'm back racing? And during my operations they contributed 13 pints of blood. It's dog-eat-dog when we're competing against each other."

Cherrix would be driving himself in New York, where the money is, ordinarily. But his "ordinarily" began changing grimly last June. It was Father's Day when he discovered this little bump on his chest. When it increased in size the next several weeks, he decided to have it checked by a physician in Salisbury, who, he said was responsible for "a terrible experience."

It was, Cherrix said, "the only bitter part of the whole thing. Everyone else has been so competent, so nice. I won't mention his name, but I couldn't get an appointment and he kept telling me over the phone that if it didn't hurt, which it didn't, not to worry about it. When I did see him, he just put a little heat and some stuff on it and sent me on my way. It got to be the size of my fist. I was told later that if it had burst, I would have been a goner."

But finally, the first Saturday in August, they cut into Bob Cherrix in the accident ward of the Salisbury hospital to remove what Bob called a "cyst."

"They didn't tell me what was wrong—said they didn't know," he said calmly. "But cancer was on my mind. My mother and my wife's father died of it last year, within 10 days. A cousin in Virginia has it. Tuesday I went back for the lab report. They said I was full of cancer.

"I will give you the name of another Salisbury physician, Dr. John Keen. An outstanding man. A couple of weeks later, he removed a kidney. It had a 15-pound tumor I didn't even know was in me. Even when they probed and pushed, I felt nothing. I hadn't been sick at all. Then I asked Dr. Keen what he would do if he were me. He said go to New York, to the big cancer place, Sloan-Kettering Memorial. What's more, he got me in. It is a marvelous place."

He was in and out of Sloan-Kettering for surgery that seemed endless. Three ribs had to be removed for one lung operation. A plastic plate was inserted. You can't graft to plastic, so they stretched Cherrix's skin across the opening and stitched it together. When he left the hospital, he could not stand up straight, not till he stretched himself out.

He put down the fly swatter and asked if I would like to see the grounds.

"We'll take it easy," he said. "If I jogged to the barn, I'd be completely given out."

He showed me a rangy, week-old foal out of his favorite mare, Myra, who had been a big winner as a trotter. He said Myra had made a horse lover of his wife, who hadn't been crazy about the animals.

I asked Cherrix how a man tells his family he has cancer.

"I never felt so sorry for anybody in my life, as I did for the kids," he said. "When I got the report in Salisbury, they waited in the car. My wife came out and she was pretty broken up. They knew then. When we got home the youngest girl, Pat, rushed right to the barn to be with her horses, and she let it all out. I followed her in and I told her this wasn't going to be that bad, because I'm a pretty tough guy."

Pat is 16. Debbie, 18, went off to junior college in North Carolina last fall but came home after one semester, to be with her father. Bob Jr., 20, a junior-college graduate, was to enter the University of Kentucky in September, but he wouldn't go. Bob Jr. was born that 1952 day his father raced for the very first time, at Harrington. He now is at Rosecroft, with the stock.

We walked on the backstretch of the hot, dusty training track. Cherrix called to a number of horses that were beyond a fence. He identified them by name and racing time. He talked of his comeback.

"I'm not racing just to be bull-headed," he said. I noted that he looks like Al Kaline, the Detroit ball player. "I wouldn't do it if it hurt me. I warm up the horses at the track, and I don't parade. I have good help. And I don't drive in the rain. If it comes up, the judges let me take myself off, and they don't fine me.

"I weigh 157. I used to drive at 175, and they hope to stabilize me at 160. I was always healthy, strong; only other time I was in a hospital was for an appendectomy. The fact I was in such good shape has helped me. I was a pretty heavy smoker, but I gave that up six years ago."

We watched a horse drink out of an old bathtub, then strolled back to the house.

"I got a little bit disgusted, the way they kept finding places to operate," Cherrix said. "But I think I'm clean now, as far as any more big things. If the Chemotherapy does what we think, there's no reason why I can't be completely cured. Who knows? I might die of a heart attack, like my dad, or of old age. I only know I'm not giving up to this cancer business."

I stayed for lunch in the kitchen with Bob, Peggy, Debbie and Pat. A most pleasant meal. Bob Cherrix said the blessing. As we bowed our heads, I think we all said a little something.

"No, No!"

A team of nine Dick Stuarts would be a baseball writer's delight. But then you'd need Dick Stuart to manage them—anybody else would go daffy. This was an interview in the spring of 1965, his only year with the Phillies. He went on to 28 homers, 95 RBIs. Not quite what he—or the Phils—anticipated.

CLEARWATER, FLA.—This is a funny story, but not to Dick Stuart. He was the guy telling it, and he was dead-serious:

"It's the last game of last season and we're (the Red Sox) playing the Senators. Brooks Robinson has finished his year with the Orioles. He leads the American League with 118 runs batted in. I've got 112—need six to tie.

"I come up in the first inning with men on first and second and nobody out, and I figure this is a good start. But Gil Hodges (Washington's manager) orders me walked. I'm steaming, but he's still in the dugout laughing his head off. He'd already lost 99 games—I guess he didn't want to make it 100.

"Later, I drive in two runs with a double and by this time the game is out of control. We're ahead like 13 to 6, but it doesn't look like I'll get to hit again.

"But in the bottom of the eighth we load the bases and I'm up. The score is 15 to 8. A home run ties me with Robinson. Ron Kline is pitching. He throws me a ball, and the second pitch is a knuckler that gets away from the catcher. Here comes Felix Mantilla dashing in from third—with one of my runs batted in! The ball is seven feet away from the catcher, but I have my hand up to stop Mantilla and I'm yelling 'no, no!' at him. But he scores and that only leaves two on. If I hit a homer, I still only got 117 RBI's and I lose by one. What good is that? I'm so teed off I just stand there and take three strikes down the middle, then sling the bat away.

"Funny thing. When I came up, I was almost tempted to tell Billy Herman (coaching third) not to send Mantilla in if it's a wild pitch or a passed ball.

We don't need the run—I do. That Kline—I don't believe he'd thrown one wild since he came to the big leagues. Oh, well."

You are tuned in to Dick Stuart, who as of April 12 will be counting his runs batted in for the Phillies. He is a home run and a runs-batted-in guy who dearly loves to talk. He talks very fast. He has a headful of figures—his own—and they are accurate.

Dick Stuart has a brand-new Cadillac with a stereo system, and he has a closet full of sharp threads, even here in Florida, and he has a platinum-blonde wife and he is—well, he is a home-run hitter. He is tall and strong and he cannot play first base very well. The name of his game is power.

You can't imagine Stuart getting any kind of pleasure out of hitting a two-out single with nobody on base. Does he?

"The run batted in is a big value," he said, relaxing in the dugout after a batting-practice turn. Stuart is a born relaxer. "I'm that kind of a hitter. I'm no leader, like Don Hoak or Dick Groat. I come up with a man on second and nobody out and with most hitters, the idea would be to hit the ball to the right side and advance the man to third base. But a guy like me is supposed to hit in the seats. I'm an uppercut hitter. I go up there to make contact as hard as I can. Theoretically, I'm going for the homer each time. I strike out a lot. But if a pitcher has something on the ball and the hitter is in shape, and has natural home-run power, which I do, the ball goes out of the park. I'd come up in Pittsburgh in that man-on-second, nobody-out situation and I'd look at Danny Murtaugh on the bench and he'd point to the seats. His theory was that if he had to use his No. 4 hitter as a bunter or a hit-and-run man, he was in bad shape.

"I'm a pretty good bunter, no good on the hit-and-run. Johnny Pesky had me bunting guys to third in Boston, and it disturbed me. One day in Fenway, we're ahead 11-7 in the seventh and the first two guys get on. I have 40 home runs, a hundred RBIs. I get the bunt sign. I don't even try. The count goes to three balls, no strikes and I get the take sign. I get mad at this and take a big swing and pop up. Pesky fines me $50. Nobody knows this, until now."

Stuart popped his bubble gum and returned to the "natural" home-run bit.

"Some guys have it, some don't. The Pirates traded me and played Donn Clendenon on first. He's been there three years and he still hasn't beaten my worst Pittsburgh year of 16 home runs and 64 runs batted in. (Editor's note: Clendenon's home-run peak is 15, and he batted in 64 runs last year.) Clendenon is big and strong. He can hit a ball as hard as anybody. We're the same size. But his power is limited to a certain pitching slot, and he will hit one in that slot only 15 times a year. I can hit different-type pitches out of the park. I've got to. The way I strike out, I've got to hit 35-40 home runs a year to save embarrassment, I've got to drive in runs—and I've driven in more the last two years than anybody in either league."

Everybody is wondering how the outspoken, so-what-fielding Stuart and the intense, no-nonsense Gene Mauch are going to get along. The prediction here is that they will get along swimmingly—as long as Stuart connects.

"Mauch will get no trouble from me," Stuart gabbed on. "As long as I start, I'm happy. A manager shouldn't resent a player who wants to play. I never said anything to any manager who took me out when I wasn't hitting. Pesky benched me for four days last year for no reason. I was up there with Mantle and Killebrew in RBIs. That's the maddest I've ever been. I don't like being taken out for defense, either, but I don't resent it. I guarantee you this—I will not let in as many runs as I will drive in. I don't think I'm a manager's problem."

The Phillies' home-run record is 43, set by Chuck Klein at Baker Bowl in the trolley-car days. Stan Lopata has hit the most Connie Mack Stadium home runs, 32. Can Stuart top this?

"I should be among the top home run and runs-batted-in men in the league, playing in that Philadelphia park. Forbes Field was a death trap. Forty-three and 32—is that all?"

The Last Dance

I didn't notice the sign outside the Grille Room till several days later. It read "Dance to Your Heart's Content."

They re-opened the Grille at the Hotel du Pont for dancing and it was very nice, except I felt a little out of place.

I always do, with my footwork, any time there is dancing on the program, but this reaction was a little different. I felt out of it because I seemed to be the only guy in the room who wasn't on a nostalgia trip.

It's not that the heyday Grille was before my time. It's just that I wasn't around here when it apparently was one of the most popular spots in town. Nice music, nice surroundings, one of those you-can't-beat-it places, they tell me.

Now the handsomely appointed room that is a cafeteria in the daytime has launched a come-back Friday and Saturday nights. It has been a good 30 years, from what I could learn, since the downstairs Grille last housed an orchestra. Almost everyone at the re-opening seemed to be recalling the names of the old bands, the staff, the original physical setup.

They were remembering when. My remember "when" about the Grille goes only back to my first visit, last Friday, and it will be an unforgettable one because of a stranger named Joe Calvarese. Dr. Joseph A. Calvarese, podiatrist.

I remembered seeing this smiling man in the good-looking jacket when I walked in.

Hal Schiff's group was playing something I thought I could handle, and I got up to dance.

"About time you old folks came out," the stranger said kiddingly as my wife and I joined the other couples.

He later introduced himself. An old sports fan, he said, and his father co-owned the T & C Arena at 3d and Scott in the days when Wilmington was a hot town for amateur boxing.

He also talked a little golf. "I like it in the winter, when they have those temporary greens with the great, big cups. Does wonders for my putting."

Joe and Louise Calvarese were with their friends Bill and Irene Wood.

I'll flash back a bit. It was Friday evening and the Woods were finishing dinner at the Marinada Inn when Mrs. Wood suddenly remembered the Grille Room. They decided to call the Calvareses to see if they'd be interested in going. Both couples had dated and courted there when the bands were led by people named Don Chattaway, Joe Fisher, Milt Katz.

Louise said hold the phone, she'd check with Joe, who was watering the lawn. He said sure, great idea. So the women decided to wear long gowns and the men changed and the Woods picked up the Calvareses in Woodbrook after making reservations at the hotel.

They had the first table on the right.

"I'm going to sit right here and greet everybody," Calvarese laughed as he and Wood faced the entrance. And if he didn't greet everybody, he came close, for he said hello to everyone he knew or recognized.

Joe and Louise danced well, and frequently. When Stu Davis, the piano player, table-hopped for requests, Joe asked for "something in the Bill Bailey line, on the lively side."

Joe brought his group over to meet mine just before closing time. The Calvareses and the Woods talked about the old layout, which hadn't changed much. Seems they had a bar then, and the dance floor was in another spot. We said our goodnights.

The Woods spent a few post-Grille hours at the Calvarese house, still reminiscing and talking about what a delight the night had been. Dr. Joe excused himself to go to bed, for he had a golf date. His usual, early-morning weekend date at Wilmington Country Club. He would almost beat Joe Cannon, the pro, to the club and Cannon once offered to give him a key.

This is why my memories of the Grille will be dominated by the night it was re-opened: It was the first and last time I met Joe Calvarese.

He died the very same night. The alarm clock he had set for his golf date went off at 6:30. Joe didn't respond.

Heart attack, the obituary said. I learned about this fine, likeable man of 55 in one pleasant evening and in a numbing death notice the next afternoon.

Joe Calvarese liked to dance, from when he was a young man dating Louise DiSabatino in the Grille. I would guess if he had had the opportunity to select where he wanted his last dance, it would have been right where it was.

Children's Nurse

I guess this one is for the ladies. Annie Reese—what a great woman. I've gone back several times to drop off jigsaw puzzles—but really to see her.

I've been around long enough to know that Mrs. Walter Reese isn't news.

There is no way the hard-line editor would go for her story.

Annie Reese is too nice. All she does is make people happy. Babies, and their parents. And herself.

A pox on the hard-line editor. Today we shall talk about Annie Reese, of Kennedyville, Md.

She is a colored lady—and the adjective is hers—of 67 years.

You see a stork hovering over a prominent family in Wilmington, you know Annie can't be far behind.

When she was 49 years old, after 32 years of domestic service as a cook, she decided she wanted to be a practical nurse and specialize in infants. With only a seventh-grade education, she enrolled in a nursing school and made it with no problems.

"She is about the best children's nurse I've ever seen," says Dr. Margaret Irving Handy, the distinguished pioneer woman pediatrician in Delaware, now 82 and retired.

They called the virtually canonized Dr. Handy the Children's Doctor. If she was that, then, from what you hear, Annie Reese must be the Children's Nurse.

"If there was a sick, or tiny child, then Annie was the nurse I especially wanted," Dr. Handy told me.

I drove down to Kennedyville, which is right next to Galena off U.S. 301, to chat with Annie. All her life she has lived in the two snug little houses that almost touch each other off the cracked hard-top road on Davis Hill. She was born in the one and now lives in the other with her husband, who is 70.

You never know. Annie comes from a family of 15 children and there were 20 in her husband's family. Yet they have none of their own, and that makes her late-blooming career even more amazing—or does it? Only two other members survive on each side—and neither has any children. Annie, the second youngest, says she had brothers and sisters die when they were but weeks old. "No doctors or pediatricians around in those days."

You must remember Bryan Field, the late general manager of Delaware Park, the horse track. Well, Annie cooked and Walter handy-manned for six years for Mr. and Mrs. Field—their last six years as a service team.

"We were part of the family," Annie recalled. "They were wonderful people, and I could never have made it as a nurse without their help. They paid for my tuition, and Mr. Field, he helped me with the books and all the new words. Mrs. Field bought my graduation clothes."

I spoke to Georgi Field, and she called Annie "a delightful and wonderful and smart woman. She was crazy about Bryan Jr. All the time we were helping her become a nurse. I kept saying to myself 'We're going to lose her'. And we did. Hardly a day goes by, I don't think of Annie and Walter."

Annie had seen this ad in the Afro-American about a nursing school in Philadelphia. "I guess I was just tired of cooking, and dinner parties. The ad said the age limit was 50. I just made it, by a year. I got interviewed, I enrolled and thanks to the Fields, I got my diploma and my cap."

The year was "19-and 56."

Classes for the Beaumont Nursing School were Mondays, Wednesdays and Fridays. Annie had only Wednesdays off from her job. She solved this problem easily—for her. She would catch the 5:18 a.m. train to Philadelphia, take a week's classes in one day and part of one night, stay overnight at her brother Bill's place and be back at work the next morning. After graduation, 105 hours of hospital training were required. Annie did this on her vacation.

Annie Reese is beautiful. A slip of a woman, 114 pounds, a kind face in rimless glasses, vivacious. Even though she was recovering from a siege of grippe this day, I could sense the devotion and the energy in her. Now and then something would strike her funny, and she would clap a hand over her mouth and muffle a giggle and break up. Her husband was puttering around outside; he apparently isn't much for this interview stuff.

They gave the Fields a year's notice and Annie turned to nursing and Walter, with Bryan Field's assistance, went to work at the racetrack as an attendant. He is still there.

Last January they celebrated their 50th wedding anniversary. It also was Annie's birthday.

Annie showed me her nursing school books, and pictures of babies she has attended. I asked her how many new-born children she had nursed. She fumbled in a drawer, brought out a sheet of yellow paper and came up with the answer: 83. "And that includes four sets of twins."

Between births, she is called to tend on "my children" when their parents need her.

"It is a nice feeling," she said. "I feel I get them started in life, somehow. The parents have confidence in me; they have no worries with me around. I always keep records of medicines and even baths. Dr. Handy, she'd assign me to a baby and she'd stop and check my book. She's been like a mother to me. I started under the very best.

"When the mother's in bed. I take care of the whole family. Dr. Handy says that's why I get so much work. Most nurses, they don't go for cooking, or housework. But that's not the way I see it. When we got our diplomas, we took an oath that we'd help around the house if we were needed."

Annie showed me an engraved silver plate that read "In gratitude, Stuart Daniel Castle, 5-6-66", a gift from lawyer Ben Castle and his wife of Surrey Park. I asked her if she remembered her first baby job. A silly question. Of course she did: Bobby Bolling, son of Mr. and Mrs. Robert Bolling of Greenville, now 17.

"I go back and visit my children, even go to their birthdays sometimes," Annie said. "Most of my work is in Wilmington, but I don't want to move there. We're not city people. We've lived in this house 49 years. Besides, it's cheaper."

When she isn't nursing, Annie works jigsaw puzzles with Walter and waits for the phone to ring. It always does. Or she will watch Marcus Welby, and weep. "That's about the only TV I watch—I even see him when I'm working. He's just like a real doctor."

Annie Reese was 9 years old when her mother first "hired me out" as a cook to help the swarming family get by. Now she says she and Walter "are lucky to have jobs, at our age." I got the feeling the people Annie works for are the lucky ones. Annie Reese is love.

Why He Stayed

Dave Nelson's decision to remain at the University of Delaware, when the college football majors were wooing him, was a great thing for our little old state. If he sounds too pure to be true in his approach to coaching—well, he isn't.

Dave Nelson afraid?

That's what the man implied.

Here he was turning down those glamorous coaching offers all those years, and one of the big reasons he refused them was because he had no confidence in himself.

This startling admission came as Nelson, who has reduced himself to one hat as Delaware's first non-coaching athletic director in 26 years, talked about his new role and his old one with a guy who wasn't around when the story broke.

"I never thought I could be successful coaching at a big school," the Admiral said. He is a great kidder and you looked hard at him to see if he was playing this for laughs. You could tell he wasn't. He had to be kidding, but he wasn't.

Here was one of the country's sharpest football brains, a master organizer, an unquestioned competitor who made copy-cats out of other coaches, confessing that there was a little chicken in his decisions not to go to Baylor, or Illinois, or Florida, or Pitt, or Iowa, or the other colleges that tried to woo him away from Delaware.

You mean that you didn't think your style would win in, say, the Big Ten?

"Not exactly," he said. "It wasn't a case of having to put the X's and the O's in the right places. That's over-rated, anyway. There is a lot more to being a successful coach. The big colleges have a different approach to football, and I didn't think I could communicate with the players the way I did in our league. It's a different game up there, played by different people. It's a business."

The Nelson approach is that you play the game within the rules, on and off the field; that you play it as a student, with morals as well as muscles, that you don't play to win at any price and that you do these things without rationalizing. Call it scoutmaster stuff, if you will. But try to say it without a tang of envy for his makeup, to say nothing of his results.

"I've never believed that you could coach at a place like Iowa the same as you can at Delaware," continued Nelson, as if both trying to clarify his feelings and to, at long last, release them. "Forest Evashevski tells me this isn't true, but I don't know . . .

"The main reason I never left, of course, is that I found a home here. I've said that all along, and I've meant it all along. But the other thing entered into it. I always was afraid that a major college was not a place where I could do a job. Somebody else could, but not me.

"I talked to boys here about things that would sound trite in the big colleges. I'm sure there would be more than a few snickers. Like telling them that drinking and smoking are strictly forbidden. I can't conceive of kicking an All-America halfback off the squad because he smoked; chances are that some All-Americans are smoking when they walk into a coach's office.

"A coach should never ask his players to do something he wouldn't do himself. While I was coaching, I tried to be an example. I'm not naive enough to think that some of our house rules weren't broken, but I will say that they weren't broken that we knew of.

"There is a professional atmosphere to major college football that disturbs me. You could say I didn't have the guts to tackle it. I was leery—I'll say that."

Nelson recalled a case of a Delaware player's not following the party line.

"We had this good lineman," Nelson said. "Let's call him over-aggressive. Anyhow, he would hit his own teammates in scrimmages—actually punch 'em. I warned him that we didn't play that way.

"Then he hit an opponent in a game. We were penalized, he was thrown out of the game. I put him on probation. I told him he had to show me he could practice for three weeks and not hit anybody, and he had to do daily wind sprints as an added penalty. At practice the next week, he didn't do the sprints, so I told him to turn in his suit if he wasn't interested.

"He turned it in. He was a first-line player. I don't think you could operate that way in the big leagues. It would be awfully difficult to try to get rid of somebody, or to convince them why you wanted it this way."

Nelson was a name-college player himself as a Michigan halfback, although he says he wouldn't be good enough by today's standards to draw a uniform.

"I was disillusioned by what I saw then," he revealed. "We would go to a country club the day before games, for seclusion. Just before my first game, when I was a soph, a bunch of the players asked me to stand guard for them outside the caddy shack. I was so much of a lamb I didn't know what was going on, and they had to explain that they wanted to sneak a smoke. Here I had waited all these years to play college football, and I see something like that. It hurt me deeply. Football is a game of sacrifices. They understand this at Delaware. I doubt that they do on the higher levels."

Now you can understand when Nelson discloses that the most tempting offer of them all came from Indiana—which wanted him as atheltic director only. "But it came too soon; I didn't want to give up coaching at 34."

When he did give up coaching, he was 45—and still at Delaware, where he was happy and secure. The feeling was mutual. Happy, secure and underrated—but only by himself.

Detox Center

A reader complained I was too flip in this column, considering the seriousness of the subject. I didn't think so at the time, but now I'm not so sure. Incidentally, a Du Pont Company draftsman saw this article and offered Erskine Caldwell a job.

The first drunk had some great lines. Let's call him Dave.

"When were you born?" asked Erskine Caldwell, pen in hand. This wasn't the Erskine Caldwell who wrote "Tobacco Road". Same name. Different pen.

"You mean I was born?" replied Dave, laughing.

"Sure, everybody was born," coaxed Caldwell.

"10-15-15," agreed Dave.

Caldwell inquired about religion. Catholic or Protestant?

"Mongrel," answered Dave, happily.

"Ever been married?"

"Are you kidding?" said Dave, dragging on a home-made cigarette. He carried a Laredo mixing outfit in a brown paper bag. "Four times. And that's not counting the ones I lived with."

Caldwell wanted to know how many divorces.

"Well," said Dave, "there's gotta be three in there some place."

I don't know how it was where you were Friday night, but where I was it was a bad night for drunks. Either that, or a good one. Only three showed up.

I was at the Detoxification Unit of the Emergency Room at the Delaware Division. This is where police bring the inebriates they find on the streets, or wherever. Or, you can come in voluntarily. It is a screening station where you get a basic medical checkup and then you are sent to the state's Detoxification Center at the Emily P. Bissell Hospital for five days of sobering-up and counseling. It's a state law. You no longer get thrown into the city jail's drunk tank, but if the cops bring you in you are hit with a "Drunk" charge.

Erskine Caldwell has been a counselor at the Delaware Division end of it for 14 months. He is a rangy black man of 22 who is very good at his position. He took it as a second job when he also was employed as an architectural draftsman. He lost the drafting job and now Detox is his living, and if there is anybody out there who has an opening for a draftsman I would like to recommend Erskine even without seeing him draw a line.

You need many extra degrees of compassion and patience for what Caldwell is doing now. They bring in these drunks and they are all kinds. Belligerent, pugnacious, happy, weepy, shouting, delirious. Caldwell has a touch for all of them and is equipped to be physical, too. He signs them in and takes their blood pressure and all the time he is making with the conversation—either maintaining it or forcing it. Trying to get the patient to relax until the doctor shows. Then, if the patient has no medical problems, he again "entertains" him until the two guys from Bissell show up with the car.

Caldwell has the 6 p.m.-2 a.m. shift on this 24-hour operation. On Friday, Dave was his first customer. It was 7:15 and Dave turned himself in. He wasn't falling-down drunk but his speech was slurred and, well, he knew he had a problem.

Caldwell almost could have filled out the form from memory. Dave told him he had been at Bissell 11 times—"and I been to Farnhurst three trips and I been to the Maryland State Hospital in Cambridge three trips."

Caldwell told me he had seen Dave only the previous night. "We had him all registered and examined. He wanted to commit himself to the state hospital. Then he changed his mind and wouldn't sign. He's one of the joyous ones."

Dave was clean and neat. He had a cheap haircut and one front tooth was missing. He said he spoke several languages, and tried to teach Erskine some Spanish phrases. The men from Bissell came in and greeted Dave by name.

"You miserable censored creeps," Dave said with a laugh as they helped him into his topcoat.

I was there four hours and the next two patients weren't joyous. The city police fetched them.

At 9:10, there was Shirley. They had picked her up—literally—on West 8th Street. An attractive married woman of 32 and she was drunk, all right, although she stammeringly denied being "tox'cated." She had what I guess were the usual defenses: "You got no grounds to hold me. I don't bother nobody. You gotta let me go home. I was walkin' down the street and somebody pushed me and I hit my head."

Caldwell had told me earlier that women patients mostly tended to be belligerent. Now he whispered to me in the corridor, "She's one of the unfightful ones."

Jerry was escorted in at 10:10, a 27-year-old found on King Street. Call him defiant. I left at 11 o'clock and he still was refusing to have his blood pressure taken.

"Don't make sense," he muttered. "I was just tryin' to go home. Second time they done this to me."

Jerry thus admitted he had been to Detox before. He sullenly tried to show his cool by lighting up to smoke, but it didn't come off because the cigarette was bent like one of those Benson & Hedges commercials.

Jerry: "You gotta force me to go to Detox. You gotta force me to take my blood pressure."

Caldwell: "Nobody's forcing you. I'm asking you. You scared of blood pressure? It don't hurt."

Jerry: "I'm scared of nothin'."

Caldwell: "All this might be in your favor. You might have got mugged."

Jerry: "I knew what I was doin'."

Caldwell: "Lotta people know what they're doing when they get mugged."

And so on. Erskine Caldwell earns his money.

He takes his work seriously but there are some light moments. Like the time he was checking in a unique, voluntary husband-and-wife team. He sat between them filling out the wife's report. Erskine looked up and there was the husband, head tilted back, draining a pint of VO.

"How come you turn yourself in and you're still drinking?" Caldwell asked, justifiably.

And the man's reply: "I just hadda have that last one. Now I'm ready."

"It Was My Son"

I love a parade, and here was a whole townful of bands. What the man from South Carolina said to me in the press box—I truly was stunned.

ST. **PETERSBURG, FLA.**—The big-band sound filled the old-time ball park and stirred the old-time blood of the Polident set in the capacity crowd of 9000.

High school bands, 18 of them, from places like Claymont, Del., Dundee, Ill., Long Prairie, Minn., Memphis, Tenn.

Al Lang Field was ablaze with 3,000 young men and women blowing, drumming, marching and dancing—themselves as finely tuned as the instruments. They bring these kids up to an event as you would athletes, and there had been rehearsals and meetings almost to the final hour.

Batons and sabers. Rifles and plumes, starting with Maryland, closing with Kentucky in the draw, they came on the lines of the 60-yard football layout like young armies, the splash of the various uniforms adding an Olympic opening-ceremony touch to the show. The strong breeze of a cool night was perfect for the flags. There were so many American flags in the 4½-hour revue that if you had to salute each, even John Wayne would have called for help.

Year after year, I had gone to this park, among others, for spring baseball training. The very day before, the Cardinals and the Red Sox had closed the practice season for the old folks. Now I was watching not the Phillies play the Cardinals or the Mets, but watching Claymont and the rest play music and each other at this annual, week-long civic outburst known as the Festival of States. The high schools call this the National Championship of Bands, and if they don't the festival committee will. I will not dispute this.

A' La Carte

I am a mark for marching bands, and have been known to choke up just at the sight of a can of tuba polish. There were 18 of America's finest school bands in competition. You had to be a palm tree not to feel yourself glow and appreciate not only their skills, but the obviously exhausting preparation. Make that 17 of America's finest. There was one clinker, a 200-member group from an all-girl school in Louisiana that was embarrassingly inept. They played "When the Saints" like the Saints were never gonna make it.

So, I was prepared for a nice little emotional tingle at this brass-in. If you like kids and parades, how can you miss?

But I wasn't ready for what happened in the press box. Most of the people up there were judges. I took a seat along the third-base line. The only other occupant there was a stocky, gray-haired fellow with a tape recorder. He came over and introduced himself as Fletcher Ferguson, managing editor of a weekly paper in Abbeville, S. C.

"Abbeville—isn't that the place where the tornado hit last week?" I asked. "Where one of the boys in your band was killed?"

"Yes," he said. "It was my son."

I think it was the band from Alabama that was performing at the time, but for me, the music stopped right there and I didn't even notice who came on next as I recovered from his stunning remark and chatted with this admirable gentleman.

The tornado struck Saturday night at 10 o'clock. Tommy Ferguson, 16 years old, a baritone-horn player in an outstanding Abbeville band, was one of a group of young people visiting at a neighbor's house. They were listening to music in a one-room building these neighbors had built for their son's use.

Tornados give no warning, I am told. "It sounded like a bunch of freight trains coming at you all at once," was Ferguson's description.

The little building literally exploded. Tommy was hurled from it as his sister, Cynthia, vainly tried to hold on to him. They found him with his chest crushed by a falling tree.

He was buried Monday—in his band uniform. Tuesday, the Abbeville Grenadiers were to leave for St. Petersburg. Nobody wanted to go without Tommy. Another sister, Dawne, is captain of the band.

"They put it up to my wife and me," Ferguson said. "We advised them to go, by all means. My wife is in the stands. I wanted her to come, too. She has been so close to this band. She makes all the trips. And I wanted her to be with Dawne, who needed help badly."

The Abbeville band had been the night's fourth to compete before I arrived. In retrospect, I am glad. I couldn't have handled that, not with the father of the missing boy sitting next to me. I was equally glad when Abbeville, its 83 members making it the second smallest band in the lineup, was voted second place. And forget any sentimental vote. Abbeville also was runnerup here in 1970 and is four-time champion of its state.

I went down to field level for the announcement of the judging. The bands had massed for a zinger of a finale, and now the first, second and third-place groups had the field to themselves. I watched Abbeville march off and, well, you ached for Tommy Ferguson and Mr. and Mrs. Ferguson and those 83 wet-eyed kids. I looked up at the press box and there was Tommy's father recording, for an Abbeville radio station, an account of the Grenadiers' fine showing.

"It was difficult to concentrate," the Abbeville band director, Leland Scott, told me. "And it has been, since Tommy's death. If it were not for his parents, we wouldn't be here. Tommy loved the band; he played his part perfectly. And you know, a lot of these kids have no homes to go back to. They were destroyed."

The Abbeville musicians finished a very tight second to a seemingly endless array of kiltie-clad Dundee Scots from Illinois, complete with a bagpipe brigade. They came to play, definitely. This was the Scots' 27th contest in six years and they've finished first in 25. Their visual effect was striking.

This is the big leagues, all right, and the Claymont band proved it belonged, even if it did no better than 9th place. I flew down with this gang and watched Kent Shaw, their 24-year-old director, and a non-teacher drillmaster named Al Sacko lead rehearsals that bordered on boot camp, and what the Claymonters were doing was being repeated around town 17 times.

I watched Ray Hearn and his fellow band boosters, whose effort financed the trip, sweat right along with the musicians. A booster named Manny Clement had rented a U-Haul truck to drive down the uniforms and instruments. I wished I had been covering the Conrad band here, too, to maybe atone for what this paper did to it, or didn't do to it, at the Presidential Inaugural Parade in Washington.

Claymont, like Abbeville, playing here for the second time, performed with class and dignity and it made you delighted to be on their side. This competition is no place for horn-carriers. Shaw and his 140 boys and girls were as uptight going into the competition, and as spent after it, as any football team you ever saw.

I have to tell you about Doy Helmick, one of the trumpet players. An hour before the band was to walk from the Hilton Hotel to the park across the street, I asked him if he was nervous. He was getting dressed.

"No," he said. "I'm not the kind to get shook up. We'll either do it or we won't."

Now it was departure time, and Shaw was giving a final talk to his troops just off the lobby. I stood in the back of the group, and somebody whispered to me. It was Helmick.

"Can I change my statement?" he said. "I'm starting to get nervous."

Gentleman John

It was time for John Quinn to go, I must admit, but I miss the guy. If he was your friend, you never had a more considerate one. Maybe it's a good thing—he never could have accepted those mustaches and hair stylings in the current line-ups.

I confess to the possibility I have been too close to John Quinn to be objective.

My Beloved Phillies go into what even for them is a calamitous skid and they replace Quinn, and I know it ripped Bob Carpenter's insides to do this and I know Quinn has to be a shaken man.

But Phillies baseball was a train wreck. The something that had to be done turns out to be a new general manager. A younger one, of course. Quinn is 64, one of the patriarchs of the executive suites. It seems as if he has been around forever, the necktied Casey Stengel.

There was the stark factor of economy, among others. Philadelphia is too good a franchise for the Phillies to offer their fans nothing more than an annual battle for last place, which has become their heritage, and a backdrop of untouchable executives. With a decent team on the field, the club would lure two million people to its magnificent stadium even without the giveaway days. This is one of the great cities in all of sports. Also one of the hungriest.

Quinn was blamed for the treadmill status of the club, a rap he understood. You win, the g.m. is a big man, and Quinn has won big in his day and almost did in his Philadelphia tenure. You lose, the g.m. is a bum. That was accepted by him, too.

But you lose in Philadelphia, the general manager is flogged and insulted and demeaned by that fortunately rare species known as the Philadelphia sports writer. They made me wince, some of the stuff they wrote about

Quinn. They drank his booze and ate his food and laughed with him and they couldn't wait to leave his parties and laugh at him and prosecute him for the felony of defeat. They looked for criminals on a playground, and Quinn was their man.

A ball player hires a schlock agent to help him deal with Quinn, and the press almost automatically sides with the schlock agent. They tore up Quinn for condemning one of his ball players in a phone call to his manager. There is a guy named Frank Lane running the Milwaukee Brewers—and he's even older than Quinn—who has been shouting insults at his ball players from dozens of press boxes for years and nobody pays any attention to him.

The old baseball man, with the hide of a rhino, never complained. I never heard him challenge the "writers" about the endlessly derogatory stories and columns.

"When somebody asks me about a certain story in the papers, I always tell them I haven't had the chance to read it," he would say.

So he would go on greeting them and shaking their hands and entertaining. Not to buy off the press, but because he felt this was the way you must do it in the public-relations department. You traveled with John Quinn, you went major-league.

Gentleman John Quinn, he should have been tagged. A Chicago reporter, I believe it was, once referred to him as the last of the baseball gentlemen. Quinn thought that was the most wonderful thing that could be said about anybody.

Family and friends, and making friends, and meeting people, were tremendously important to Quinn. He is beautifully devoted to an ailing wife. He insisted the Phillies be represented at the funeral of a Philadelphia sports writer's father, and he meant representation besides the automatic appearance of himself and his wife.

Last year, during spring training, they surprised him at the annual Governor's Dinner in St. Petersburg with a plaque saluting the Quinn family for its long and dedicated service to baseball. His father had been president of the Boston Braves. One son is a general manager in the Pacific Coast League. Another heads the Milwaukee farm system. A daughter worked in the California Angels' office and even a son-in-law is the in-effect general manager of the Chicago White Sox.

Quinn proudly hung this plaque in his office at Veterans Stadium. The only one there, and he must have received scores.

"You get something like this," he told an interviewer, "you can stand a lot of the other stuff."

That night in Florida, there wasn't a Philadelphia reporter present to share and record one of the warmest hours in Quinn's life. They all had been informed about the surprise presentation, but they obviously didn't think it newsworthy. The only Philadelphia media man there was Byrum Saam.

I know all this doesn't make John Quinn the greatest baseball man in the world. I know the fans would accept Charles Manson as g.m. if they thought he could bring them a championship. But there are other things to be considered, I believe, if you are going to crucify. The whole man.

I guess John Quinn was too loyal in the long run, too loyal to his club owner and to the game itself, his version of the game. I did not savor his long contract hagglings that would leave both Quinn and the ball player limp and grumpy. He rarely fought hard with the established player, the guy who had it made. The player still trying to make it, he had to prove it to Quinn and prove it hard he was worth the buck he wanted. This, Quinn felt, was his duty as the g.m.

"It is very easy to spend someone else's money," he told me. He was not about to dilute his traditional approach to negotiations just because he had the key to the Carpenter vault. This last winter, he signed almost everybody so quick and easily after all their bad years that I truly believe he didn't know what to do with himself the first few weeks of spring training.

John Quinn should be understood as a top baseball man. A shrewd man, who authored some phenomenal player trades at some phenomenal times, like at 3 o'clock in the morning with another drink in his hand. His shop literally was open all night. He would be up bright and early in a fresh collar, willing to make more. Sure, there were some clinkers. Still, Quinn is in the first division of the traders.

But what has he done for you lately? Nothing, if you go by the standings, which is the only way a baseball club can go. Quinn, in his last summer before retirement, couldn't get the Phils out of the quicksand. You can blame it on the pitchers and the batters, but it is the general manager's personnel. He is the one who gets the players.

Quinn obviously didn't get them. It is incredible to me that at this stage of their "rebuilding" the Phillies have only two regulars and one starting pitcher they can call their very own: products of their development program. And now you have the irony of the farm director replacing the general manager. I am not sure this is the answer.

But it was time for a change of some sort. No question about that. Carpenter's decision was that new thinking in the head man's role was required. So he sat down with his right-hand man of 14 years. I would not have sat in on that scene if you had paid me.

John Quinn could be a fiery, screaming loser and he had unswerving ideas about how a ball player should dress and how he should be paid and how people should conduct themselves. He was much, much more than a nice guy who finished last, which is the way the baseball guides will print him. What pains me is that he is a fine human being who didn't even finish.

By Tom Winsett

How would you feel about a newspaper's decision to run editorial-page columns written by a convicted murderer? Opinions flooded our Letters to the Editor department. Some pro, mostly—and pardon the pun—con. This is how I felt.

I was sitting here trying to think of something funny to say about the remarkable case of Tom Winsett, if only to preserve my reputation for trying.

But the laughs wouldn't come. Something told me to forget it, after typing lines like:

—Who's the next women's editor—Marilyn Dobrolenski?

—How about a travel column by Sirhan Sirhan? Reminiscent, of course.

—What has Tom Winsett done lately that qualifies him to write a column? Why, he hasn't slain anyone in 10 years.

—How about Burt Lancaster to play "Word Man of Smyrna?"

—Or, how can they make Tom Winsett write a column? Didn't the Supreme Court knock out capital punishment?

None of them came across as anything but distasteful, because anything that has to do with Winsett is no cause for amusement.

I gave up because I kept thinking of the man that made it all possible for Tom Winsett to write columns in prison and have them published on the editorial pages of The Morning News. The man that made it all possible was a law officer and he is dead because Winsett shot him, and that is the reason Winsett is in a position to write a one-sided column. Equal time? Bob Paris long ago stopped having equal life. He was 28 years old.

Winsett was trying to steal television sets from a motel. I might say that monumental caper could have been the hint of the intelligence that was to lead him into columning, but there I go again.

A' La Carte

Winset was convicted of the shotgun death of Paris, the state trooper who had been sent to the robbery scene.

Winset got life. The two-time paroled loner from Long Island became not a jailhouse lawyer, but a jailhouse scholar, and journalist. He became editor of the prison magazine. He earned his high school diploma. He earned off-campus college credits at the University of Delaware.

I think that's fine, what he has done for himself as the inmate of a penal institution—if that is what the sentence had to be. The part about the University is a little disturbing, though, to anyone who has undergone the piratically expensive punishment of educating their kids. It also has to disturb anyone who knows that one of the law officer's daughters now is attempting to make it—financially—through college.

But the point is that Tom Winset indeed did not surrender to majoring in license plates. I give him much credit for that.

Writing for the Delcor Diamond, that being the name of the prison publication, is one thing. Laying his opinions, his observations on my morning newspaper's subscription is gallingly quite another.

I do not blame the publication of the column on him. He'd have been crazy not to accept this. But the decision to print Tom Winset's angles on "the forgotten man—the prisoner", as he termed himself, was an arrogant one and it makes me angry. Sensitivity should be as vital a part of printing a newspaper as the ink. Whatever happened to it?

There is no place in my conscience for the Tom Winsetts; least of all there is no place for him in my business.

I do not want Winset telling me about prison life. In the first place, I wouldn't believe him. In the second place, I go back to his qualifications—he is an expert by reason of the homicidal death of a lawman. The paradox is intentional.

I read Winset's first two columns and it was difficult to remain angry, for they were embarrasingly vapid. Serves 'em right, was my first impression. Embarrassing, I would think, to those who decided a column by a convicted murderer would be—well, whatever it was supposed to be. Newsworthy? Humanitarian? Progressive? A Sociological All-Timer?

We have a dozen guys and girls around here who could have written on the same two themes and done it brilliantly, without benefit of a record. I can only suspect, if the paper knew what it was getting, that exhibitionism was a dominant factor.

Winset will get around to charging, I would presume, that prison life does not deter crime. He is on safe ground there. It never stopped him.

I will guarantee you one thing. Tom Winset's column is not going to deter any crime. It might stimulate it. The by-line possibilities are endless.

I await with rather a seething interest his future subjects. If he is scraping for ideas, I can suggest a few:

—Interview the trooper's widow.

—How does it feel to kill and have killed a man?

—What were the circumstances that led to a career of crime? What, or who, did the leading?

—You have written that "people really don't care about the good a man does". Try us.

His writings on those might make Tom Winsett readable, and possibly justifiable. But I still will believe the thinking that made him a columnist for one of our papers was cold.

I am an eye-for-an-eye man when it comes to crime. I do not want his glamorized "I" for his victim's eye.

If you are asking if all this means I oppose the publication of Tom Winsett columns simply because he is a convicted murderer of a policeman, the answer is yes.

The word "simply," though, is yours.

Class of '84

I was looking for something pleasant to write about, an escapist change from the bloody news coming back from the 1972 Olympics in Germany. I found it in the first grade as a new school term began.

I wanted to get as far away as possible from the madness of Munich, and for a few hours I made it.

I went to school. To first grade yesterday. To watch 5-and-6-year-olds their very first day in their very first elementary class and in a new school, too. Oh, to be able to trade places with Shawn or Leonard or Regina or Tommy.

They didn't know the beautiful mood they were creating on this exquisitely clear morning. Stop the world—I want to get on again.

I was smitten 22 times. That's how many boys and girls there were in Mrs. Leah Mechell's big, bright room. I would have adopted 25, but there were absentees.

Room 7, it was, at the Pennsylvania Avenue Elementary School in Claymont. The teacher was there a half-hour ahead of her little troops.

"I'm like the children, I'm sure—I had trouble sleeping last night," Mrs. Mechell said. "I've been teaching 15 years, and I love it, but you never get over the first-day anticipation. You lie awake wondering if the children will take to you. Should I use the motherly approach, or what? It puts some at ease. Others, especially the boys, that's not the way to reach them."

Mrs. Mechell excused herself at 8:10. She had bus duty. I wandered around the room that was about to come out of hibernation. 30 desks and their pastel chairs were steeling themselves. The blackboard was brown. I looked out the window and watched mothers and an occasional father leading some children, the "walkers" as opposed to the bus riders, up the hill and into a new world. The September sun cast long shadows in front of them.

I checked out the Girls and Boys bathrooms. I was tempted to raise the seat in the Boys. I figured it might have been just a small help to some very nervous young man.

A mother came in with her son and asked if this were First Grade 7. I assured her it was, and she sat on a bench with her boy. She told me she had another boy, a second grader, who wasn't going to make it because he fell out of a tree Tuesday, and broke both arms.

A boy with a fat notebook and the remnants of a summer black eye came in silently and sat on the bench. Then a doll of a girl, wearing a long skirt. It said Woody Woodpecker on her lunch box. Soon there were five sitting there, scrubbed and silent, and the mother said goodbye to her son when she heard the halls come alive with the sounds of the riders.

Mrs. Mechell shepherded her bus contingent into the room and they looked around, hesitantly. She told them to take any seat they wanted. Later, maybe in two weeks, she will re-arrange the desks in clusters of five or six to form small work groups for the balance of the semester.

One girl, her name was Tammy, had a sprained right arm in a sling and Mrs. Mechell knew of it and she told Tammy to stay with her during recess, so she wouldn't get bumped.

"Good morning," she greeted her charges once they were seated. She got a few weak but brave responses. She introduced herself, and she told several children she had taught their brothers or sisters in previous years. She was putting them at ease, and she is very good at it. Talking with her, I noticed she never referred to them as "kids" and this impressed me.

"You've got to get all the worries out of their minds—that's the first thing to do, and it is most important," she had told me.

She set about chasing their worries. She told them about the cafeteria and gym and polled the lunch moneys and the lunch carriers. One boy's big sister showed up with his lunch money and I know he had to feel better. Another boy said he forgot his money.

"Don't worry about that. You'll get your lunch and I'll give you a note for your mother and you can bring the money tomorrow," he was assured.

She told them the bathroom operation. "You don't have to tell me or raise your hand—just leave your desk and go."

A boy raised his hand. "And if there's somebody in there, you're supposed to wait in line," he announced, thus earning the first "A" in plumbing.

Mrs. Mechell put a card with each student's name on his desk and went around the room asking what they preferred to be called. Then she asked if anyone would like to say anything.

"I do," a boy said. "My sister plays in the dog's water."

Another informed his teacher and his new friends he liked to jump out of closets and scare his mother. Another boy raised a hand but, when called on, said "I forget the words".

A' La Carte

They pledged allegiance to the flag which Bobby held on opening day. Mrs. Mechell told me she eventually would follow this with a moment of silence, in which those boys and girls who learned prayers in Sunday School could pray to themselves if they wanted.

"It's no use having them do this right away, though," she said with a smile. "It would take me 15 minutes to explain what a moment of silence is."

She led them on a six-minute tour of the school, and they walked wide-eyed past that institution known as The Office. They tried out the cafeteria chairs and bounced their voices off the gym walls.

Back in the room, the warm scene was interrupted by an incident that would make your heart ache. The school nurse came in with a little girl. "Does anybody know her name? She won't talk. She was in another school, and nobody knew her and we're trying to find out where she belongs."

One of Mrs. Mechell's students knew the silent girl's first name, and a call to the former's parents helped solve the mystery, I was to discover later. The girl is retarded. I hope somebody remembers her when they get around to moments of silence.

I spent two hours in Room 7 and Mrs. Mechell was progressively loosening and warming her audience.

"You try not to upset them," she disclosed. "Anything personal, so early, turns them off. Like the little girl with the long skirt. She is so cute, but long skirts can be dangerous on stairways. I'll remind her, but certainly not today.

"Some of these children look brave, but deep down inside I know they are awed. It's a huge building to them. They are worrying if they would get lost if they left the room without me. They're thinking about maybe they'll miss the bus."

The books can, and did, wait. I spotted the first sleepy yawn at 9 o'clock. After recess, Kelly had trouble with the zipper on her white boots. Jeffrey had trouble re-tieing his sneaker laces.

Mrs. Mechell took a head count.

"The walkers who live near the school, some have been known to have had enough at recess and go home," she said. "You've got to recognize this possibility or you'll have the parents on your back, and rightfully so."

Tragedy: One boy came back from recess with tears in his eyes. A buddy from another room had kicked him in the shins. He went off to the nurse's room down the hall and proudly came back with a trophy, an ice pack. Two dabs, and he had cured himself.

They were counting, when I left. They only had to count to 10, but many went to 20 and one little guy, concentrating mightily, eyes on the floor, got all the way to 23.

Only 12 more years, gang. The Class of 1984 will be even farther from madnesses like Munich. Let's all have a moment of silence for that.

All-Star Frank

Every city has its sandlot baseball characters. My favorite is Frank Crawford. Or was, before he followed Casey Stengel into retirement. The Crawford All-Stars twinkle no more.

For years, there have been these little items about the Crawford All-Stars on the summer sports pages.

The Crawford All-Stars will practice. Or meet. Or play a game.

The Crawford All-Stars are a Negro baseball team.

Up until just now, they have been managed by their founder. But Frank C. Crawford—the middle name is Columbus—is retiring.

"I'm quittin' as the field manager," he announced. "I got high blood pressure from players not showin' up, and things. From here on, I'm just the general manager."

Frank C. Crawford is one of the great characters of this sports community, or any other. He is 63. He is an operator—part hustler, part rascal, part charmer, all organizer.

Frank's big body is always garnished with a neat suit and a tie and white shirt and panama hat and carnation. This was his on-the-field dress, too, no matter what the thermometer said. He never forgets the carnation. "I just walk into McCready's every morning and they have the flower waitin' for me. I leave a dime on the counter, like buyin' a newspaper."

Crawford also wears horn-rimmed glasses and a gold-toothed smile. There is a diamond ring on each pinky. "These white people raised me in Greensboro, Md., and when Tom Hobbs died, he left me these rings."

Frank Crawford cannot read nor write. He has been jailed a couple of times. He shrugs off both situations as not really important.

He laughs when he discloses his philosophy: "You don't need an education—you need money."

The Crawford All-Stars have been twinkling since, as the g.m. puts it, "nineteen and thirty," and they are funded by what you might call public subscription.

"Rich sponsors give me money to keep the team going. People have died and left the team money. Big people like me very much. Personality and manners mean a lot."

Crawford displayed a check, fresh out of the mail. It was from a du Pont, for $25.

The All-Stars are always solvent. This year, they have new uniforms and, Crawford claims, 500 bats. There has been a slight hang-up, though. It is almost August and the season hasn't opened.

"That's where the high blood pressure comes in," Crawford said. "Had a little trouble linin' up the players. But we're all set now. Ken Miles is goin' to run the club, and he'll keep on playin' first base and catchin'. Freddie Mason will help out."

Crawford estimates he has shepherded a thousand players with the All-Stars. Their home diamond is at Fourth and Church, where home runs sail into the Christiana River. Mostly, they play away, visiting the Elkton Hornets, the Kenton Hawks, the Cordova Eagles, the Denton Tigers.

"Teams like us to come to their place because we draw so well and they give us the benefit of the doubt," said Frank in his best Crawfordese. A couple of seasons ago he was telling me about a game in which one of his pitchers became very wild, "so I called time and went to the mound and had a press conference."

There always are a couple of ground rules, Crawford variety.

First, all games are seven innings. "If it's a tie, that's it. The players, they got TV's and families, at home."

Second, the players don't get paid. "I get a lot of players from over in Penns Grove, and they get gas money. Nobody makes a fuss because I treat 'em so good. We play away, we'll stop somewhere and get a $10 bucket of chicken and some beer. I always said the sandlot players are better to work with than the big leaguers, because they give you all their services for nothin'.

"I got that leadership," Crawford declared, "so I don't have to worry about buyin' players."

Frank Crawford cannot read nor write. Yet he sells advertising and authors a sports column for the weekly tabloid, the Delaware Valley Defender. "I dictate the stuff to my girl secretary, Barbara Hicks. Then Herman McKinney types it. He's my analyst—he catches any mistakes. I got a good knowledge of sports, all the news and views. Most of the people at the paper don't know about my education."

Frank Crawford cannot read nor write, yet he sells TV sets. "I always carry my business cards. I go to a home and they want a set, I take 'em right to the store, which is Gus's. I'm pretty good on figures—I've never been a penny short."

The business cards tell the story of Frank C. Crawford in classic terms: "Top Sportsman, TV Man and Bondsman, Out at 7, Back at 12."

The inventor of the Crawford All-Stars also recruits farm help. He has been a chauffeur, the manager of shoe-shine stands and pool rooms, a promoter of beauty contests, proprietor of hot-dog counters at places like the Harrington Fair and camp meetings.

"Life has been good to me," he said. "I got 25 suits and I've had these great ball teams. Harry Scott, he's the greatest I've ever managed. Great outfielder and hitter, always on time and very neat. Miles and Scott and Mason and Scrappy May, the greatest sandlot players that ever lived."

The All-Stars, past and present, are a membership. Crawford, a widower, lives alone at 929 Spruce St. and "my downstairs is fixed up like a club, a bar and pictures and everything, and all the players have keys."

Speaking of keys, Frank, how about those jail sentences?

"I drew four years in 1949 and served six months," he said. "All because I picked up a hitch-hiker who had a stolen watch on him. Let that be a lesson to you—never pick up strangers. That was my only time up, unless you want to count 10 days I got in 1927 for non-support."

There was another "incident" in 1962. "This guy tried to run over me with his car and I dashed into the house and got a pistol and took a shot at him. I don't know how I missed him.

"But all that is nothin' now. A lot of cops have played for my teams. It means a lot when you can manage cops."

Frank said in all those games, all those years he never encountered any racial strife. "Why, my All-Stars were even all-white teams a couple of years in the '50s. I've never had any black-and-white trouble. A few times, I detected some before the games started. I just took the other managers off to the side and told 'em, 'Gentlemen, the ball game is over.' And we left."

That's Frank C. Crawford, Top Sportsman, Open All Night.

Ace On Wheels

You see and talk to a Tom Brown, it makes all the able-bodied athletes seem like impostors.

BALTIMORE—Tom Brown and his bride, Susan, will leave for a two-week vacation in Denver, Colo., June 22.

They could go now, but Brown has a date to play a basketball game in Wilmington the previous night. It will be his last one, ever, with his team. When he returns to work, it will be to Richmond, Va., and a new job.

You'll see Tom Brown that night, Friday, June 21, at St. Mark's High School.

He is a wheelchair basketball player, perhaps the best, an All-American. In fact, one of the best wheelchair athletes in the world.

Brown is player-coach of the Baltimore Ravens, who will go to St. Mark's to play to the first annual Delaware All-Star High School Basketball Game—a program the sports pages have been flagrantly secretive about—for the benefit of the Easter Seals Society.

I drove down to the Baltimore-Central Maryland League for Crippled Children and Adults to learn something about wheelchair basketball. This organization and the Maryland Rehabilitation Center sponsor the Ravens, who work out and play some of their games in the league's gymnasium.

Tom Brown is 26 and he is a congenital amputee. This means he was born without legs. He told me he began playing wheelchair basketball in Denver when he was 13. He went on to graduate from the University of Illinois and to get his master's in therapeutic recreation. He has been recreation supervisor at the Maryland Rehab Center for two years and is going to Richmond for a similar position. The Ravens and Richmond are in the same conference, and Brown probably will swing the balance of power in the Virginia entry.

I watched the Ravens scrimmage, a workout they put on just for me.

Wheelchair basketball is an amazing, difficult, strenuous activity that those fellows make look easy. They play under slightly modified rules. You can dribble the ball as you spin a wheel, or carry the ball for two spins only and then pass, dribble or shoot. The endurance, the power needed to propel the chairs about the court, to break, to brake, to pivot, to shoot sitting down—well, it is hardball basketball.

Tom Brown was scrimmaging with players like Tony Hewitt, an inner-city kid who is 15, Two years ago, Hewitt was shot in the back while riding his bicycle, by somebody who had a grudge and mistook Tony for his enemy.

Rodney Allen, 19, has a hip condition. Allen can walk. The rules say a player is eligible who is disabled in the lower part of the body to the extent he would be denied the opportunity to play standup basketball.

Bob Ardinger, 24, is post-polio, a University of Maryland graduate and a special-education teacher. Carl Younkin, 27, an electronics worker, married with two children, became a paraplegic when he fell from a silo.

They play in sports-model chairs that cost $500 apiece; light in weight, designed for balance, special bearings. All hand-propelled.

There are 92 wheelchair teams in the country and the Baltimore Ravens are third-best. That's where they finished in last winter's national tournament at Illinois. The University has a complete wheelchair program, and it was there as a student that Brown also competed in track and field, softball, football.

"I was in all of 'em," said Brown, after wheeling his way to the sidelines after the workout. "Basketball I like best, by far. Football was fun. They play it only at Illinois, on a Tartan surface in an armory."

Sure-handed, sure-shot, husky Brown holds nine scoring records in tournament competition. He averaged 22 points last season, with a high of 46.

"We have a rule here that anybody who comes out for the team, makes it," he said, sipping a can of soda. He sat there with half a body, double a heart. "But the first five guys do almost all the playing.

"Maneuverability is the whole game—you saw that. Coordinating the movement of the chair with the dribble is the toughest fundamental. It takes a lot of work. We can block and screen better than the normal guys—thanks to the chairs."

Brown holds the world record for the 100-yard dash, 19 seconds flat. He has been to two Pan-American Games, in Buenos Aires and Jamaica, coming back with a total of four gold and four silver medals. He threw the discus, the javelin, "ran" the relays, among other events.

Brown invited me on the court with him to try my luck at wheelchair basket shooting. I am not too bad at this on my feet, but I must have hit .093

and my driving rating was even lower. The basket looked five feet higher and the ball seemed pounds heavier.

"Think higher," Brown shouted. I thought higher, but my arms didn't; thus the ball still kept bouncing off the rim. I was the helpless one in the wheelchair, several times riding right into the wall trying to field a rebound. It took me forever to get position. Brown never seemed to miss either a basket or a bounce, layups, 15-footers, back-handers—the works—always shooting to the proper spot.

I asked him if he ever played against an able-bodied team.

"One time in Denver," he said, "our gang played some guys from Northern Colorado U. We spotted them 75 points and beat them, 98 to 97."

Brown was married, nine months ago, to a teacher of the hearing impaired. They met at a summer camp in Colorado.

As I left the gym, Brown was shooting baskets—and making them—from the middle of the floor and Susan was fielding them. Wheelchair teams rarely shoot, he had told me, from beyond the foul circle. They are as disciplined as any strong basketball unit.

Come out and see for yourself June 21. The All-Star schoolboys will be following an extremely tough act.

Barber Test

I had been seeing these ads in the paper for years, about tests for barbers' licenses. So, I went to one of the auditions. Hair truly has become a major industry. But they are not getting rich on me.

"**L**ook at that backhand," Lou Mauro whispered. "Marvelous."

I looked. It was a sharp backhand, all right.

"You can see the man is an old pro," Leroy Gaines said. "Pressure means nothing to him," added Ernie DelleDonne. "He is an artist."

Wimbledon? Forest Hills? The Walnut Street Pool Room?

Wrong. The scene was a barber shop, and Mauro, Gaines and DelleDonne were watching a guy shave another guy. After hours.

They are members of the State Board of Examiners of Barbers, and they were on duty, examining.

Actually, they were watching four guys. And a girl. All candidates for a master barber's license.

The arena was The Shaving Mug in the Bank of Delaware Building. This is the home grounds of Mauro, who is president of the board. Some barber shop. I thought I was walking into Joe Namath's subterranean nest. What it is is a European Unisex Hairstyling Center For Men & Women.

To qualify for the state exam, you must be of good health and have one of three backgrounds, all of which were represented this night. The old pro with the Chris Evert backhand with the razor has an out-of-state license (Maryland) and is thinking of moving to Delaware. The other four applicants either were barber-school graduates with one year's apprenticeship in a shop or non-graduates with three years apprenticeship.

Thus armed, you pay $50 and you take the test. A two-parter. One is practical: Haircutting and shaving. The other is written, 100 questions. Get 25 wrong and you flunk.

The candidates bring their own customers, or subjects, and their own equipment. The veteran from Maryland brought two platoons. That's class. He trimmed the hair of a boy too young to have a beard, then laid a shave on a friend who had been sitting in the waiting room, beneath the poster of Raquel Welch.

"Why a shave?" I asked. "I thought barbers cut out shaving."

"Most shops have," Mauro replied. "But a barber still should know how to shave. Otherwise, he's like a bricklayer who doesn't know how to mix cement. Shaving, that's the toughest part of the exam. I've only flunked three applicants in my seven years on the board — we get about 25 a year — and all were for chopping up their subjects in the shave. One time, I thought we were going to have to call the ambulance. But the guy took the test next time around and did fine. I think the subject recovered, too."

The candidates clipped away under the scrutiny of the roving examiners and one fixed deerhead. Mauro is a bow-and-arrow deer hunter. The Muzak played softly.

There was no time limit. DelleDonne silently spun one subject's chair to examine his haircut, and nodded his approval. Earlier, the young barber had been told he was depending too much on the clipper. "Show us a little more scissors work, all over."

The candidate behind the fourth chair lighted a cigarette, took a drag, parked it on an ash tray and resumed clipping. Judge Gaines quietly reminded him that wasn't a recommended practice.

"Sorry, just a habit," said the rookie. Later, he sat in the barber chair and smoked as he took the written test.

It is a basic haircut-and-shave test. No fancy stuff, like contouring, styling, honing, stropping.

"They can learn the scientific parts on their own," Madro explained, "at seminars, barber shows. We're doing less-and-less clipper work, going more to the scissors and the razor. It's hardly worth it to hone a razor any more; we all use replaceable blades."

One candidate wore a Pinkerton Security Service shirt. He said he was Bill Delancey, 25, of Stanton, a guard at the telephone company. Mauro predicted that the candidates were understandably nervous, all but the old pro, and Delancey admitted he was.

Delancey said he was a barber-school alumnus with a year's experience in Larry Timmons' parlor in Newark. "I've been interested in barber work since I was in high school. I like the pay opportunity, meeting different people, the conversations. Some day, I'd like to have my own place."

The girl was a left-hander, and a cutie. She wore a body shirt and short-shorts. She asked Mauro to check out her haircut effort and he suggested she "be more definite on the hair line; make it a little neater around the ears." She did.

Melody Oberly is 19. Now a resident of Newark, she dropped out of Claymont High School because she wasn't interested in going on to college or getting into secretarial work. She chose barber college. She is one of three lady barbers at Chuck Faulkner's shop in Ogletown. I wasn't about to knock her decision, but I wondered why she elected to fuss with men's hair instead of women's.

"Because men are easier to work with," she said. "Women complain too much; I couldn't put up with them. And my job is working out even better than I had imagined. You wouldn't think there were as many gentlemen around as there are. My customers are very polite. I make more money than I would as a secretary, and working conditions are so much better."

While the candidates were taking the written test, which includes questions dealing with the vascular system and dermatology, Mauro told me confidentially all had passed in chairwork. He was to notify them of the results in a week, or so. I sneaked a look at the exam and the last question was "In men's haircutting, what is the one implement that a barber could not do without?"

"I know that one," I said. "It's either a Band-Aid, or a conversation."

Mauro didn't exactly break up, but he did tell me the answer: A comb. I don't buy that. My barber hasn't used one on me in years. Check his license, men.

Kitty Scats

Bless you, Mike Douglas. His show in Philadelphia is a great source of column material, and his staff is most cooperative in making the interviews available. Ten more minutes of this one, and I would have fallen in love with Amanda Blake.

PHILADELPHIA—Miss Kitty is such a mature dish that I'm afraid I stared. It's a good thing Marshal Dillon wasn't around to beat on me.

But if the marshal could be so distinterested as to let her hang up her bustle and depart the Long Branch Saloon, never to return, then why worry.

Gunsmoke's loss is Africa's gain.

Africa?

"That's right," said Amanda Blake, all red-haired and long-skirted and purty in her Mike Douglas Show dressing room. "How do you feel about a documentary on East Africa, from a woman's viewpoint? That's what I have in mind. I'm leaving for Nairobi this week to do some research.

"This project is one of the reasons I decided to leave the show, after 19 years. I figured there had to be something going on besides Gunsmoke. My husband and I have long been active in animal work, the preservation of wildlife. We're mainly interested in endangered species, particularly the cheetah. This documentary would be both about the people and the animals of East Africa.

"Friends say I'm crazy to walk away from a lucrative thing like Gunsmoke. True, it has made us all rich, and it's been nice work. But the last 2½ years were a struggle. Very tiring. I did a lot of commuting from my home in Phoenix, and there were all those weeks of getting up at 4:30 a.m. to get ready to shoot at 8. And I could no longer rationalize that the world began and ended with Gunsmoke.

"I want to do my animal work and I want to get involved with other TV and movie companies. In other words, I am blowing my mind.

"I just finished an ABC Movie of the Week. Modern dress—boy, it was neat!" said the luscious redhead with the hearty laugh and the throaty voice.

So they are filming the 20th successive year of Gunsmoke without a feminine lead.

Gunsmoke. A miracle of the grim and dull reaper that is TV. A western that is the longest-running dramatic series in the history of the tube.

"It was my own idea to get out," said the ex-Kitty Russell. "But it was fun, for the most part. And we really were one big family. I know Jim Arness has this thing about the press, but he is one fine man. And very funny. He breaks me up."

She told of the day she had her pet lion, 16 weeks old, on the set. The lion behaved splendidly, except when the marshal had a line. Then he would roar and they'd have to start all over again. He wouldn't make a peep when Kitty or Doc or Festus spoke. He only reacted to Arness. Finally, after the fifth roar and the fifth re-take, Arness yelled "Okay, I've had it! Get that critic off the set!"

Miss Kitty and Matt Dillon. I don't think the lawman ever laid a glove on her, that you could see. Surely, she would have liked some heavy romantic stuff now and then.

"Jim and I made this decision, not to present our situation blatantly," she said. "We think we conveyed the picture—that Kitty was a hooker who progressed to a madam and that all these years, she and Matt were having an affair. You had to figure that out for yourself. We weren't about to spell it out and have parents tell our young audience they couldn't watch. We played it straight. Call it a thinking man's romance."

There were episodes that Amanda Blake, actress, wasn't ecstatic about.

"They had a problem with Miss Kitty," she said: "She was so well protected within the confines of Dodge City, by the marshal and his friends, that they had to get her out of town for stronger roles. So, they'd stick me in a runaway stagecoach or have me kidnaped or attacked. They'd come to me and say, 'Have we got a great part for you this time!' and I'd answer, 'Oh, yeah? What is it this time—kidnap or rape, or both?' "

She was most proud of an episode called Mannon.

"Steve Forrest was Mannon, a psychopathic killer who rode into town. Come to think of it, this was the only time they didn't protect me in Dodge City. Anyhow, Mannon attacked me and punched me around and I got the chance to assault him verbally. I loved it; Forrest was such a fine actor to work with."

"Did the marshal get him in the end?" I inquired, breathlessly.

"Of course!" Miss Kitty laughed.

I wondered what would have happened to Amanda Blake of Hollywood if Arthur Godfrey or Jack Lescoulie, or whoever it was, had not invented television.

"Probably not much," she frowned. "My movie career wasn't going that well. My first two years, with Metro, were quite unproductive. Then I had a year at Columbia that was a complete disaster. I made a couple of pictures that weren't even B's. They were Z's. Can you believe "Counterspy Meets Scotland Yard"?

"I eventually ran away and hid, in New York. It was breach of contract, but I got what they wanted. They let me go.

"I was working live TV, things like the My Favorite Husband series, when I heard about this Gunsmoke casting. I had been a fan of its radio show. I was a real pushy broad. I got myself all gussied up and sat in the producer's office till I got tested."

And as the sun slowly sinks on Festus' stubble, Miss Kitty sidesaddles away from the hitching post. I don't know about you, Marshal, you big oaf, but my heart is broken. The old saloon won't seem the same.

Just Like Rudy

Well, not quite. The next day, I couldn't have done a tango step if you had paid me. That is no reflection on Nancy's teaching. It is just that I do not have very retentive feet.

Move over, Marlon.

I have taken a tango lesson, and I'm ready for action.

The offer came from the Arthur Murray people, by way of New York. They said they would set it up at the Wilmington studio at 12th and Market.

The last time they had a poll, I was voted one of the six worst dancers in the tri-state area. However, I decided to guts-out the lesson because while I haven't seen "Last Tango in Paris", and do not intend to, everybody is talking about the movie and I recognize its topical value, or something.

A guy told me Brando really doesn't dance the tango. Near the end of the picture, he is smashed and he butts into a tango contest with his reluctant companion, thus completing their decathlon. It seems the tango is the only maneuver they haven't tried. Brando finally stumbles around the dance floor by himself, slaloming among the contestants, and for a sock ending he drops his pants and, back to the judges, bends over and salutes them. This is appropriate, in my book. Having butted in, he butts out.

Brando's finale almost tempts me to go see the movie. I have never seen a guy tango with his pants around his ankles.

Anyhow, to get back to the lesson, I figured I could do as well as Brando. I even offered to get smashed, but the lady from New York said that wouldn't be necessary.

"I am a terrible dancer," I warned her. "Please tell the local staff to be gentle."

"Don't be afraid," she cooed into the telephone. "I want you to experience the comeback of the tango. The tango is special. It has had a varied career—sometimes sexy, sometimes a caricature of what is sexy. But no matter how it is danced, the tango invariably sends out waves you just don't get from the waltz."

"I don't know about that—you haven't seen my waltz," I said. "I used to teach it in the Navy, to the sailors. I kept sending out Waves to dance with them. Little bit of service humor there, doll. Hello . . . hello . . ."

She was gone. But her local store followed through, and there I was sitting nervously on a divan in the second-floor studio, feeling not nearly as flip as I had over the phone. Two male instructors were teaching two young suburban housewife types some intricate steps and twirls and the ladies were so good they could have passed for teachers. This did nothing for my morale. I hoped all this fancy stuff wasn't the tango.

One instructor introduced himself to me. Sam Rivera, the manager, a Cuban.

"Oh, yes, we've been waiting for you," he said. "Nancy is giving a private lesson in another room. She'll be right with you."

I told him not to rush her. I didn't mind waiting another four or five hours, or maybe I could come back in a year or so. And come to think of it, I had better go get my gaucho boots, which, I just remembered, are in my car. And the car is parked in Bayonne, N.J.

But Rivera shushed aside my excuses and went back to his pupil and sure enough, here comes Nancy.

I will now digress and tell you something I had read about the tango. It started out as a sedate English country dance, in the early 1800s. It traveled to France, then to Spain, still very proper. Spanish sailors introduced it to South America, particularly Argentina, where the cowboys of the pampas made it a dance of passion. Rudolph Valentino in "Four Horsemen of the Apocalypse", started an American craze for the dance.

Got the international picture?

So there I was, bracing myself to learn a dance that has roots in England, France, Spain and South America—and who walks out to teach me but a girl of obvious Japanese parentage. There must be some mistake, I came to learn the tango not the kabuki.

Nancy Nakao, and what a doll. She told me later she is married to the guy who owns the studio, Bill Godsell, "but I look more like a Nakao. That's my maiden name."

"Konichiwa," I greeted her, thus exhausting one-fifth of my Japanese vocabulary.

"Oh, you've been to Japan?" she said, wide-eyed behind the granny glasses.

I studied my nails. "Twice. Olympics '64, Orioles '71."

"Gee, I haven't," she said. "I was born in a relocation camp in California right after the war. My parents originally were from Hiroshima. We all moved to Seabrook Farms in New Jersey, the food processing plant. I was clerking in a supermarket when I heard Arthur Murray was looking for teachers. I always loved to dance, so I applied in Philadelphia and was hired and trained. That's where I met my husband. We live here, in the Woodlawn Apartments."

It was a delightful conversation, but I couldn't stall any longer.

"Are you ready for the lesson?" she asked. "The other people have finished."

I was glad for that. I was hoping for no spectators.

She put on a record "My Heart is a Violin," by the Dancing Strings. I embraced her with my version of the Valention clutch.

"The lady in New York was right," I said. "This really is a sexy dance."

"Uh, we usually stand a little apart from the learners," Nancy smiled, "because they are always afraid of stepping on the girl's toes."

She taught me the basic tango step. Forward left, forward right, forward left, a long side step to the right and a closing step left with no weight on the left foot. Then all over again.

"The first three are simple walking steps forward," Nancy said. "And the pace for the five steps is slow-slow-quick-quick-slow."

We tangoed. It was easy. I was sensational.

"The simple way to remember it," she said, "is to associate the word 'tango' with the five steps. Spell it out as you go. T-A-N-G-O."

That helped, but I was glad we weren't dancing the scottische. I dance extra poorly while carrying a dictionary.

I was moving forward all the time and eventually there was an obstruction. The wall.

"Obviously," Nancy said. "We cannot go forward any more."

I agreed, because it was a tough looking wall. She showed me how to get out of the predicament. We took several walking steps to my left, side by side, and she gracefully spun back into my clutches, and then we resumed the basic step. I was giddy with success. Eat your heart out, Hal Leroy.

She changed the record to "Hernando's Hideaway". We tangoed, basically. I asked her to show me something a little more intricate. She did. I blew it. Back to the basic.

There are endless variations to the tango, I learned. It could take months to learn them all. You think Arthur Murray is crazy?

I settled for the basic and the little escapist thing Nancy taught me, to elude walls and burly Argentinians.

Nancy said there had been no great rush on the studio since "Last Tango" came out. She, too, has not seen the movie. "But there is a general trend back to ballroom dancing, and the tango is included in this revival. The young people now are getting away from the discotheque dances, and want to learn the steps their parents did—the jitterbug, the fox trot, the cha-cha, regular slow dancing."

I thanked Nancy Nakao for the lesson and the commentary, then laid a "Sayonara" on her.

"You are welcome, Mr. Cartwright, and goodbye to you."

"Just call me Mr. Valentino," I said. "I must go. My llama awaits."

I tangoed down the steps. Slow-slow-quick-quick-slow. T-A-N-G-O. I stumbled over the "G." I walk much better to music.

Caught Short

I like to fish when I get the chance. However, not much ever happens. But thanks to Frank Powell and his trust in the neighborhood, this trip at least was something to write home about.

It long ago was established that as an organizer of fishing trips, Frank Powell couldn't lead you to the herring at Grossinger's.

The Foulk Road Phillie, the club's sales director, is a way-back Eastern Shoreman who keeps organizing these informal little fishing excursions each year to his version of God's country. For headquarters, Frank uses the charming house in Newark, Md., hard by Snow Hill, in which he was born and now maintains as a weekend retreat. From there, you get up early and go out and attack various tributaries of the Chesapeake Bay from their banks.

Everything is wonderful except that nobody ever catches any fish, hour after hour, year after year, backlash after backlash.

The dogged Powell never is nonplused, which is a nice way of saying he is iron-willed.

"So maybe we didn't hit the tide at the right time," he will shrug. "But you will admit that you cannot beat the fun, and the fresh air and the fellowship. And the great people you meet down here."

His sales pitch this morning, as the group hit the highway, was hospitality.

"These Shore folks would do anything in the world for you," he said. "You just wander around and fish off their property, and it is taken for granted. They're happy to have you."

Well, the first stop was somebody's place along the Wicomico River and the somebody wasn't up yet. The group that included Jim Gallagher, the former Cub and Phillie executive who now is on the baseball commissioner's staff, and Dick Porter, the former American League slugger who is a watery old Shoreman himself and keeps telling Powell he should know better than to fish so haphazardly, parked on the guy's lawn. Salty as all get-out in their boots, they clomped to a point in the marshes and threw lines in the silent and bored waters and fished for a couple of hours. Nothing.

When the group returned to the car, the somebody was up—and the group was out.

"We bought this property for privacy," he said. "This fishin' bit is getting out of hand. If anybody ever had any privileges, they are hereby canceled."

Powell bowed and scraped in apology, turning on his best Eastern Shore twang, the one that makes "fesh" and "orsters" out of fish and oysters. As the party headed for another and equally empty river—public property was featured, from here on in—he explained. "That fellow is no native. He moved down here from Yonkers, or some place."

The day wore on and the fish stayed away by the millions. Gallagher had his dog along, and he was the only one that had a bite. "You have to expect these bad days," Powell said on the drive back to Newark, the original Quiet Village. If the Phillies had as many bad days, he'd be out of a job.

"But this is some kind of country, isn't it? Makes it all worth while. And such beautiful people—makes me proud to be one of them. Everybody knows everybody else. Why, nobody even bothers to lock up their houses. I could put a $50 bill on my kitchen table and leave the back door unlocked and the money would be there a week later."

Powell, aglow with humanitarianism, steered his car into the driveway. He headed for the house as his weary associates, so healthy they were ill, went through the motions of reclaiming their gear.

Powell suddenly reappeared, walking briskly—but not so briskly that you couldn't detect a face that was even redder than the day's winds had toned it. What gives?

"I locked the kitchen door when we left," he coughed, "and left the key in my other shirt in the house. But we'll get in. I keep another key with a neighbor across the street."

It's a good thing he does. The house was locked up tighter than Kate Smith's support hose. Some windows were both locked and painted shut. You got the feeling that Powell had consulted the CIA before he left the key with anyone.

"Now we're all set," Powell said when he returned. "I have a great idea for next year. We'll go down to Crisfield—great people—and charter a boat and—"

Minnie the Hat

Quite a change from the hat-check girls you used to see in Warner Bros. movies, is this lady. A nice change.

Hang on to your hats. Minnie Piazza will be back in September.

Hang on to your coats, too.

Oh, if there is a blizzard between now and then, she will return to action.

Mrs. Domenica Piazza is the hat-check lady in the Brandywine Room at The Hotel.

Over the years, she has handled almost as much clothing as Robert Hall. Hats, coats, capes, stoles, galoshes.

Umbrellas, briefcases. And an occasional dog. No, nobody was wearing the dogs, but she checked them anyhow.

Tyler McConnell's water skis. Tommy Lane's 8-iron. Jack van Urk's stirrups. Harvey Smith's microphone. John Hickman's megaphone. Dorothy Travers' pizza pan. Joe Hukill's barbells. Not really—I'm just kidding. But if such checkables ever did appear, you can be assured Minnie would have taken them in stride and might even have spent her spare time polishing them.

It seems as if Mrs. Piazza has been fielding garments and paraphernalia and unfailingly returning them to the rightful owners ever since Stetson—or was it Rex Harrison?—invented the hat.

Well, not that long, but pretty good. Minnie is 61 and for 34 years she has worked all the stations in the hotel. For the last 15, though, she has been a Brandywine Room fixture.

People remember Minnie checking for them when they went to high-school proms in the ballroom. Now their sons and daughters use her service. And if their clothes look familiar, Minnie is too nice a lady to mention it.

I learned something. The hotel does not operate the check rooms. Minnie's first employer was the late Vietta Scheckinger, who had the concession for the ballroom, the Brandywine Room, the Green Room, the Georgian Suite, all of them. Minnie worked for her for 21 years.

When Mrs. Scheckinger died, the hotel ran the checking but several years ago the lease was taken over by Herman Cole. Cole is a bartender in the hotel.

Mrs. Piazza thus is not a hotel employe, and does not come into Du Pont Co. benefits. But in point of service, she is one of the leaders. She has outlasted four managers.

"It is a nice second job," said Minnie, who lives comfortably with her husband in Newport Heights. Mike Piazza is a security guard at the Beneficial Building, and they have two grown daughters. "I couldn't support myself with it, but in my situation it has worked out well. It is no job for a younger person. I've worked with young girls off and on, but they didn't like it. The hours cut into their social life. You can't leave except for an emergency. You've got to be around until every item is accounted for."

Minnie works a split, lunch and dinner, a six-day, 40-hour week. Playhouse nights are her big ones. She can handle 200 coats on a full night—"without a lot of fur coats".

Button off? Lining ripped? Minnie will fix them. And she prides herself on her accuracy and her memory. Regular customers don't need checks. She remembers their items.

"My own little secret with the men," she said, "is neckties. I sort of memorize a man's tie, and connect it with what he left with me, and I don't have to give a check. Those I don't know, I must insist they reclaim their things with checks. Many just don't feel like looking for them—women especially—but I have to be firm, in a nice way.

"So many briefcases look alike, I have to be extra-careful numbering them. One fellow told me when he picked his up that it contained a $1,500 diamond bracelet. I guess that's about the most unusual item I've had, unless you want to count the two Afghan dogs an actress from the Playhouse left. Can't think of her name. But I get to check for a lot of celebrities—I remember Joe E. Brown, Eddy Duchin, Dorothy Kilgallen, Tyrone Power, Eleanor Parker."

You hand a tip to Minnie, it's hers. You put it in the saucer, it belongs to the concession. Her record tip is a 10-dollar bill. "The man handed it to me folded up—it was just before Christmas. When I found it was a ten, I telephoned him to tell him maybe he had made a mistake. No, he said, it was my Christmas present."

It is seasonal work, of course. Like, nobody is going to check an overcoat in July. So Minnie has the summer off, roughly from the end of April to mid-September. In late spring, when the weather is fickle, she makes her own judgment whether it might be cold enough to go in and open the room.

Have a good summer, Min. She'll be back in the fall, men, to get you off the hook.

Camp Handicap

Fairlee Manor is the kind of thing that happens when you buy Easter Seals. I took a picture one morning of the crippled campers pledging allegiance at the daily flag-raising, and wondered why they looked blurry through the camera's viewer. I had tears I didn't even know about.

FAIRLEE, MD.—The first-timers, Sandy Kother said, are the hardest to get matriculated.

"They think of camp as something for kids," she said. "Once we get them here, though, they fit right in."

The camp IS for kids. Crippled kids. But it also is for adults. Crippled adults.

The two-week session for adults is under way at Camp Fairlee Manor, which is where you help send a handicapped person each time you buy Easter Seals. Mrs. Kother, the program director, was speaking about the first-time adults, and there were 20 in this record group of 64.

They are like no other campers you ever saw. Most trundle about in wheelchairs, powered either by battery or by one of the remarkable teen-age counselors. They even dance in wheelchairs. The wheelchairs go right into the swimming pool with them, down a ramp.

They have been stricken and marked by cerebral palsy. Or multiple sclerosis. Or they are mentally retarded. Or they have Parkinson's disease or muscular dystrophy or rheumatoid arthritis or elephantiasis. One has had a brain tumor operation. The black man without the legs is a diabetic. And I learned about spina bifida, which is what they call it when you are born with a gap in your backbone.

So what was that you were complaining about this hot summer? The way it makes your skin dry? The endless grass-cutting? The price of corn?

They almost literally live for these two weeks, these twisted and gnarled and physically or mentally short-changed studies in courage. I heard it in their voices, saw it in their faces this first full day in camp. They had taken their choice of four activities, and now they were relaxing in clusters under big trees. The impossible word that comes to mind is carefree. They are sunny people. If Sandy Kother's first-timers were edgy, you couldn't spot them. As she said, they already had "fit in".

"They are adults and that is the way we treat them," said Guy Miller, the executive director of the Delaware Easter Seal Society. "We encourage them to do things, but we don't push nor regiment them. If they just want to sit in the shade and enjoy the day that way, fine. This is their vacation. We tell the children what to do; the adults can do their own thing. If they want a beer with their dinner, they get one. They're grown ups."

Jane Cox is not a first-timer. She is a seventh-timer, a radiant 22-year-old from Secretary, Md. When there are no more camp applicants from Delaware, and there is room then crippled people from neighboring states are considered.

Jane was born with arthro-gryposis. The ligaments and tendons in her arms and legs did not form normally. She lives with her parents, and works as a payroll clerk and receptionist at the Chesapeake Rehabilitation Center in Easton. She gets around in a wheelchair. Her hobby is poetry and painting. She holds the brush in her mouth.

I talked to jolly Jane Cox about why she so obviously enjoyed coming to this leafy retreat. It formerly was the estate of Mrs. Louisa d'A. Carpenter of Wilmington, who donated its 269 acres and its manor house to the society two decades ago.

I guess it's because I like to be around people with lots of handicaps," said the girl with the undeveloped forearms. She is on vacation. "It's so inspiring to see them, these people a lot more unfortunate than I. I consider myself lucky. I like to be with them and I like to do things with them. Square dancing, that's my favorite."

I asked Miss Cox if she would make any improvements in the camp, were she in charge. She thought for a while.

"Yes," she replied, "but it would cost money. I'd build more resident facilities, so more people could come."

I walked by Gardner Hitchens, who is the dean of the campers. He is 85, he has rheumatoid arthritis and he lives in the Governor Bacon Health Center. Gardner, he likes to park his wheelchair and wear a wild beret and chat with whoever is available. The young staffers, they love the old guy.

Guy Miller and Ray Kother, who is Sandy's husband and the camp director, had mentioned the amazing relationship between the counselors, whose average age is 19, and their adult charges.

"The kids on our staff, they develop a feeling for these people," Miller said, "and it is the rule rather than the exception. They visit them during the winter months, in their various homes. The kids come from as far away as Virginia to call on their campers over Christmas, at places like the Delaware Home and Hospital in Smyrna, the Home of Merciful Rest, Stockley, Governor Bacon."

Kother thought his counselors "enjoyed" the adults more than they did the very young campers, even though the work was more tiring. "The grownups, they like to stay up nights talking or visiting each other, and the counselors stay up with them. And they're always waiting on them, getting them something—a Coke, a drink of water, a cigarette. Transferring the adults is more physically exacting, too. From the wheelchair to the john to the pool to the bed."

Mrs. Kay Davis, 56, has been coming here from the Smyrna home for 11 years. She bears the scars and the lumps of rheumatoid arthritis, in all four limbs. Kay and her late husband formerly operated a store at 22d and Carter in Wilmington. She sat in her wheelchair puffing a cigarette with a little smile of contentment on her freckled face.

"All winter long, I live for this," she told me. "I guess I like the counselors the best. I love young people who are considerate of handicapped people. They fascinate me. They come see me in the winter, take me out to dinner.

"I've loved this place from the start. When I started coming here, we only had seven women in our dorm and there were only 20 in camp all told. I've seen it grow. There is nothing about it that I dislike. I have never heard one complaint. I tell outsiders how they teach us modified swimming and modified bowling, and they can't believe it. I do a lot of ceramics work at the home and I have an exhibition coming up in October. But here, I made arts and crafts my third choice. I'd rather be outdoors."

For Bill Grablis, who is 48, life in a wheelchair began 10 years ago, after he slipped and fell backward on a steel bar while doing maintenance work at an auto assembly plant. He told me discs began going bad, and one after another he had to have a number removed. There were 11 operations. He lost the use of his legs. He cannot eliminate the pain.

"This is my third year here and there is nothing like Fairlee Manor," said the husky one-time welder. He lives alone in Richardson Park and asked me to say something about the "ace" neighbors who take care of his shopping and his laundry. "I'm only sorry I didn't hear about it sooner. They treat you like a king. For me, it's a real treat to get away from my own cooking and dishwashing for two weeks."

Grablis' pet activity is archery. He brings his trap equipment, and his enthusiasm for target-shooting may see it develop into a programmed event. At the Mancus Center in Wilmington, he teaches woodworking—"I don't know who has more fun, the class or me."

They turn nobody down at Fairlee Manor. There are no qualifications concerning degree of ambulance, bladder control, medication, or ability to feed one's self.

In Miller's opinion, this is the best camp of its kind in the nation. I think of it as a personality camp. The adults here, in their wheelchairs or with their crooked walks, provide a great share of it.

Mgr. Bunning

Jim Bunning wouldn't tell me his timetable for Big Leagues or Bust as a manager, but I would guess if he doesn't make it by 1975, he'll go back to stocks and bonds. This column was picked for the 1974 edition of Best Sports Stories.

READING, PA.—I hope the sports department won't mind if I borrow Jim Bunning for the day. I promise to return him.

Sports fame is fleeting, and all that, but you must remember Jim Bunning. It ain't that fleet. He's only been away from major-league baseball since the end of the last season.

Last year, on opening day with the Phillies, Bunning pitched the first game ever at Veterans Stadium. Won it, too, before 55,000 people. It was the largest crowd ever to see a ball game in Philadelphia.

Last night, Bunning opened up another season—as a minor-league manager. That tall, lanky body he regimented almost fanatically was out there in the third-base coaching box for the Reading Phillies against Trois Rivieres, which is Canadian for Three Rivers. The crowd was 1,900. This is the Eastern League.

I drove up to see how he felt going into his new career, because you don't find Jim Bunnings managing any more in the minor leagues. Bunning was a superstar, you see, and superstars, when their playing careers are over, do not head for the bushes to manage. Accustomed as they are to the good life, they either get out of the game or stay in the majors as coaches and occasionally managers.

Take the Eastern League. The other managers have names like Len Johnson, Joe Klein, Karl Kuehl and Bob Cox. Matter of fact, the name manager is becoming rather extinct in the major leagues, largely because the names don't want to undergo the agony of managerial apprenticeship down on the farm. This is why clubs hire guys like Frank Lucchesi, Earl Weaver and Dave Bristol.

So why Jim Bunning, Mr. Class of pitching, a sure-fire Hall of Famer? He can't need the money. He always drew big salaries and he has nine kids and they can't begin to eat what they amount to in exemptions.

Bunning, who retired as a player a few months from his 40th birthday, was in his Holiday Inn room catching an Orioles game on TV. He turned off the sound and we watched the silent screen as we chatted. I give Bunning a rating of nice-guy-when-you-get-to-know-him. He has a veneer you must penetrate.

Pitching, he was such a dedicated, private professional that young newspapermen approached cautiously. He could immobilize a stranger with a glare and a bristling answer. He pitched like an iceberg and sometimes he acted like one. He was all business, and the business included key roles in the ball players' association as a pension expert. Gene Mauch once called Bunning the most organized man he ever knew.

"I came here to manage," Bunning said, answering my question, "so I can manage in the major leagues some day. That is the reason, absolutely. I have to learn to manage, and I would rather make my mistakes in Reading than somewhere else."

I wondered how long he was prepared to wait for the "some day".

"I have a timetable," Bunning replied. "I'm not going to say what it is. My wife and I discussed it and decided on it. There is no sense in staying in the minors longer than necessary. If after a certain period of time I feel I am ready for the big leagues, and nobody in the big leagues feels I am ready, then I'll go back to selling securities."

Bunning is a gent of definite opinions. I asked him if, as a player, he had looked upon his managers, or some of them, as necessary evils.

"They have to contribute something," he said. "You can't play without one. He makes the moves. If nothing else, he picks the line-up. It depends on the individual, just how much he contributes.

"Sure, I've played under bad managers. You can bet your life on that. Some didn't know how to win. Some couldn't handle pitching. Some couldn't handle men, especially young men. Some were just putting in time—they didn't have the dedication that managing requires.

"Gene Mauch was the strongest individual I ever played for. He was able to do most of those things, and he wasn't a great player himself, which is a little plus for him."

Yeah, Jim, but I know ball players who hate Gene Mauch's insides.

"He had some faults, too," Bunning admitted, "but he was able to get more out of more people than any guy I ever played for. He had a knack of keeping all the people on the club in the game, of keeping them ready. He always seemed to have his best pinch-hitter up when he was most needed, of having his best relief pitcher in at the right spot.

"He was able to control a game. If Mauch had a problem, it was with fringe players. His rapport with them wasn't too good."

So how does Jim Bunning figure to get along with his eager young troops?

" 'Get along' is not the object—that's the wrong term," he corrected. "What I have to do is get the best ability out of each individual rather than treat them all the same. I sound like a psychiatrist, I guess, but that's how you must be. Some kids need more direction than others. I spent most of spring training trying to get to know my players personally. Knowing them as personalities will help get the ability out of them.

"If I don't have the respect of the players, I won't get things done. They'll listen, but they won't do it. I'm fortunate in having my own record to start with—I think they respect me for that. But the name Jim Bunning will take me only so far. You can't con them. Now that I have their attention, I must manage them."

Bunning claims there are a lot of "mysteries" in baseball that managers should clear up.

"I'm trying to be honest with my club—and believe me, that's not a common practice. I have told them who's pitching, who's playing, and why. I have five outfielders. I told my three regulars why they're the regulars, and I told the other two guys why they are not the regulars. When I was pitching, I was always in the regular rotation and I knew I was going to work. But I felt for the guys who weren't secure and never got any explanation. Bickering by these types can lead to malcontent on a club."

Bunning was thrown into the managerial waters in a couple of dozen spring-training games.

"I wondered how it would feel coaching third, and I found it fascinating," he said. "But I always had the feeling everybody was stealing my signs. I felt conspicuous giving them. I know nobody was stealing them, though—I had a little difficulty getting through to my own players.

"One thing I must adjust: I kept expecting more out of my pitchers than I should. Maybe that's the mark of an old pitcher, but I know I'm less tolerant than I should be. I intend to give the starting pitchers every chance to stay in the game. I won't have a quick hook, I know how I felt when a manager came out to get me."

Can this new manager judge the caliber of farm-system players on such short notice?

"You'll have to ask the powers in Philadelphia," he said. "In Florida, the staff rated all the players on a major-league scale. I don't know how my reports compared with the other coaches and managers. I know I can judge whether a kid pitcher has a big-league arm. And I know this, too: I've got an outfielder named Iorg who is the best hitting prospect in the whole organization."

I had to bring up manager-press relations. In the big leagues, a manager spends almost as much time with the poets, before and after a game, as he does during it.

"I had a good experience in Philadelphia," said Bunning with a smile which indicated that was the true test. "No hates. When I came over from

Detroit, somebody said I had a reputation of not getting along with the press. That's a lot of garbage. One thing as manager, though—I believe you must weigh your words more than as a player."

It was time for Bunning to manage. He got up and turned off the TV and headed for his ball players. 22 years ago, he was a newly signed ball player heading for his first manager in Richmond, Ind.

Good luck, skipper, and give my regards to Pawtucket. If you like bus rides, you've got the job half-licked.

To Have and Hold

Columns happen in many ways. I met Doug Looney of the National Observer when he came to Wilmington to cover a Scrabble tournament. Seems Looney interviewed Dan McGowan and mentioned my name. McGowan said he was looking for information on a Du Pont-possessed $10,000 bill. How did Looney know I am a Du Pont?

The guy called me long-distance and wanted some information on a $10,000 bill.

"Sorry," I told him. "I've run up some tabs in my time, but that's preposterous. You've got the wrong man. What's the name of the joint? I'll even take a handwriting test and—."

He meant the kind of $10,000 bill that is money, he explained. The kind you spend, if you have one.

That was even more ridiculous. Me, with a $10,000 bill, the kind you put in a wallet? How could I be expected to have one—a week from payday?

Dan McGowan patiently told his story. He wants to rent or buy a $10,000 bill, just to have and to hold, and he was calling to ask for a little research. I was to discover his quest has not gone unpublicized. He started out with a tiny ad in the Wall Street Journal and the National Observer spotted it and Dan McGowan has become their boy. If he succeeds, they will get the break. Shucks.

The guy is a college professor. He is 29 and he teaches a course in money and banking at Hobart and Smith Colleges in Geneva, N.Y. and therein is a partial reason for his search. He thinks the sight and feel of a $10,000 bill would jazz up what he admits is a dull subject. Personally, I think the students won't care less. You see one 10-grand bill, you've seen 'em all.

But mostly, Prof. Daniel F. McGowan wants a $10,000 bill just to be able to say in his old age he once fondled one—"like your father saying he used to have a Pierce Arrow".

He came to the point of the call. "Remember that big Du Pont coin robbery in Florida a few years ago? Well, somebody told me there was a $10,000 bill involved, one the bandits forgot, or something. I wondered if you would look up the story, and get back to me."

I did, and he was right. In October of 1967, five masked baddies invaded the Miami estate of collector Willis Harrington du Pont and left with a haul valued at $2.4 million. And one clipping said "The bandits dropped a $10,000 bill in their haste to leave."

So Willis Harrington du Pont, son of the late Lammot, has, or had, a $10,000 bill. So?

So, he can expect to hear from Dan McGowan. He says he has located a philanthropist in Pittsburgh who will lend him the money to either rent or buy a bill, at an annual interest rate of 10 percent or $79 for 30 days.

The current owner is not going to get rich, or richer, dealing with McGowan.

"I might pay an additional $100 to buy it, or $80 to rent it, and that's it," he said. "Anybody who has such a bill doesn't care much about money anyway, because if they kept it in a safety-deposit box they'd be losing $800 interest yearly."

They don't make 'em any more, the 10-granders, the largest denomination of U.S. currency ever publicly circulated but now near extinction. The largest they print now is a $100 note.

The picture on a $10,000 bill is of Salmon P. Chase, which sounds like a W. C. Fields alias but who really was Secretary of the Treasury under Lincoln. To further help you identify the bill, should u question it, it takes 900 of them to weigh a pound.

In 1933, there were 3,600 of the $10,000 bills in circulation, McGowan learned from Federal Reserve.

"There are 409 out there now, as of February," the young professor said, "and I've got a lead on three. The Horseshoe Casino in Las Vegas has a hundred on display, behind bullet-proof glass. I wrote them—I thought it would be a great idea, great publicity for them if they gave me one. I never got an answer."

Perhaps a dozen of the big ones are outstanding, but they never are publicly circulated and are used only in inter-bank deals. The Federal Reserves told McGowan, in effect, to drop dead; that if a $10,000 bill gets into their system, it would be destroyed. Banks also are unsympathetic when McGowan inquires about loans, but now he has this live one in Pittsburgh going for him.

"I'm really hung up on this," said McGowan, who comes across through the persistence as a fun guy. "It is fun, for a professor to be doing this, but in the business world, they think I'm weird. I've become a focal point for phantom $10,000 bills. People contact me and say 'Try this guy', and I always answer them and follow through like I'm doing now.

"I'm even thinking of producing a 30-minute documentary, on the history of the bill.

"One guy called and told me to forget the $10,000 bill, that he could help me make tons of dollars. He took me out to a lavish dinner, and then I sat in his great big motor home and he told me how I could become a success—by selling household products. I burped politely and left."

I asked if he was prepared for a possible yawn from his class, once he proudly displayed his hard-earned $10,000 bill, if any.

"Some won't be thrilled—there are students like that," he said. "But there will be others with a bit of the romantic in them. But it really doesn't matter. What will matter is that I will have a real negotiable, liquid, legal-tender $10,000 bill in my possession. Isn't that reason enough?

"Hey, wouldn't it be fun to streak with a $10,000 bill? No, not me. Maybe some girl, streaking the campus with the bill on her. It would be interesting to see if anybody recognized the denomination."

They won't, Prof. They'll be too busy recognizing the statistics. And be very careful the girl isn't on the cross-country team. You might never see her—or the 10 grand—again.

Kids and Kubs

You can have Disneyworld, although I will give it second place. The most delightful attraction in Florida is these old guys playing softball. I caught them during Casey Stengel's reign with the Mets, who train in St. Petersburg. Thus, the reference to "amazin'", the adjective Casey used when he lied about his club.

S**T. PETERSBURG, FLA.**—Harry K. Hyland is having a bad spring.

"I've got four triples and a home run," he complained, "but I'm really not hitting. I think maybe I'm getting too old."

It could be, for Harry K. Hyland is 87. So what's your excuse, Jackie Brandt?

Hyland is the only player from Delaware in the 35-year history of a remarkable group known as the Three-Quarter Century Softball Club and its two teams, the Kids and the Kubs.

You think the Mets are amazin'?

Walk a few blocks from the Mets' playground here to North Shore Park right on Tampa Bay, and you will see the most amazin' ball clubs and ball games of them all—in Florida, in the United States, in the world.

You have to be 75 years old before they'll even let you try out. And if you show them you can play well enough, you must "make written application, stating age and other qualifications to the club secretary and receive a majority vote at a regular meeting of the club".

Three times a week, 4 months each winter, they appear on a regulation softball diamond in 7-inning games that are guaranteed classics. They have drawn as many as 5,000 people to a game. There is no admission charge. There couldn't be. The games are priceless.

Hyland was catching for the Kubs this day. They are the ones with the red caps. The Kids wear blue caps. Otherwise, the uniforms are the same—white shirts, white ducks, black bow ties.

The Delawarean moved here from Bellefonte 15 years ago. For 30 years, he was a foreman for National Vulcanized Fibre. He's from Wilmington High, class of '97.

At 87, he had to be the oldest player on the field. But only because an 89-year-old named John Maloney, from Madison, N.J., was out of action.

"He's a pitcher, and we form the oldest battery in history," said Hyland, a spry, little man with a powerful handshake. They're all spry, as you might imagine. "John pitched a few innings this week, but he had the doctor last night and he was advised to lay off for a day or two. So he's the announcer today."

The average age of the Kids and Kubs this season is 80.54 and it says in the program that "75 per cent of the players do not use tobacco in any form."

With Maloney temporarily sidelined, Hyland had to warm up a pitcher who was only 79, O. K. Miller, a retired dairy farmer from Great Falls, Va.

Think of gentlemen in their 80s playing ball and you immediately think of coronaries, or at least fractures. The somber thought was relayed to Hyland.

"Oh, some of the boys get pulled muscles and sore thumbs," he said. "Three years ago, we had a pitcher drop dead. He was 76, named Leo Swanson. He fielded a ball, collapsed and never regained consciousness."

The Kids and Kubs don't worry over things like this. If they did, they'd never be out there. You get the feeling that at their age, they think it would be a beautiful way to go.

They have a little ritual before each game that is mighty touching, with the teams lining up on the basepaths with a flag bearer and singing "My Country 'Tis of Thee" and then giving a rousing cheer, something to do with "What's the matter with 75"?

The Kids and the Kubs are no place for the feeble. There were some good stops and some good arms in the infield. There were some bad arms in the outfield; base-runners went wild on them. There were four or five "home runs"—and never mind the scoring—and now and then a fan would offer a dollar bill for one.

The action was hilarious at times. The Kids had an 84-year-old shortstop, Walter Lebengood, of Orwigsburg, Pa., who had a fascinatingly luxurious beard, nice and white, clear down to his bow tie. He looked like one of the Seven Dwarfs. Once he made a fine lunging stop of a ground ball and sprawled on his back as he flipped the ball to second for a forceout, one leg in the air. He had a tough time getting up, and then looked a little rocky. O. K. Miller raced out a home run the first time up and three teammates led him to the bench and clowned around rubbing him down. Next time up, Miller grounded to the pitcher with a man on third. The play was made to the plate and O. K. turned around to watch it while he was on his way to first. He got going again too late and it was a double play.

Fielders pursued everything but obvious line-drive home runs, which were casually retrieved against the fences. One disgusted old rooter yelled at the Kid outfield to play deeper. "What are you doin' out there—playin' in for a bunt?"

The senior citizen sitting next to us in the bleachers said he was a regular spectator. "They have some arguments that are dandies. Once Lebengood, the guy with the whiskers, accused a runner of interference and got so mad it took four of 'em to get him off the field."

After 3½ innings, "intermission" was announced and the players came into the stands passing the hat. They went back to work and the Kubs beat the Kids 27-13. The winning catcher was Hyland. And he came out of his slump. It was amazin'.

The Prison Bus

The day before Christmas, and you have to figure the shopping centers are crowded. So, unfortunately, are the prisons. This was visiting day, via the prisoner dependents' special bus. There are a lot of un-Merry Christmases.

Promptly at 8:45 a.m., Jim Reed put the bus in motion. It lumbered away from the car barn and through the wet, cold, scarred city.

The day before Christmas. A Sunday.

First stop, Fourth and Broom: Two women got on and sat in separate seats up front.

Fifth and Market: Nobody on the corner.

Tenth and Market: A pale girl with big glasses, long hair and a maxi coat boarded. So did a girl in a blue leather coat, red shoes and a patch on her Levi's that said something about sex. She sat down before I could read it.

Kingswood Center: The busiest stop. Eight women and three little children. They added some life to the scene. There were teen-age twins, one carrying a Password game.

And so on. By the time the bus hit the Du Pont Parkway, there were 28 riders.

All women, plus the kids. On their way to see their men. Their men in prison. For an hour of Christmas in a cage.

The sign in the window of bus 823 said this was the Smyrna Special. Each Sunday, it goes to the Delaware Correctional Center. One dollar for the round trip. A bargain organized by the center, DART, the Episcopal Diocese and the Delaware Council on Crime and Justice. But if you don't have to go at all—that's the bargain.

The bus has been running since October, as an experiment. This might have been its biggest group.

The pale girl with the glasses looked like Sandy Dennis. She said she was riding it for the first time, and was on her way to see her husband. Two years for burglary. A drug addict. They have a son, 3.

"I've been going to Smyrna weekends for two months," she said, "always trying to promote rides. I'd call everybody I know, Monday through Friday, but it's such an inconvenience for them. There was no way I could get a ride today, with everybody busy with Christmas. But I don't have to worry now, because of this bus."

A child cried. His young mother pacified him with a bottle of orange juice. A plump, pleasant grandmotherly type did an expert job braiding another child's hair. The bus was too warm. People drowsed as it crossed the bridge at St. Georges.

Jim Reed discharged his passengers at the gatehouse. They picked up their visiting reservations. It was a short walk through two sliding metal doors. There are visiting hours at 8:30, 9:30 and 10:30. The bus riders get first call for the 10:30 shift.

Robert Johnson was the officer at the reception desk. He sat beneath a sign listing "Articles You May Bring". Articles like two sweatshirts (must be plain white or gray). Three handkerchiefs. One pair sneakers. Money (any amount). One belt (not over 1 inch wide and must have a small buckle).

The officer checked in the packages and made out receipts for money. The prisoners would get them later. The reception room and the visiting room were bright and decorated with bunting, tinsel, lights.

I chatted with Ed Carpenter, the officer in the visiting room, and watched as Sandy Dennis took a seat in the back of the room. There are small, low tables between the prisoner's chair and two visitors' chairs.

A red-haired prisoner in T-shirt, dungarees and blue sneakers—hospital garb—came in the opposite door and sat down near the front. This was her husband. Short, a featherweight. They sat there for some seconds before she saw him. They didn't embrace, but they immediately went into a nonstop conversation. They looked like two freshmen in a Student Union lounge.

A prisoner sat in one of the visitors' chairs. A robust, handsome young man with one bare foot, the big toe bandaged. The officer told him he had to sit in the single inmates' chair. The prisoner didn't budge. Carpenter told him again. The boy picked up the chair next to him. I got scared. I thought he was going to throw it. But he put it on the other side of the table, making two on that side, one on his. The officer told him he couldn't do this, either, and finally "Warren" obeyed the rules. He sat there for five minutes and when no visitor appeared, he knocked on the door and left. This happens. Visitors have car breakdowns, etc., en route, and are unable to contact the prison.

Warren's visitors appeared later, and they sent for him. I was happy for him.

The overall scene was not as emotionally heavy as I anticipated.

"Some times a person's first visit is pretty tearful," Johnson said. "Then they get to know the setup. As you can see, they can hold hands and kiss and generally, it is a cheerful mood. Visitors are limited to two at a time, but there is no limit for the children. I know a lot of people think of the old Bogart and Cagney visiting hours. Talking through a metal screen, a guard with a big club sitting on a stool. The closest we have to that is closed visiting."

Closed visiting is for the "naughty" prisoners. Johnson used that word. It takes place in an adjacent room, and there is a window between the visitor and the inmate. Conversation, but no contact.

Sweatshirts and hankies for Christmas. I wondered about gifts like jewelry.

"Inexpensive watches are okay," Johnson said. "Usually the deputy warden passes on these. He's off today, so I took it on myself to okay a couple of Timexes. Expensive watches, they can only lead to gambling and fighting and stealing."

I watched a cute little girl in a red and white outfit stand on a table and balance herself by clutching her father's hair. Her prisoner father. Several women were wet-eyed as they stopped at the reception desk to make new appointments.

Not all of my bus riders were in the visiting room. I learned that this room was for pretrial, maximum and medium security. There was another, in a dining hall in another building, for minimum security visits.

My grandmother-type lady had been visiting in minimum, she told me on the way back. Her son, 30. Three years. Burglary. She said she hoped they would change the visiting hours in minimum, which are 10 to 11, because the bus doesn't arrive till 10:15.

She has been riding the special since it started. "It's a godsend. I had to go a month without getting here, because I couldn't find a ride. And when I could I'd have to pay the driver $5 or $10. First time I rode the bus, there were only four other people."

She told me about the woman and her husband who missed the bus one Sunday. "So they rushed around and got a cab. Cost them $26.80 to get here and then they found out visiting hours were over. Not only that, the cab wouldn't wait for them. They came back with us."

I asked her what she would have given her son had he been home for Christmas.

"At his age, just money," she said. "$10 or $15, so he could buy something for himself. I wish we could bring food on a holiday. They used to let us at the New Castle Workhouse." Yes, she said, her boy had been in the workhouse, too. I asked about her husband.

"He won't come down here," she laughed. "He don't like it. I don't either, but—well, it's my son."

The bus was quieter on the way back. The women isolated themselves in fresh thoughts of their men. The signs above them were incongruous. "My

Man Wears English Leather." "The Happy Vodka." "Pick A College, Any College. Send Money."

The driver and I had the last few blocks to ourselves. Jim Reed is 40 and he's been driving a bus since he was an 18-year-old in Winston-Salem, N.C. This was his first Smyrna trip.

"While you were inside, I stayed in the bus," he said. "I'll admit it, I'm scared of those places."

He took the sign out of the window and drove the Smyrna Special into its garage. A Christmas trip was over. I wondered how, or if, the women and their men had exchanged Merry Christmases.

Hey Grandpop!

Judging from the reaction to this piece, a lot of people must have gone through the same experience before accepting grandpaternalism. Or isn't that a word?

Let's face it. I'm a grandfather. This is a true confession.

I have been, for five years. I know that will come as a shock to all my fan clubs. Not everybody knows it. You'd never have guessed—right?

I wasn't ready for the grandfather bit, which is why it was classified information. But the battle is over. The swinger has gone down swinging.

I don't know which was the bigger blow: The eye doctor's telling me I had better get bifocals before I walked into a train, or my daughter-in-law foaling before I was ready.

Twins, of all shocks. Boys. With one delivery, I became a grandfather twice. Two years later, another son, and I hadn't even gotten around to forgiving her and her equally inconsiderate husband for the first affront.

How dare they make an ancestor out of me?

What a blow to my image. If those waitresses, and the girls in the office, should find out—who wants to be leered at by a known grandfather?

Grandmother, she couldn't wait to become one. A grand mother has followed form and become a grand grandmother. She loves the little ones. I guess I did, too, right along, but did they have to be related to me?

But I now accept the inescapable fact, and it only hurt for a short while. I salved it with the knowledge that some of my best friends are grandfathers. Most of them aren't, but what the heck. That's their breeding problem, not mine.

I accept the fact because the kids wouldn't let me do anything else. They drove it home to me. It happened during The Summer of '73. They are gone now, back to California, their first extended and communicable visit over.

They drove it home in subtle ways. Like at the seashore:

They have preceded me to the lazily busy beach this first afternoon, and I am walking towards them. I am like a three-base hit away.

Steve spots me and greets me with a voice that belies his skinny body. "HEY, GRANDPOP! C'MON IN THE WATER! C'MON GRANDPOP!" carries across the sands.

Scott joins in the reception. He, too, sounds like a chip off the old Ethel Merman. "HURRAY FOR GRANDPOP! HERE COMES MY GRANDPOP!"

Greg is the litte one, but in altitude, not volume. "YAY, GRANDPOP!" is his contribution to the destruction of an ego.

I give it the old "Who, me?" routine. I look around, while mumbling epithets, but there is no one else on my stretch of sand. It has to be me. I am trapped.

But "Grandpop"? Isn't there another way to refer to a grandfather, preferably something without the "grand"? Pop-Pop? Ugh. How about just plain "sir"? No, I guess that wouldn't sound so good, coming from small children. ("Hey, sir! C'mon in the water, sir! Hurray for sir!")

I consider the adoption of a pretense that I don't know these loudmouth kids. Perhaps wrapping the beach towel around the lower half of my face, like a displaced Berber, and strolling right by them. But I doubt this will work. I have the suspicion I have grandfather legs, and will be recognized anyway.

To my amazement, other people on the beach have not been alerted by the shrieks of "Grandpop" and are not staring at the obviously unlikely owner of that title. They are snoozing, sunning, reading. They don't even look up as I approach. What's another grandfather to them? I take a quick check and do not recognize any waitresses, or girls from the office.

The indoctrination continues. I flop on the sand and the twins flop with me. Steve begins to examine my head. He apparently has not seen one like it at close range.

"Grandpop," he says, "did you get a haircut?"

"No," I tell him.

Steve goes to the front and takes a better look at the top of me.

"Then where is the rest of it?" he puzzles.

I sigh, defeatedly. Grandpop indeed has arrived.

The last several days of their trip, they shared our home. They left mementos. The dining-room rug needs some stain-removing. The mauled miniature dachshund's spirit may be shattered for weeks. The TV doesn't seem to work as well. The screen doors are bellied, and I swear I can hear them panting.

And a memento of an unfrocked grandfather.

At the airport, they were fascinated by the baggage man as he ticketed the suitcases on the sidewalk. I bent and hugged each boy, and said goodbye, but they squirmed to get a better look at the ticketing and they weren't interested in the amenities of departures.

Hey, kids, this is me! Remember? I'm your Grandpop!